CONFRONTING CIVIL WAR IN AFRICA

Vulnerability & Resilience in South Sudan & Sudan

LUKA BIONG DENG KUOL

A Note from the Publisher

The publisher wishes to acknowledge and thank Dr Douglas H. Johnson for his invaluable help and support for Africa World Books and its mission of preserving and promoting African cultural and literary traditions and history. Dr Johnson and fellow historians have been instrumental in ensuring that African people remain connected to their past and their identity. Africa World Books is proud to carry on this mission.

© Luka Biong Deng Kuol, 2021

Email: luka.kuol.civ@ndu.edu
lukabiongdeng@gmail.com

Paperback ISBN: 978-0-6451469-7-4
Hardback ISBN: 978-0-6451469-6-7

Cover design, typesetting and layout : Africa World Books

Dedication

To my beloved mother Anyiel Acouth
who died in Abyei on 21st July 1976

Contents

·····-·-··-·-··-··-··-■-👓-■-··-··-··-··-·-··-·····

Abbreviations and Acronyms

FEWS   Famine Early Warning System
GOS   Government of Sudan
ICG   International Crisis Group
NDVI   Normalised Deviation Vegetation Index
NGOs   Non-Governmental Organizations
NIF   National Islamic Front
OLS   Operation Life-line Sudan
SPLA   Sudan People's Liberation Army
SPLM   Sudan People's Liberation Movement
SPSS   Statistical Package for Social Sciences
SSIM   Southern Sudan Independence Movement
SSIA   Southern Sudan Independence Army
UNICEF   United Nation Children's Fund
USAID   United States Agency for International Development

Preface

························◆◆◆························

W hen I finished my Doctor of Philosophy (PhD) some years ago from the Institute of Development Studies (IDS) at the University of Sussex in the United Kingdom, I opted to publish various chapters of my thesis in various peer-reviewed articles rather than publishing it into a book. Some of these peer-review journals include Journal of Disasters (Deng, 2008), Journal of Civil Wars (Kuol, 2014), Journal of African Affairs (Deng, 2010a), Journal of Eastern African Studies (Deng, 2010b), IDS Bulletin (Deng, 2002), Overseas Development Institute (ODI) Humanitarian Practice Netwrok (Deng, 2013) and peer-reviewed chapter (Deng, 2007). Over the years, I observed a considerable increase in the citation of these articles. The recent surge in food insecurity, vulnerability and famines caused primarily by violent conflict in the world and particularly in Africa might have increased demand for better understanding of vulnerability and resilience during civil wars. Based on this growing need, I decided to put my thesis into a coherent book that provides a framework for analyzing household vulnerability and resilience during armed conflict and climate change.

In an attempt to unravel and better understand household vulnerability, this book sets out a framework called the Risk-Livelihood-Vulnerability Framework that links risk events in a systematic way to household livelihood strategies and their outcomes in terms of vulnerability and resilience. The formulation of this framework was informed by gaps in the literature and various approaches to vulnerability such as Coping Strategies Approach, Asset-Vulnerability Approach, Livelihood Approach, Entitlement Approach,

Complex Emergencies Approach, and Social Risk Management Approach. This framework was tested through comparative empirical inquiries at household and community level in Bahr el Ghazal region of South Sudan, the then southern Sudan, which was exposed in the 1990s to a protracted civil war and climate change.

The first element of the framework provides a better understanding of the risk events faced by rural households and their interdependence. Given the growing link between armed conflicts and climate change, the implications of such interconnected risk events for household vulnerability need better understanding. The assumption that the risks events such as drought are generic and exogenous to household livelihood strategies may need to be revisited. Based on perceptions of the research communities, it is shown in this book that drought is positively correlated with the counterinsurgency warfare at the community and household levels. This finding complements the growing empirical evidence at a macro level of the positive correlation between armed conflict and rising temperature in Africa. The implication is that the "standard vulnerability pattern" that assumes risk events as exogenous and links vulnerability only to the level of household assets ownership may need to be revisited.

The second component of the framework analyzes the livelihood strategies adopted during the civil war. While it is generally recognized in the development literature that rural households are proactive in confronting risk events such as drought through livelihood strategies including diversification, households living in armed conflict environment are generally perceived, because of the dearth of evidence, as passive or unable to confront the effects of civil war on their livelihoods because of the chaotic nature of civil war. The results of comparative empirical inquiries show that households exposed to exogenous (from outside the community) counterinsurgency warfare do indeed adopt proactive and innovative ex-ante livelihood strategies to confront civil war, while those exposed to endogenous (from within the community) counterinsurgency warfare tend to adopt rather ineffective livelihood strategies. Unlike households exposed to drought who usually adopt a livelihood diversification strategy, such strategy is not the best option for those exposed to counterinsurgency warfare except in social assets in the case of exogenous counterinsurgency warfare. Surprising, investment in social capital and diversification of social assets increased among the households exposed to exogenous counterinsurgency warfare.

The third element of the framework assesses the level of vulnerability and resilience as outcomes of household livelihood strategies. The household vulnerability is measured in this book in terms of exposure to risk (susceptibility), the intensity with which the risk event is experienced (sensitivity) and the capacity to resist downward movement in well being as a result of the occurrence of a risk event (resilient). The results of comparative empirical inquiries show the curse of assets as such assets like livestock, the mainstay of rural livelihood in Bahr el Ghazal region, became increasingly susceptible to counterinsurgency warfare with non-poor becoming more vulnerable during the civil war. However, the households exposed to exogenous counterinsurgency warfare were surprisingly more resilient not only than the households exposed to endogenous counterinsurgency but also those exposed to drought.

This framework may be needed at the time when many African countries are likely to continue sliding into a trajectory of violent conflict that will be increasingly caused by interplay between the violent conflict caused by governance deficit and decaying democracy and climate change. This book will act as a guide to have a better and coherent approach to improving understanding of and responding to household vulnerability and resilience during the prolonged violent conflict and climate change environment that are becoming increasingly bunched.

Acknowledgements

This book is based on my four years' Doctor of Philosophy (D. Phil) study at the Institute of Development Studies (IDS) at the University of Sussex, United Kingdom that was a breathtaking and transforming experience. I owe special thanks and deepest gratitude to Stephen Devereux, my supervisor, who has not only diligently and meticulously supervised my research, but also sustained me with much-needed encouragement and support. I benefited a great deal from his exemplary supervision and I was overwhelmed by his endurance, active engagement and prompt, insightful and conscientious feedback on some of my lengthy drafts.

I am especially grateful to my research enumerators (Martin Mawien, Nyang Chol, Joseph Majok, Thomas Deng and Moses Mawien) who helped me, not only in collecting households survey data and participating in community focus group discussions, but they also managed to allow me to interact amicably with their communities. I owe special thanks to my nephew, Longar Awour, who provided me with much-needed support when we got stuck in the mud and rains with our bicycles on our way to one of the research communities in Abyei area. I owe special gratitude to Ayen Deng (Achethedit), who nursed and provided me with the necessary care when I was struck down by severe malaria during my fieldwork where there were no health facilities. My sister Akuet with her daughters (Nyandeng, Alai and Nyalang) were also an important source of inspiration and support during the writing up of my thesis.

I am grateful to Neil McCulloch, Sarah Cook, Martin Greeley, Howard White, Robin Luckham and Chris Stevens for their guidance and encouragement during my research work. My DPhil colleagues, Colette, Paul, Isatu, Katsu, Naomi, Anne, Camillo, Jo, Edward, Marie-jo, Jonathan, Mila, Fang, Tony, Marc and Asha were great in providing me with encouragement and support. Also, IDS administration was very supportive in providing me with a much-appreciated position of the IDS resident warden during the writing up of my thesis. Last but not least, I would like to thank my external examiner, David Keen and internal examiner, Jeremy Swift for their valuable academic feedback and advice during my PhD viva.

My research was generously funded by many agencies, particularly the United States Agency for International Development (USAID), Hugh Pilkington Trust, Avenue Charitable Trust, Operation Lifeline Sudan (OLS)/World Food Programme, Christian Aid, Catholic Relief Services, Norwegian People's Aid, Sudan Relief and Rehabilitation Association and a personal friend, Paul Murphy. In addition, I received considerable support and encouragement during the course of my research from various individuals. I would like to thank Brian D'Silva, Elijah Malok, Gen. Salva Kiir, Dr John Garang, Arthur Akuien, Justin Yuac, John Steele, Ken Miller, Robin Shawyer, Karen Glisson, David Astor, Simon Maxwell, Zacharia and Santina Deng, Francis and Dorothy Deng, Deng Alor, Sue Lautze, Dr. Lual Deng, Pieng Deng, Ring Biong, Gordon Wagner, Maker Ayuel, Fred Wekessa, David Deng Athorbek, Lian Yak, Deng Mading, Arop Deng (Awal), Atiob Acouth, and Isaiah Chol.

First and foremost, I owe special and deepest gratitude to my wife (Esther Tindilo) and our children (Bulabek, Anyiel and Achai), whose love, unwavering support, inspiration and tolerance of my protracted absence from them have undoubtedly been a great source of strength and encouragement that brought my thesis to a conclusion. In particular, I owe my greatest debt to my younger daughter (Achai), who was born during this difficult period of my studies and to whom I failed to accord the fatherly care and affection. I thank my daughter Anyiel, a trained journalist, for proofreading and editing of the first manuscript of this book.

CHAPTER ONE

Introduction

----------------◈----------------

C ivil wars have become pronounced and endemic to many African
countries since the end of the Cold War. The population in sub-Saharan Africa now live in countries that are at war with themselves
and low-intensity conflict and coupled with impacts of climate change have
become endemic to many other African countries. This upsurge of civil
wars in Africa has a considerable negative impact on the socio-economic
structures of the rural communities, resulting particularly in the apparent
weakening or even breakdown of organised society. This gradual decay
of organised society in much of Africa leads to Africa being described as a
doomed continent with a degenerative social disease that threatens to infect
the rest of the world (Kaplan, 1994). In comparison to other regions, Africa
has the highest incidence of intense civil wars, this trend is increasing, while
it has fallen or remained static in other regions. In the last five years, there
has been considerable increase in conflict in Africa with 2015 and 2016 re-
cording the highest incidents of violent conflicts since 1946 (PRIO, 2018).

The risk of civil wars in much of Africa stands now as the leading contributory cause of vulnerability and has overtaken the long dominant role
of ecological risk (Deng, 2007). The main causes of African famines have
changed from being drought to civil wars (Devereux, 2000 and De Waal,
2018). For example, during the 1990s Von Braun et al. (1998) identify only
one famine out of a total of eight famines in Africa that was mainly caused
by drought, while the rest were mainly triggered by civil wars. In the last

thirty years, there have been no calamitous famines but new famines largely caused by civil wars emerging in Africa (de Waal, 2018).

Globally and at the close of the 20th century the serious food emergencies and famines were almost always due to civil war rather than to natural disasters. Devereux (2000:6) found that two-thirds of all the major famines since 1900 were primarily caused by political instability or civil wars. Conflict continues to be the main driver of food insecurity and accounted for about 60 percent of global food insecure population (WFP, 2018). By the end of 2017, a record high of 68.5 million people were forced to flee their homes due to wars, violence and prosecution with Africa continues to host the largest number of forced displaced population (UNHCR, 2018). Africa has the highest number of war-related deaths per year compared to other regions with social services have also been forgone for military expenditure. Emergency assistance for zones of armed conflict continues to hijack foreign assistance flows that overall is shrinking in response to economic downturns and domestic pressure to cut budgets and welfare spending.

This upsurge and prominence of internal wars over interstate wars in the world and specifically in Africa, in particular, has posed a compelling need to improve understanding of how people survive in such violet environment for better policy direction and intervention. Though there has been increasing academic interest in studying civil wars, most of the current studies tend to focus mainly on macro issues with limited relevance and conceptualisation at micro (community and household) levels. The risk of civil war is pervasive with increasing trends and concomitant vulnerability in many rural areas of sub-Saharan Africa. Risk and risk-related behaviours, despite their complexity, have been the dominant field for research inquiry in economic theory.

Risk and Vulnerability Literature: Concerns and Gaps

Risk and uncertainty and human reactions to them have played an important role in shaping and explaining the values of economic institutions and systems in developed countries. Arrow (1971) developed a theory of risk aversion that shows that individuals tend to display an aversion to the taking of risks and that such risk attitudes guarantee the optimal allocation of resources. Risk attitude is crucially important as it is related to rational behaviour and efficient management of assets and livelihood strategies, particularly at a household level.

Despite the apparent recognition of the prevalence of risk aversion attitudes and rational behaviour towards risk management in developed countries, there are conflicting views about the evidence from low-income economies. Some studies suggest that farmers in low-income economies are burdened by an extreme aversion to risk, while others found moderate risk aversion and some even found evidence of risk neutrality. These conflicting views about risk attitudes indicate disagreement about rational behaviour and efficient asset management of self-provisioning households in low-income economies.

The vast and still growing literature on 'coping strategies' as short-term household responses to the adverse effects of drought in the 1980s has clearly shown evidence of rational behaviour and the prevalence of moderate risk aversion attitudes among rural households in low-income economies. Recent studies have also assessed household longitudinal responses to economic shocks in the urban context of low-income countries and found that urban households exhibit not only rational behaviour in their asset management but are also managers of complex asset portfolios (Moser, 1998). These findings allow linking the observed level of vulnerability in low-income economies with the level of asset ownership rather than with irrational behaviour of households.

Though there is now agreement and consensus over the prevalence of rational behaviour among households exposed to drought and economic shocks, there is little evidence about their prevalence among households exposed to the risk of civil wars. In lieu of empirical evidence of household responses to the adverse effects of civil war, there is a growing perception that the very nature of civil war causes households to be burdened with extreme risk aversion attitudes that will inhibit any rational behaviour and adoption of proactive livelihood strategies.

This apparent gap in the literature of risk makes many studies on livelihood and vulnerability to lump together various shocks as exogenous with the implicit assumption that they will trigger a similar pattern of household responses (Farrington et al, 1999; Siegel and Alwang, 1999; Moser, 1998; Sen, 1981). The dearth of understanding of risk-related behaviours in the civil war has made existing studies in risk and livelihood literature unwittingly equate these behaviours with the risk-related behaviours in the context of other risky events or has even ruled out any rational risk behaviour in the context of civil war. It is questionable whether such assumptions are empirically proven, as there are limited conceptualisation and application of risk theory to the context of civil war. It is also unclear whether the risk management strategies adopted by households exposed to the risk of civil war- where people struggle not only for economic survival but also for physical, social and political survival – will be similar to those adopted in the context of ecological and economic shocks. It is also unclear how far households exposed to the risk of civil war diversify their primary livelihood activities, to what level their social capital has eroded and whether the current asset-vulnerability debates are tenable in the context of civil war.

These questions constitute a considerable gap in risk literature and have stimulated this book. Chambers (1989) recognises the effects of civil wars on household vulnerability as a gap in the literature and Buchanan-Smith and Davies (1995) also note that famines caused by conflict are increasingly common, but are as yet poorly understood. Swift (1989) also emphasises that though civil wars are treated as exogenous, they are crucial to understanding household vulnerability and famine in Africa. De Waal (1993a) recognises that civil war, compared to other contributory causes of famine such as drought, receives far less attention than it deserves. De Waal argues that this apparent gap in the literature is due to the hazards of doing field research during wars, which means that household vulnerability related to civil wars will remain poorly understood and will continue not to receive sufficient analytical scrutiny. Some researchers attempt to fill this gap (Swift, 1996; de Waal, 1996; Keen, 1994, 1997, 1998; Goodhand et al., 2000; Cliffe and Luckham, 1999) by focusing either on understanding the causes and dynamics of civil wars or on their effects on rural livelihoods with limited analysis of household livelihood strategies.

With the upsurge of the risk of civil wars in rural areas of Africa, there is a compelling need for more information on households' risk-related behaviours that cannot be provided by economic theory alone. This book recognises this fact and adopts a wide range of approaches and disciplines to study and understand the risk of civil war and household risk-related behaviours. Specifically, the major thrust of this book is to contribute to the process of understanding the complex household livelihood strategies adopted during the prolonged civil war.

The Primary Objective

This book is based on my doctoral thesis titled "Confronting Civil War: A Comparative Study of Household Livelihood Strategies in Southern Sudan". The primary objective of the research stems from the apparent concerns and gaps in risk literature and approaches to vulnerability, and the compelling academic and policy need to improve understanding of risk-related behaviours of households exposed to prolonged civil war. The research intends to contribute to the process of narrowing the existing literature gap by thoroughly and rigorously assessing the livelihood strategies adopted by households to reduce and/or avoid the anticipated and actual adverse effects of civil war. The key hypothesis of the research is that "households exposed to the risk of civil war consciously take rational courses of action and livelihood strategies to reduce and/or avoid the anticipated and actual adverse effects of civil war." In addition, the research examines the following four sub-hypotheses that attempt to qualify the above main hypothesis as presented below.

- As civil wars are sustained by greed, the conduct of civil wars and counter-insurgency warfare is more important to the rural communities than the conventional civil war between government and rebels.
- Given the nature of counterinsurgency warfare, livelihood diversification may not be the best livelihood strategy option during the civil war.
- Depending on the nature of counterinsurgency warfare, social capital may be a causality or valuable livelihood asset during the civil war.
- Depending on the characteristics of counterinsurgency warfare and livelihood strategies adopted during the civil war, the non-poor households may not be necessary less vulnerable than the poor households.

Empirical Context: Field Research and Methods

Sudan was geographically the largest country in Africa and a land of extraordinary cultural diversity until South Sudan seceded in 2011. It is justifiably considered as a microcosm of Africa because of its central location reflecting within its borders all the racial, ethnic, religious and cultural diversity of the continent. Since its independence in 1956, Sudan has been embroiled in devastating civil wars and wasted long years of its independence in the following major civil wars: (1955–72) in Southern Sudan; (1982–2005) in Southern Sudan, Nuba Mountains, Blue Nile and Eastern Sudan, the civil war that erupted in Darfur in 2003 and Southern Kordofan and the Blue Nile states in 2010. South Sudan that separated from Sudan in 2011 slid into civil war in less than three years in 2013.

The costs of the civil wars in Sudan and South Sudan were exceptionally heavy, especially on the civilian population. For example, the 1982–2005 civil war resulted in an estimated death toll of more than two million, and about four and a half million people being uprooted from their homelands in Southern Sudan (World Bank, 2003). The first civil war that erupted in 2013 in the newly independent South Sudan resulted in a death toll estimated to be around 400,000 (Checchi et al, 2018).

The recurrent civil wars and drought in Sudan resulted in chronic food shortages and widespread famines, most notably in 1984, 1988, 1992 and 1998. Southern Sudan, which was not prone to famine during the first civil war in 1952–72 and post-civil war period in 1972–82, has experienced two major famines during the second civil war, in 1988 and 1998, with excess famine mortality of more than 300,000 persons (Deng, 1999). Even after its independence in 2011, South Sudan experienced famine in 2017 and persists susceptibility to severe food insecurity and famine.

The second civil war started in 1982 in Southern Sudan and gradually reached most rural areas by 1990. Bahr el Ghazal is one of the three regions of Southern Sudan that had been the epicentre of counter-insurgency warfare. This counterinsurgency campaign was being waged by the government militias, mainly composed of northern Arab pastoralists who live just to the north of the internal frontier of Bahr el Ghazal region, and later on during the 1990s by the southern militias composed of the major ethnic groups (Nuer and Dinka).

The situation in Bahr el Ghazal region worsened during the 1990s after political divisions erupted in 1991 within the forces of the main rebel movement, the Sudan People's Liberation Movement (SPLM), which resulted in a splinter group (mainly composed of Dinka and Nuer). This splinter group joined the government forces to further intensify counter-insurgency warfare in Bahr el Ghazal region, a stronghold of the SPLM. Unlike the raids of the Arab militia that were exogenous and occurred during the dry season, the counter-insurgency warfare that was waged by the splinter group (Dinka militia) was all-year-round and emerged from within the Dinka communities.

The unique characteristics of the Bahr el Ghazal region and its experience in the 1990s made it ideal for conducting a vulnerability study on communities who have had different experiences and exposure to different types of counterinsurgency warfare. The period covered by the study is the 1990s with the pre-war period used as a baseline to gauge changes and trends in the level of vulnerability and resilience. The years 1988 and 1998 when famines occurred in Bahr el Ghazal were used as benchmark years to help interviewees refer to events that are vividly remembered by their communities.

The study distinguished between two types of warfare, namely insurgency and counter-insurgency. While insurgency warfare refers to the guerrilla warfare waged by rebels against the state, counterinsurgency warfare refers to that carried out by militia forces used by the state to oppose insurgency warfare. Given its importance, counterinsurgency warfare is used interchangeably with civil war. For easy reference, the counterinsurgency warfare that was waged by government militia using members within the targeted communities (such as Dinka militia) is termed as 'endogenous counterinsurgency', while the counterinsurgency warfare waged by government militia using members outside the targeted communities (such as Arab militia) is termed 'exogenous counter-insurgency'.

The primary data were collected from May 2000–March 2001 during fieldwork in three villages in Abyei (Kiir Kou village), Gogrial (Alek village) and Cuibet (Langdit village) counties of Bahr el Ghazal region as shown in the map overleaf and in Table 1.1. The size of sample households as provided in Table 1.1 is sufficient to warrant statistical analysis of vulnerability and resilience during the civil war. The three sample research areas were purposively selected to represent different risk events. The actual selection of sample villages was guided by a set of predetermined criteria, such as population concentration, geographical spread, representation of various socio-economic groups, level and nature of vulnerability and a longer period of settlement in the village. In order to avoid cultural and ethnic differences, the research areas were exclusively resided by Dinka ethnic community.

Map of South Sudan and Research Areas

Source: *United Nations*

Red Circles indicate the research areas of Abyei (Kiir Kou villages), Gogrial (Alek village), and Cuiebet (Langdit village)

Table 1.1

Characteristics of Research Areas in Bahr el Ghazal Region

Basic Data	Abyei	Gogrial	Cuiebet
Total Population★	32,641	113,341	33,950
No. of Households★	5,440	18,890	5,658
Sample Households	211 (4%)	205 (1%)	99 (2%)
Ethnic Community	Dinka (Ngok)	Dinka (Rek)	Dinka (Rek)
Location	North	Central	South
Main Risk Event	Arab Militias	Dinka Militia	Drought

★*Source: World Health Organisation (1999)*

Abyei area, being located at the northern end of Bahr el Ghazal, represents communities exposed mainly to exogenous counter-insurgency warfare, while Gogrial area, being located in the central Bahr el Ghazal region, represents communities primarily exposed to endogenous counter-insurgency warfare. The village in Cuiebet area, being located to the southern end of Bahr el Ghazal, represents communities that had been mainly exposed to drought. The Cuiebet sample area is included for comparison, but it does not represent the main research focus and it is used interchangeably, or on some occasions not considered in the analysis at all when it is not necessary.

The research fieldwork used various approaches to collect the necessary qualitative and quantitative data for assessing vulnerability. Because of the lack of secondary socio-economic household data in Southern Sudan, questionnaire-based household surveys and community surveys were used as the most relevant and best-suited field methods to investigate changes and trends in the level of vulnerability. The use of a hybrid framework consisting of the two methods—sample surveys and participatory methods—is necessary as each provides a separate emphasis but complements the other within the overall research into the changes and trends in vulnerability (Ellis, 2000, p. 198).

Other participatory methods, such as 'participant observation', were used including staying as much as possible within the research communities, which allowed me to obtain information that I could not solicit through other formalistic methods. Besides providing additional information, the 'participant observation' method was also helpful in triangulating the data gained through other methods. The Statistical Package for Social Sciences

(SPSS) was used for quantitative data analysis (Puri, 1996; Rodeghier, 1996; Norusis, 1997; Nachimas and Nachimas, 1996; SPSS, 1998).

The stratification of sample households according to wealth is complex as the understanding of poverty or wealth varies considerably across cultures and disciplines. Despite this apparent variation, it is assumed in most research that 'the poor' can be identified by using a single measure (Ellis, 2000). Many economists favour a universal or 'objective' measure, such as minimum level of consumption or income, while a 'subjective' measure that is based on the community definition of poverty or wealth is preferred by participatory approaches (Bevan and Joireman, 1997). The most commonly used poverty measures, such as household surveys of wealth and consumption poverty, provide systematic differences in wealth ranking, while subjective measures such as personal and community wealth ranking provide minor differences (Bevan and Joireman, 1997, p. 320).

One major disadvantage of the personal wealth ranking measure is that it is subjective, with the head of household making an overall judgment of the wealth status of the household. Another limitation of this measure occurs in communities that have been recipients of food aid, where respondents may be tempted to conceal their real wealth status. Despite these disadvantages, the personal wealth ranking measure takes account of both economic and non-economic aspects as well as relative deprivation, which can be aggregated across research communities (Bevan and Joireman, 1997, p. 324).

Given its relevance and appropriateness in the context of civil war, the personal wealth ranking measure was used in the study by specifically asking household heads to describe the wealth status of their households both before and during the war, with pre-coded possible answers (poor, middle and rich). Instead of using community wealth ranking, households were asked about the community perception of their wealth status. Besides these two questions about the wealth status of the household, household heads were specifically asked about the number of livestock owned as a proxy indicator of wealth. Both community perception and the number of livestock owned by households were used as appropriate measures for determining the wealth status of households.

The Organization of the Book

The book is organised into seven chapters, beginning with this introductory chapter. Generally Chapter 2 reviews and critiques the various approaches to household vulnerability in rural communities. Prior to the review of these approaches, the chapter provides the definition and contextual understanding of the main concepts and terms that are used in this book. The chapter then reviews each of the most important approaches to vulnerability and its distinctive contribution to understanding it. The chapter also assesses the common themes cutting across various approaches to vulnerability and concludes with the relevance of these common themes to the context of civil war.

Chapter 3, on the basis of the preceding chapter, anchors these approaches to vulnerability in a theoretical and conceptual framework, which helps to ask the right questions and to relate the processes of vulnerability to a wider context. The chapter presents the framework to be known as the Risk-Livelihood-Vulnerability Approach and discusses its main components. It continues by analysing each component of the framework in the context of civil war, intending to provide and clarify the main hypotheses of the research. Towards the end of the chapter, the hypothetical livelihood outcomes of civil war, in the light of civil war causation discussion, are drawn from the household vulnerability models. These hypotheses are compared with the outcomes normally observed in the context of drought, particularly across different wealth groups.

Chapter 4 takes further the arguments in the preceding chapter and discusses in more detail the conduct and sustenance of civil war in the context of the Sudan's second civil war. The chapter starts by tracing the evolution of the military doctrine of counter-insurgency warfare in contemporary Sudan. After presenting a detailed account of the counter-insurgency warfare, the chapter then presents and analyses the perceptions of sample households of the main risk events to which they were exposed in the 1990s. The chapter then compares the main characteristics of the most important sources of risk, as identified by sample households in the 1990s. Towards the end of the chapter, the research communities are then compared on the basis of their exposure to the main risk events in the 1990s.

Based on the characteristics of risk events in the 1990s and the level of communities' exposure to these risk events, chapter 5 assesses the livelihood strategies adopted by households to confront the effects of these risk events. On the basis of the empirical fieldwork data, the chapter starts by discussing, analyzing and comparing the ex-ante risk reduction livelihood strategies adopted by sample households and research communities in the 1990s to reduce their susceptibility to these risk events. The chapter then examines the ex post risk mitigation livelihood strategies across research communities and sample households. In particular, the chapter pays special attention to diversification as one of the most important livelihood strategies adopted by rural households to reduce the potential impact of risk events. The chapter then examines and analyses separately the status of and investment in social capital as one of the important livelihood strategies adopted by rural communities.

Chapter 6 attempts to provide an understanding of the level of vulnerability and resilience, as possible livelihood outcomes of the risk management strategies adopted by households in the 1990s. The chapter recognizes the complexity of measuring vulnerability, particularly in the context of civil war, and provides the most relevant indicators to assess the three elements of vulnerability, susceptibility, sensitivity, and resilience. In particular, the level of susceptibility is measured in terms of frequency of displacement, while sensitivity and resilience are respectively measured in terms of depletion of assets and consumption level. Based on the fieldwork empirical data, each of these three elements of vulnerability is then analysed and examined across research communities and sample households. The most distinctive feature of this chapter is that the three elements of vulnerability are associated with the main characteristics (sex, initial wealth, education, age, marital status) of household heads to provide a nuanced understanding of the type of households who were most vulnerable in the 1990s.

Chapter 7 summarises the major findings from the empirical chapters. The chapter starts with teasing out the implications of the empirical findings for understanding and research, by referring to the theoretical framework provided in Chapter 3. The chapter then concludes with lessons drawn for policy and practical implications for intervention.

CHAPTER TWO

Vulnerability Approaches:
Review, Critique and Gaps

T his chapter focuses on reviewing and critiquing various approaches
that analyse the determinants of household vulnerability in rural
African communities. Prior to the discussion of these approaches,
Section 2 provides definitions and a discussion of the main key concepts and
terms that will be used throughout the book. The approaches are discussed
in Section 3 and include quantitative approach, food insecurity approach,
entitlement approach, complex emergency approach, asset-vulnerability
approach, social risk management approach and livelihood approach. These
approaches have in common the fact that they attempt to provide an understanding of the level of vulnerability of households exposed to external
shocks and risk events. Interestingly most of these approaches consider the
assets available to individuals or households as crucial in understanding the
options available to them, the strategies they adopt for survival, and their
vulnerability to adverse trends and events. Despite the common themes
that are shared by these approaches, each approach distinctively focuses on
specific aspects of the determinants of household vulnerability. The chapter
then concludes in Section 4 with the relevance of some arguments provided
by various approaches to vulnerability analysis in the context of civil war.

Concepts and Definitions

The identification and definition of the main concepts that will be used in this chapter are crucially important in providing some foundations and in setting the key contextual considerations that inform the rest of the book. The main relevant concepts and definitions that need further elaboration are risk, livelihood, assets, social capital, diversification, vulnerability, civil war and household. Though these concepts are widely used in contemporary writings on risk management, their meanings are often elusive due to their vagueness or due to various definitions being used by different sources.

Risk and Uncertainty

Generally, risk is a commonly used term as it is applied to nearly every human action, yet it remains poorly understood and defined not only because of semantic definition problems but also because the analysis of risk management hinges crucially on its definition. The difficulty in defining 'risk' has been emphasised by Stiglitz (1974), who compares 'risk' to 'love' in that we have a good idea of what it is, but we cannot define it precisely. In an attempt to avoid a precise definition of risk, some economists (Rothschild and Stiglitz, 1971; Arrow, 1971) tend to define risk as 'what risk averters will pay to avoid'. On the other hand others (Anderson, 1973; Dillon, 1971) adopt a finance theory approach in using the variance of returns on investment as a proxy for risk.

The word 'risk' is originally derived from the early Italian word 'risicare', which means 'to dare' and presents risk as a choice rather than a fate (Bernstein, 1996:8). Most British English dictionaries focus on the unpleasant side of risk and define risk with words along the lines of the possibility of suffering hazard or exposure to this. For example, while risk in the United States and the United Kingdom is defined according to their dictionaries as 'the chance of disaster or loss', the term means in Australia 'variability in possible outcomes' (Dillon, 1971). In the context of the Dinka – the research community - the Dinka words that are synonymous with risk are ngwel (Ngok) or angol (Rek), words that are associated with exposure to hazard or disaster. Unlike other disciplines, finance theory focuses on the pleasant side of risk and views risk as potentially profitable. Carter et al

(1996) argue that risks are not all bad as it is not uncommon to deliberately take a risk that potentially has a significant desirable outcome.

Despite the ambiguity in the definition of risk, most economists tend to refer to 'risk' as uncertain events (probability of occurrence) and outcomes (expected utility) with known probability distributions, while 'uncertainty' is referred to as uncertain events with an unknown probability distribution. Though a distinction is made between risk and uncertainty, economists continue to use 'risk' and 'uncertainty' interchangeably, but in most cases, the term 'risk' is widely used to refer to 'uncertainty'.

Psychologists, on the other hand, challenge any definition of risk that is based on risk aversion, as other subjective values are equally important (Bem, 1980). They argue that humans do not behave according to the mathematical formula because they have their subjective notions of probabilities (Bem, 1980; Cohen, 1964). Many psychologists have shown that these subjective probabilities are largely influenced by the characteristics of the decision-maker and the social settings that can predispose an individual to take greater or lesser risks in pursuit of desirable outcomes (Kogan and Wallach, 1967; Bem, 1980; Cohen, 1964).

Generally, the common denominator in all definitions of risk is that a risk is fundamentally composed of a cause, about which there may be some uncertainty and an effect or impact about which there may also be some uncertainty. In light of this discussion, the following definition of risk (uncertainty) is suggested to describe the meaning of the term as it is used throughout this book:

> *'Risk is understood, in the context of rural livelihoods, in terms of the exposure that is fundamentally caused by uncertain events that are accompanied by uncertain effects (outcome) on livelihoods'.*

As the probability distribution of the occurrence of civil war, particularly counter-insurgency warfare as the focus of the study, is unknown, the terms 'risk' and 'uncertainty' will interchangeably be used throughout this book. The people exposed to violent conflict and counterinsurgency warfare have their notion of probabilities of such risks. The managerial aspect of this definition is that risk is decomposed into manageable and unmanageable components. While the causes of risk (risk events) are generally perceived to be beyond human influence, its uncertain effects (outcomes) on livelihoods can be influenced by human actions. There is a growing recognition that human action through collective global actions, rather than a mere individual household's actions, could influence risk events such as global warming. Such an argument is even more relevant and plausible in the case of risk events such as civil war and economic shocks. In the context of civil war, community exposure to the risk events is well captured by the manner in which the civil war is being conducted, particularly counter-insurgency warfare, rather than a conventional war between rebels and states as discussed in Chapter 4.

Livelihood

The concept of livelihood is central to risk management approaches, particularly in rural areas. While the concept of livelihood is gaining recognition in development studies, it is less accepted in most economic studies, as they tend to focus on income and consumption as net results of a living, rather than on the general concept of livelihood. Also, the distinction between assets, livelihood activities and income is somewhat blurred. Though livelihood and income are not synonymous, they are apparently inextricably related, as income constitutes the result at a given point in time of the livelihood process (Ellis, 2000:10) or the processes of its components, such as activities and access. Interestingly both livelihood and its components, such as activities and access, are all processes that are hard to separate or measure.

Like risk, the concept of livelihood has dominated the writings on poverty, risk management, social protection and rural development, but it has a rather elusive meaning (Ellis, 2000:7). Swift (1989:11) provides, without explicitly using the term 'livelihood', a comprehensive description, linkages and end results of the main components of livelihood in terms of assets (endowments), production (activities), exchange (access) and consumption (end result). Chambers and Conway (1992:2) later explicitly defined livelihood in terms of its main components such as capabilities, assets and activities. As the meaning of 'capabilities' overlaps with that of assets and activities, Ellis (2000:10) modifies the definition of livelihood to emphasise livelihood as process and access and defines livelihood in terms of assets, activities including income, and access to these assets.

The confusion in the concept of livelihood stems from whether livelihood is a process or an outcome and the overlapping and inextricably interrelated meaning of its components. The Oxford English Dictionary definition of livelihood reflects such confusion, as livelihood is referred to as a 'means of a living' or an 'occupation or employment'. In the Dinka language, the term livelihood is synonymous with 'peer', that literally means 'a living'. As this definition of livelihood as a 'means of living' is more comprehensive and directs attention to the way a living is obtained, the definition that emphasises 'occupation' is somewhat limited, as it focuses on only one component of livelihood. Consistent with the framework provided by Swift (1989:11) and the definition provided by Ellis (2000:10) and in the light of the literal Dinka meaning of the term 'livelihood', the following definition of livelihood is used throughout this book:

> *'A livelihood consists of the assets, the livelihood activities and the access to these, that together constitute a means to a living (peer) of the individual or household'.*

Assets and Social Capital:

Assets are generally described as resources or stocks of capital that can be used directly, or indirectly, to generate the means of survival of the household or to sustain its material well- being at different levels above survival (Ellis, 2000:31). The distinctive feature of assets is that they either exist as a stock, giving rise to a flow of output, or they are brought into being when a surplus is generated between production and consumption, thus enabling an investment in future productive capacity. Though assets are commonly accepted as essential components of livelihood, there is disagreement over the definition and composition of assets. Swift (1989:10) defines assets to include investment (human, physical, natural), stores (liquid and non-liquid stocks) and claims (social capital – horizontal and vertical, including the international community). Other researchers (Scoones, 1998; Moser, 1998; Ellis, 2000; Siegel and Alwang, 1999) later rearranged Swift's (1989) categorisation of assets into various groupings, but mainly into natural, physical, financial, human, and social capital. Alternatively, assets are categorised into tangible assets (natural, human, physical, financial) and intangible assets (social, location and infrastructure, and political and institutional assets). While most economic analyses focus on productive tangible assets (physical and human), sociologists and anthropologists often focus on intangible assets (Siegel and Alwang, 1999:10).

While natural capital refers to the natural resource base (land, water, forest, pastures and fisheries), physical capital includes productive assets (tools, equipment, work animals), basic household assets (housing, household goods, storage and utensils) and stocks (liquid and non-liquid stocks such as livestock, food, cash and jewellery). Human capital, on the other hand, refers to household composition and size, education, skills, knowledge, ability to labour, health and nutritional status, while social capital includes social ties and networks, association and intra-household dynamics.

The debate about the definition, coverage and efficacy of intangible assets, such as social capital, in the context of risk management, is far from being settled. While Fine (1999) describes the concept of social capital as ambiguous and chaotic as it draws its meaning from abstract studies, others provide different definitions; many of them refer to the manifestations of social capital rather than to social capital itself. Putnam (1993), for instance, defines social capital as the informal and organised reciprocal networks of trust and the norms embedded in the social organisation of communities. Fukuyama (2001:7) defines social capital as informal norms that are rooted in traditional virtues and promote co-operation between individuals and groups.

In the context of the rural Dinka community, people attach considerable value to personalised social networks and ties, as an essential asset that requires investment as part of their risk management strategies. These social networks, trust and ties are intertwined in the Dinka way of life and the ideal of human relations known as 'cieng', which is traditionally guided and reinforced by ideals of human dignity (dheeng) (Deng, 1999:59). Whether or not this accords with particular definitions of social capital, social networks, trust and ties do play an important role in rural livelihoods. In the light of this discussion and the definitions provided by Putnam (1993) and Fukuyama (2001), the following definition of social capital is proposed as describing the meaning of the term as it is used throughout this book:

'Social capital is the stock of informal and organised reciprocal net-works of trust and norms that are embedded in a traditional way of life (cieng), guided by traditional ideals of human dignity (dheeng) and that promote co-operation between individuals and among groups'.

Diversification

The term diversification is one of the few concepts that is widely recognised and dominates most writings on risk management approaches, poverty reduction and rural development, but with no or limited consensus on its meaning and uses. While economic development literature uses the term diversification to define the structural transformation of the economy, the popular use of the term diversification tends simply to mean either changing or increasing the number of assets or activities at the household level (Siegel and Alwang, 1999:23 and Ellis, 2000:15).

Most of the current uses of the concept of diversification are based on finance theory that uses the term diversification to describe the allocation of financial assets to maximise returns on a portfolio of assets, subject to a given level of risk. Siegel and Alwang (1999:23) recognise the misconceptions about the meaning and use of diversification and attribute much of the confusion to attempts at drawing parallels from the finance literature, which is not entirely appropriate in the case of non-financial assets.

Ellis (2000:14) also recognises confusion over the terms diversity and diversification and clarifies this confusion by referring to 'diversity' as the existence, at a point in time, of many different income sources, while 'diversification' interprets the creation of diversity as an ongoing social and economic process. Even with this clarification between diversity and diversification, the term diversification continues to be used in the limited definition of livelihood that focuses on assets or incomes. Ellis (2000:15) provides a relatively comprehensive definition of rural livelihood diversification that emphasises the increasingly diverse portfolio of activities and assets. This definition falls short of incorporating the notion of access as an important component of livelihood. The definition also focuses only on an increase in the number of assets and activities and ignores changes in assets and activities as an important component of livelihood diversification. It is important also to make a distinction between diversification related to livelihood activities

(Ellis, 1998) and that related to assets portfolio (Dercon, 1993). Though both types of diversification refer to the main components of livelihood, their distinction is important in understanding rural livelihoods and the risk-related behaviours of households faced with shocks and risk events.

In the light of these discussions and the current definitions of livelihood, the following definition of rural livelihood diversification is suggested below and will be used throughout this book:

> *'Rural livelihood diversification is the process by which rural households change or increase their number of assets, activities and the means of accessing these as part of their risk management strategies'.*

Vulnerability

The term vulnerability is a central concept in risk management, but it requires a concise and precise understanding if it is to be a useful concept. There is often confusion, though it is gradually fading out, in perceiving vulnerability as a synonym for poverty, although there is an inextricable interrelationship between them. The differentiation between vulnerability and poverty was made clear by Moser (1998:3) who emphasises that while poor people are usually among the most vulnerable, not all vulnerable people are poor. Despite growing recognition of the important distinction between vulnerability and poverty, there is still no common consensus over meaning and definition of vulnerability. In most of the writings on poverty and risk management, the term vulnerability is often used to refer to exposure to risk events and the household's capacity to confront these risk events.

Swift (1989:9) was among the first researchers who articulated the concept of vulnerability by identifying its determinants (proximate and primary variables), as well as by linking the concept of vulnerability to external and internal factors. Chambers (1989:1) articulates further the concept of vulnerability by defining it, differentiating it from poverty, as well as by encapsulating both the process and the state of being within the concept of vulnerability. Chambers (1989:1) defines the concept of vulnerability in terms of exposure to risk events or shocks (external factors) and the capacity to cope with them (internal factors). Other definitions of vulnerability that developed later were shaped by the initial contributions of both Swift (1989) and Chambers (1989).

The concept of vulnerability is now gaining momentum in studies on poverty and rural development, but with no agreement on the meaning of vulnerability. Some researchers define vulnerability in terms of exposure to external shock, while others emphasise either internal factors or both external and internal factors. For example, Glewwe and Hall (1998) refer to vulnerability as exposure to specific shocks or changes in socio-economic conditions, while Holzmann and Jorgensen (2000:6) define vulnerability as the likelihood of being harmed by unforeseen events, or as susceptibility to exogenous shocks. In the field of food security, a well-accepted definition of vulnerability is 'an aggregate measure, for a given population or region, of the risk of exposure to food insecurity, and the ability of the population to cope with the consequences of the insecurity' (Downing, 1991). Others emphasise the impact value of risk events in defining vulnerability. This definition of vulnerability in terms of exposure to external shocks or impact value is consistent with the Oxford English Dictionary definition of vulnerability, that refers to the likelihood of being physically or emotionally hurt, or exposed to attack.

Siegel and Alwang (1999:5) define vulnerability as both an ex-ante and ex-post state, associated with the probability of falling into a state below the minimum level of survival or destitution. Bayliss-Smith (1991:7) and Davies (1993:62) show the process through which exposure to external shocks unfold into internal dynamics (resilience and sensitivity) that largely determine and explain the level of household vulnerability. While resilience refers to the capacity of households to deal with shocks and resist downward movement in well-being, sensitivity refers to the severity and intensity with which the shock is experienced, particularly the extent to which the asset base of the household is prone to depletion following adjustment to risk (Davies, 1993:62).

In the context of the Dinka, there is a clear distinction between a poor person and a vulnerable person. While in Dinka a poor person is referred to as ayur or angang, which literally means 'poor', the vulnerable person is referred to in the Dinka language as raan nyop, which means a 'soft' or 'weak' person. The opposite of nyop is ril, indicating the kind of strength, energy and enterprise that a young man is expected to exhibit after initiation. The Dinka term of nyop expresses weaknesses in the face of strong forces and clearly captures the internal dimensions of vulnerability, particularly lack of resilience and high sensitivity. So a weak person (raan nyop) in Dinka is not necessary poor (angang)

In the light of the preceding discussion, the concept of vulnerability is the product of an interaction between risk and livelihood, with risk capturing the external dynamics of household vulnerability, while livelihood captures the internal dynamics and process in confronting shocks and risk events. Making use of the definition provided by Chambers (1989:1) and in the light of the preceding discussion, the following definition of vulnerability is suggested to describe the term throughout this book:

> *'Vulnerability is defined as exposure to risk (susceptibility), the intensity with which the risk event is experienced (sensitivity), and the capacity to resist downward movement in well-being as a result of the occurrence of a risk event (resilience).'*

Civil War and Counterinsurgency

The term 'civil war' is widely used but rarely defined. The few researchers, who dare to define it, tend to be selective to suit their argument, disciplines or research interests. As a result, the meaning of 'civil war' becomes elusive, either because of vagueness or due to different definitions being encountered in different sources. For example, the term civil war refers to various terms, such as internal conflicts, political violence, armed conflict, civil strife, civil conflict and 'new wars'. These terms reflect either an emphasis on specific aspects of civil war or disciplinary biases or an unsettled debate about the causes of civil war. This elusive and vague definition of civil war allows some researchers to come up with some astonishing empirical findings that hardly reflect the reality and the context of civil war.

Most economists use the definition provided by the Stockholm International Peace Research Institute (SIPRI) and Sivard's World Military and Social Expenditures that define civil war in terms of any violence resulting in more than 1000 conflict-related deaths per annum within a country (Luckham et al., 2001). Green (1997) defines a civil war as 'generalised, sustained violence afflicting most or all of a State…' Stewart et al (1997) define civil war in terms of major participants or groups within a state with the political goals of challenging or upholding government authority and involving large-scale violence.

Gurr (1970:4) defines political violence as collective attacks within a political community against the political regime that involve the use of violence to attain ends within or outside the political order. Gurr (1970:11) identifies three forms of political violence, namely turmoil (relatively spontaneous, unorganised political violence with substantial popular participation); conspiracy (highly organised political violence with limited participation); and internal war (highly organised political violence designed to overthrow or to secede from the authority of the regime with widespread popular participation).

The term 'war' is generally defined in English dictionaries as fighting between nations, conflict or contest, while the term 'civil' refers and relates to the citizens of a state as opposed to the armed forces. This literally makes the term 'civil war' describe the war that is waged by citizens against the state, as opposed to war between nations. In the Dinka language, the term 'tong' is similar in meaning to 'war', but it literally means 'spear'. While the term 'tong' encompasses all types of war, the term 'civil war' is literally translated as 'tong baai' that means 'people's war' or 'war of the country'. With the increasing effects of civil war over time, the Dinka have gradually changed the term tong baai to that of tong riak (war of disaster or destruction).

In light of the aforementioned definitions, the term 'civil war' is here defined as:

> *'An organised armed conflict that has (i) caused death, displacement and loss of assets; (ii) challenged government authority; (iii) widespread popular participation; (iv) occurred within the recognised international boundaries of that state; (v) involved the state, including its militia, and rebels as the main combatants.'*

This suggested definition is used throughout this book to describe the meaning of the term 'civil war'. Unlike other definitions, this definition captures the main features of civil war as risk events particularly its outcomes, such as death, displacement or the loss of assets. Besides civil war, the conduct of civil wars is more important to rural livelihoods than civil wars themselves. In particular, two types of warfare are important, namely insurgency warfare and counter-insurgency warfare. While insurgency warfare refers to the guerrilla warfare waged by rebels against the state, counter-insurgency warfare refers to the warfare carried out by militia forces used by the state to oppose insurgency warfare. Given its importance, counter-insurgency warfare will be used interchangeably with civil war throughout this book.

Household: The Livelihood Unit of Analysis:

The appropriate unit for livelihood and poverty analysis has not been con-clusively established. Sen (1981) recognises the difficulty that arises from the fact that the family rather than the individual is the natural unit of poverty and consumption behaviour analysis, because of different preferences and the contribution of each member and the importance of economies of scale. Generally, economists use the household as a single decision-making unit (unitary model) with the inherent assumption that household behaviour could be adequately described by the single set of preferences of an altruistic household head (Ellis, 2000:19).

This assumption of the household head acting as a 'benevolent dictator' has been challenged by Haddad et al. (1997) who recognise that deci-sion-making within a household involves a complex interplay of conflict and co-operation of individuals with separate preferences (collective model). Crehan (1992) also argues that the household is an infinitely variable social arena that is difficult to define in many cultural settings and may not even exist in some instances. In recognition of the importance of kinship net-works for household survival, it has been argued that the family rather than the household is the appropriate social unit for livelihood research (Bruce and Lloyd, 1997).

Despite the criticism of unitary household models, alternative models of the household remain limited by the abstract nature of their formulation (Hart, 1995). It is recognised also that the predictive capability of collective models of the household in analysing and explaining household responses to adverse trends and risk events is not different from that of unitary models (Haddad et al., 1997). A large body of research has clearly shown the advan-tage of using the household as a unit of analysis to detect variation within and across household responses to risk events and shocks (Ellis, 2000:19). For example, Baber (1998) uses the concept of the household as the basic unit of analysis and then disaggregates it into analytically tractable sub-groups for livelihood analysis.

Despite the recognition of the problems associated with the household as a unit of analysis, the distinctive feature of the household as a social arena in which intense social and economic interdependencies occur between a group of individuals makes it a relevant unit of social and economic analysis. Generally, the household is conceived or defined as a social group which resides in the same place, shares the same meals, and makes joint or co-ordinated decisions over resource allocation and income pooling (Ellis, 1993). Naeraa et al. (1993:14) use the approach of a 'common pot' to define a household as a group of people who regularly eat together on a daily basis. Similarly, the International Crops Research Institute for the Semi-Arid Tropics (ICRISAT) defines a household as a group of individuals who share a residence and eat from a common pot (Carter, 1997:558). Though this definition of household places the emphasis on co-residence, there is a need for a more spatially extended understanding of household, without invoking the concept of the entire extended family. In operationalising the entitlement approach, Seaman (2000:136) uses the household, a nuclear family or a much larger group, as the smallest coherent unit of analysis for the food economy approach and defines it as a group of people who contribute to a common economy and rely on the income from that economy.

Generally local concepts of 'household' often differ significantly from any fixed academic definition and the set of derived terms developed by social scientists to define a 'household' can rarely be directly applied to particular cultural contexts. Even within the discipline of anthropology, definitions of a household are by no means standardised (Messer, 1983). For example, Bender (1967:496) recognises the need to define family in terms of a kinship relationship but ended up defining a 'household' simply as a residence group that carries out domestic functions. It is apparent that although households contain one or more features, such as co-residence, joint production, shared consumption, and kinship links, no particular single feature or combination of these features constitutes a universal definition of the household (Gittelsohn and Mookherji, 1997). Instead, the concept of the household is context-specific and varies from culture to culture and probably within cultures as well.

In the context of agro-pastoralist communities, such as the Dinka of Southern Sudan (the research community), the concepts of household and family are complex and intertwined. For example, anthropologists classify the social structure of Dinka, using English expressions, into main tribal groups, tribe, sub-tribe and section (Liendhardt, 1958). For Dinka, the social units (tribe, sub-tribe and section) below the level of tribal group are called wuot (i.e. are all associated with the subdividing of grazing land (wut) that means cattle camp). A dry-season cattle camp (wut) contains a number of gal (singular gol), that are dung-fires around which an individual lineage tether their cattle and hence each wut contains different and many lineages. In order to differentiate between tribe, sub-tribe and section, one has to understand the cultural context, which is hardly captured, by the fixed and standardised classification. The cattle camp (wut) is the analogy used by the Dinka to refer to both the territorial and lineage make-up of society. Crosscutting the concept of wut is the concept of dieth or (dhien) that literally means birth but is used to refer to clan or lineage. Just as wut can be seen in the dimension of space, so dhieth links a person back in time with his/her ancestors. Then each dhien/gol consists of families, which are usually known in Dinka as baai, referring to residence, or as mac thok, which implicitly refers to shared pot and closer lineage and kinship links. Also each family consists of a number of wives with their children, which is known as hoon thok, literally means the 'door of the house'.

As the Dinka gradually move from purely pastoralist livelihoods to agro-pastoralist livelihoods with a permanent settlement, they adapt their pastoralist social structure and organisation to their permanent settlement (baai) that is synonymous with wut. For example, in Dinka language, the term 'baai' refers to the spatial definition as co-residence (homestead), but it also made up of several and different lineages (dhien). The distinction between household and family becomes complicated in the context of polygamous societies, as all members of such families share the homestead (co-residence) but do not necessarily eat from the 'common pot'. In the context of polygamous societies, the head of the family (invariably a man) makes or co-ordinates decisions regarding resource allocation and income pooling, particularly cattle, with each individual wife (hoon thok) taking her own decisions on crop production. The situation is even more complex, as the grown-up children in the larger family share food and meals and in most cases, women share as well. In such social settings children, though they 'belong' to their mothers, are generally considered as the children - particularly the grown-up children - of the larger family and receive indiscriminate treatment and care from all members of the family as a way of nurturing a sense of togetherness.

This clearly shows that the conventional definition of a household that places emphasis on spatial proximity and the sharing of meals will not be appropriate in the context of polygamous societies. In order to overcome this overlapping between the extended family and the polygamous household, Devereux and Naeraa (1996) identify a compound (co-residence) as a larger extended family that consists of a number of households (a man with his wives and children), with each household divided into sub-households (a wife with her children). In such polygamous settings, there are specific asset and livelihood activities that will require using the larger family, or even the community, as units of analysis, while in other specific cases a household or the individual members of the household could be used as the units of analysis. In the context of the Dinka of Southern Sudan, it is more appropriate to use the definition of the household that is flexible enough to incorporate some aspects of extended family, particularly issues related to livestock ownership and management. For this book and in the context of agro-pastoralist Dinka society, the term 'household' is defined as follows:

> 'Household refers to the smallest coherent, productive and consumption socio-economic unit that is composed of either a woman with her children or a larger family, who share livestock and food and make joint or co-ordinated decisions regarding resources allocation, income pooling and livestock management.'

Risk Management and Vulnerability Approaches

> "The revolutionary idea that defines the boundary between modern times and the past is the mastery of risk: the notion that the future is more than a whim of the gods and that men and women are not passive before nature" (Bernstein, 1996:1)

Risk is a central feature and part of the life of all communities and its management has been one of the most challenging preoccupations of mankind. The concept of risk, particularly its understanding, measurement and management, has been central to the work of a group of thinkers who have managed to improve understanding of risk and to convert risk-taking into one of the prime catalysts that drives modern society. The modern conception of risk is rooted in the Hindu–Arabic numbering system that reached the West seven to eight hundred years ago (Bernstein, 1996:3). The discovery of the theory of probability, the mathematical heart of the concept of risk, in 1654 by a French mathematician, Blaise Pascal made it possible for people to make decisions and forecast the future with the help of numbers (ibid.).

This discovery was followed by the derivation of the Law of Large Numbers and methods of statistical sampling in 1703 by Bernoulli, the Law of Averages and normal distribution by de Moivre and eventually the theory of risk aversion and rational behaviour in 1730 by Bernoulli (Bernstein, 1996:5). While the Law of Large Numbers and the Law of Averages are essential ingredients for quantifying risk, the theory of risk aversion and the dominant paradigm of rational behaviour laid the groundwork for the modern principles of risk and investment management. In 1875 Galton discovered regression to the mean, and this was followed by Markowitz's discovery in 1952 that demonstrated mathematically why "putting all your eggs in one basket" is an unacceptably risky strategy, and why diversification is the most effective risk management strategy (Berstein, 1996:6).

It is widely recognised that risk, human reactions to it and the transformation in attitudes toward risk management largely explain economic growth, the improved quality of life, and technological progress in contemporary Western societies. By formalising a theory of choice and rational behaviour and by defining a rational process of risk-taking, these theorists have managed to provide the "missing ingredient" that has propelled economic progress; through the emergence of insurance and of stock markets thus permitting a reduction in the social amount of risk-bearing (Arrow, 1971). As argued by Bernstein (1996:3), the capacity to manage risk, and with it, the appetite to take risk and make forward-looking choices, are key elements of the energy that drives forward the economic system.

Despite the apparent improvement in risk management in capitalist societies, rural communities in developing countries are still prone and vulnerable to risk events, such as natural disasters, bad weather, health-related problems, socio-economic shocks and civil war. The important question is: why are rural communities in pre-capitalist societies vulnerable to these risk events that seem not to pose major threats in capitalist economies? In an attempt to explain the current level of vulnerability in the rural areas of developing countries, various approaches to risk management are reviewed with their relevance to the context of civil war. These approaches include a quantitative approach that is based on rational behaviour paradigm, food insecurity, entitlement framework, complex emergencies, assets–vulnerability framework, social risk management approach and livelihood approach.

Quantitative Approach: Rational Behaviour Paradigm

> *"...all men, or the generality at least, wish what is honourable, but, when tested, choose what is profitable." Aristotle (adopted from Cook, 1966).*

Risk and human reactions to it have played an important role in shaping and explaining the values of various contemporary economic institutions and the systems of various communities at different levels of economic development. The developments of choices among probability distribution and the modern theory of statistical inference have widened understanding of choices and rational behaviour under uncertainty and risk. These developments have undoubtedly shaped the modern risk management that is increasingly driven by mathematical apparatus.

There are conflicting views about the prevalence of risk aversion and rational behaviour, the basic premises of risk management, in low-income economies. There was a sterile debate in the 1960s among anthropologists, with an occasional contribution by economists, about the level of rational behaviour in pre-market societies. One group of anthropologists, the 'substantivists', argued that choices and behaviour in pre-market societies are not economically 'rational', as individuals are not motivated by selfish propensities for economic gain, but by simple, unadulterated subsistence needs (Dalton, 1961). The group also argued that a pre-market society is based on two principles of behaviour, reciprocity and redistribution, which order the process of production and distribution and result in the economic system being submerged or embedded in social organisation (Dalton, 1961; Cook, 1966).

The main argument of this group is that the motive of material gain or profit is not 'natural' to human beings but is operative only under special circumstances of time and space, and it is not surprising that human behaviour in pre-capitalist society is inherently irrational, altruistic and devoid of the pursuit of self-interest (Cook, 1966). The other group of anthropologists, the 'formalists' argue that individuals in pre-market societies are capable of rational maximising behaviour and that conventional economic theory is fully applicable to pre-market societies (Cook, 1966). Posner (1980) argues that the rationality of 'economic man' is a matter of consequences, not of states of mind, and concluded that people in pre-capitalist societies do not consciously calculate the costs and benefits of alternative courses of actions, any more than the modern consumer does when buying one good instead of another.

It is interesting to observe that the social organisation, institutions and values of the societies, particularly reciprocity and social redistribution mechanisms - the bases of survival in pre-capitalist societies - are largely blamed for the irrational behaviour, sluggish economic growth and rudimentary risk management approaches and vulnerability in pre-capitalist societies. It has been shown that the distinctive institutions (social capital) of pre-market societies, including reciprocal exchange, marriage, polygamy, the size of kinship groups and the value placed on certain traits such as generosity, can be explained as adaptations to uncertainty and high information costs (Posner, 1980). The views expressed by some anthropologists, particularly substantivists, concerning irrational economic behaviour in pre-market societies, prompted many researchers, economists and non-economists, in the 1970s and 1980s to reassess the prevalence of risk aversion attitudes among rural communities in low-income economies.

Some economists carried out experimental studies to assess risk aversion and preferences towards risk in pre-capitalist societies as a way of assessing their rational allocation decisions. The findings of these studies generally support the existence of moderate risk aversion and rational behaviour ((Moscardi and de Janvry, 1977; and Hazell, 1982), while other studies (Binswanger, 1980; Sillers, 1980; Walker, 1980; Grisley, 1980; and Antle, 1987) suggest that a small proportion of farmers demonstrate either risk neutrality, risk preference or extreme risk aversion.

Although these studies found rational behaviour in low-income environments, Alderman and Paxson (1992:5) criticised these studies as they ignored other factors such as market imperfections, particularly asymmetric information that may respectively overestimate or underestimate the level of risk aversion. Alderman and Paxon (1992:1) argue that the well-known problems of moral hazard, information asymmetries, and deficiencies in the ability to enforce contracts, may explain why households in developing countries will not effectively manage risk as a result of incomplete or absent insurance markets. The findings of these studies provide inconclusive evidence about risk preferences and rational behaviour in the allocation of resources in pre-capitalist societies.

This unsettled debate about rational behaviour in pre-capitalist societies encouraged non-economist researchers in the 1970s and 1980s, when famine was becoming recurrent in many low-income countries, to engage in understanding better household responses to drought as a major risk event. Based on empirical work in India, Jodha (1975) shows how households facing food deficit adopt various coping strategies, including curtailment in current consumption or 'choosing to starve' rather than selling their assets. This study was then followed by various studies in relation to African famines in the early 1980s that contributed to the compilation of a vast literature on 'coping strategies'. These studies show that households faced with food deficit tend to follow a sequenced response in which the conservation of assets that would permit them to resume their previous livelihoods is a key tactic (Watts, 1983; 1988; Corbett, 1988; Swift, 1989; Devereux, 1993). These sequences of responses to food deficit or shocks are usually referred to as coping strategies (Corbett, 1988; Davies, 1993; Ellis, 2000).

Corbett (1988) formulates, on the basis of four detailed case studies, a three-stage model of 'household coping strategies', namely insurance mechanisms (undertaken to minimise the risk of production failure); disposal of productive assets (coping); and destitution (failure to cope). Davies (1993:62) makes a distinction between coping strategies (means to bridge the food gap) and adaptive strategies (designed to facilitate bounce-back to normalcy and to resist shocks). Devereux (1993:53) also makes a distinction, on the basis of empirical evidence, between consumer protection strategies (market and non-market transfers) and consumption modification strategies (designed to reduce or diversify consumption or to reduce the number of consumers of the household's food).

The large literature on 'coping strategies' as short-term household responses to the adverse effects of drought in the 1970s and 1980s has provided evidence of rational behaviour among rural households in pre-capitalist societies. This clearly shows that people are not passive victims but take a proactive response to shocks and risk events. Though the early literature on 'coping strategies' focused on consumption rationing, it shows that such austerity measures are a strategic response to livelihood shocks, as it is related not only to bridging consumption deficits but also to balance this priority against longer-term economic and social costs (Devereux, 2001a:249). Watts (1983) shows that the sequencing of these coping strategies is determined by the effectiveness of each strategy (in terms of bridging consumption deficit) and the cost and reversibility of each action. Devereux (1993) shows empirically that coping strategies with low long-run costs are adopted first, while those with higher costs, which are difficult to reverse, are adopted later. Recent studies have also assessed household longitudinal responses to economic shocks in the urban context of low-income countries and found that urban households exhibit not only rational behaviour in their asset management but are also managers of complex asset portfolios (Moser, 1998).

These studies clearly indicate that coping strategies, such as the decisions to ration food consumption, are not only rational but can be understood as risk management strategies that aim at managing the current endowment set (assets) to maximise the household's long-term entitlements in a way that will minimise vulnerability to future risk events. These findings allow the linking of the observed level of vulnerability in low-income economies with the level of asset ownership rather than with the irrational behaviour of households.

Though there is now agreement and consensus over the prevalence of rational behaviour among households exposed to drought and economic shocks in pre-capitalist societies, there is little evidence about whether the behaviour of households exposed to the risk of civil wars is rational or not. As coping strategies literature was developed in relation to drought, and given the fact that civil war is now a major cause of rural vulnerability in Africa, the real research question is: do drought coping strategies apply to war? There is apparently a dearth of information and empirical evidence about the risk-related behaviours or 'coping strategies' of households exposed to protracted civil war. In lieu of empirical evidence on household responses to the adverse effects of civil war, there is a growing perception that the very nature of civil war burdens households with extreme risk aversion attitudes that would inhibit any rational behaviour and proactive livelihood strategies.

Entitlement Approach: Tangible Assets and Markets

As the argument about irrational behaviour among rural communities in pre-capitalist societies was refuted with empirical evidence, some economists came up with arguments that impute the causes of famine vulnerability to poverty. Taking famine as an outcome of vulnerability, Sen (1981) formulated his entitlement approach that provides an analytical framework for examining famine, as well as putting forward a 'new' theory of famine causation (Devereux, 2001a:247). The main argument of the entitlement approach is that vulnerability to famine is largely attributable to one's ability to command food through all legal means and that such ability is determined by one's ownership of tangible assets and the rate at which one can exchange these for food (Sen, 1981:45). In other words, vulnerability to famine is a direct function of the relative poverty that is determined by a household's ownership of tangible resources (labour, land, animals) (Swift, 1989:10).

According to the entitlement approach, vulnerability to famine is a result of relative poverty and/or a failure of households to use their ability to avoid it. This is subsumed in Sen's (1981:45) argument that 'a person starves either because he cannot command enough food or because he does not use his ability to avoid starvation'. As the entitlement approach focuses on the former, it explicitly favours a restrictive view of famine as an 'economic disaster' (Devereux, 2001a:256, Sen, 1981:162) that imputes the root causes of vulnerability to famine to poverty and market forces (Keen, 1994:4). Besides its restrictive view of vulnerability to famine as an 'economic disaster', the entitlement approach fails to consider the concept of risk as an important factor in the analysis of famine causation.

Risk events such as drought and civil war are generally considered as exogenous to the entitlement model, as the determinants of entitlements are only confined to economic factors, such as the level of tangible assets ownership and terms of trade. According to the entitlement approach, vulnerability to famine is static and is synonymous with relative poverty that is measured in terms of tangible assets. Failure to distinguish vulnerability from poverty, as argued by Chambers (1989:1), blurs the distinction and sustains stereotypes of the amorphous and undifferentiated mass of the poor. In examining the causes of the Sahelian famine in the 1970s, Sen (1981:119) attributes the causes of famine to the decline in income and purchasing power of the rural communities, without apportioning any cause to the severe drought in the 1970s that resulted in the food availability decline in the region.

Implicitly, the entitlement approach assumes that exposure to risk events, such as drought, is generic (covariate risk) across households, while relative poverty is the effective variable that would explain differential household vulnerability to famine across households and community groups. As such susceptibility to risk, according to the entitlement approach, is measured in terms of income variability that affects poor households more than non-poor households, in terms of their efforts to smooth consumption and vulnerability to famine. The omission of the determinants of entitlements from the entitlement approach has been criticised by Watts (1991) as a deliberate way of avoiding engagement with the highly politicised context within which famines invariably occur (Devereux, 2001a:256). However, it is crucially important, as discussed in Chapter 5, that the characteristics of risk events and their determinants largely explain and differentiate the level of household vulnerability. The generic and amorphous labelling of risk events blurs a clear understanding of their dynamics and of how they unfold in terms of vulnerability at community and household levels.

One major omission from the entitlement approach is the role of intangible assets, such as social capital, in the famine causation analysis, as assets are narrowly defined in terms of tangible productive assets. Entitlements, as defined by Sen (1981), include all the productive resources owned by a household, including its labour-power, and all its tangible assets. In his detailed analysis of various famines, Sen (1981) focuses almost entirely on the relative role of production and exchange failures in causing particular famines, with no reference to the role of social capital. This increasing reliance on formal markets as the centre-piece of famine causation analysis has generally exposed the entitlement theory to much criticism. Devereux (2001a:255) argues that the entitlement approach has limited relevance to the context of traditional pre-capitalist societies, that are the domain of non-commodity exchange (gift) through reciprocal dependence and social capital.

Besides the inapplicability of the entitlement approach to the context of pre-capitalist societies, the relevance of the approach to the context of civil war created unresolved debate. Sen (1981:49) completely excludes civil war from the entitlement approach and concedes that the approach is defective in the context of civil war, which he considers as parasitic and abnormal.

> *'...while entitlement relations concentrate on rights within the given legal structure in that society, some transfers involve violations of these rights, such as looting or brigandage. When such extra-entitlement transfers are important, the entitlement approach to famines will be defective. On the other hand, most recent famines seem to have taken place in societies with 'law and order', without anything 'illegal' about the processes leading to starvation.'* *(Sen, 1981:49)*

Surely by excluding the role of civil war from the entitlement approach, Sen (1981) must have gravely misjudged and misread the dominant role being played by civil war in causing massive damage to rural communities in Africa, even during the time he was writing his popular book 'Poverty and Famines'. Edkins (1996:559) raises concern about the exclusion of civil war from the entitlement approach, which is formulated to provide a framework for understanding vulnerability and famine causation, and argues, as rightly mentioned by Sen, (1981:49) that the entitlement is 'defective'. De Waal (1990:473) also asserts that the entitlement approach is irrelevant and has no place in the context of civil war.

Devereux (2001a:257-8) emphasises the need to unpack the impact of civil war, particularly its distributional impact on rural livelihoods, prior to any outright rejection of the entitlement approach as a framework for understanding such livelihood shock resulting from civil war. Devereux (2001a:257) recognises the need to treat civil war like other risk events, such as drought, despite their varying level of effect on entitlements and livelihoods. Devereux (ibid.) assesses the effects of civil war on all sources of entitlement and categorises these effects into three clusters; namely disruptive effects (conscription and contraction of local markets); extra-entitlement transfers (requisitioning of grain, raiding of livestock, seizing of food aid); and unruly practices (siege and denial of access). He argues that while the first cluster (disruptive effects) could be incorporated within the entitlement approach, the other two clusters are beyond the scope of the entitlement approach.

The last two clusters are the main characteristics of civil war that determine the severity and intensity of its impact, and such characteristics are similar features of other risk events, such as drought or economic shock. As the entitlement approach treats all risk events as exogenous factors, excluding the main characteristics of civil war from the entitlement approach is not exceptional, as Sen (1981), for example, excludes the severity and intensity of drought from the Sahelian famine causation analysis. As rightly highlighted by Devereux (2001a:131), the entitlement approach seeks to analyse how famines happen rather than why they happen. The emphasis, however, on treating civil war like other risk events is extremely important, as it allows putting civil war in the general framework of risk management, rather than seeing civil war and its characteristics as chaotic and anarchic with effects beyond the household's management.

Complex Emergencies Approach: Political Vulnerability

The term 'Complex Emergencies' itself is not offered as a basic concept to be theorised, but simply as a convenient heuristic framework to help understand post-Cold War disasters (Cliffe and Luckham, 1998, 1999; Goodhand and Hulme, 1999:17). The new global interdependence that emerged after the Cold War in the 1980s has been accompanied by the increasing frequency of large-scale and complex disasters, that are highly politicised and have eluded international humanitarian intervention (Duffield, 1993:131). One main aspect of these complex disasters is that national governments resist humanitarian intervention to reach the needy and victims, and this has resulted in international NGOs filling the gap by establishing an exclusive parallel system that has gradually supplanted indigenous structures (Duffield, 1993:132). Sudan is a case in point, as successive regimes during the mid-1980s and the 1990s have denied access to the needy population and have obstructed emergency operations (Cater, 1986; Deng, 1999). In such a complex context, vulnerability to famine is seen as a complex socio-political crisis and as part of a new post-Cold War phenomenon.

The roots of the 'complex emergency' approach lie in the inadequacies and limitations of the entitlement approach and the coping strategies approach. Entitlements or coping strategies as approaches for understanding famine vulnerability are inadequate to explain the phenomenon of political survival in the context of complex emergencies, as they neglect the issue of power, and consider only the victims of famine. Duffield (1993:134) argues that despite the fact that the literature on coping strategies has informed policy debate about proactive responses taken by people exposed to crises, the literature fails to recognise the underlying power dynamics, as some coping strategies may involve the transfer of assets away from those in distress. Keen (1994:213), on the basis of detailed accounts from Sudan, argues that the real roots of vulnerability to famine may lie less in a lack of purchasing power within the market, than in a lack of people's access to the means of power, political representation and lobbying power.

Interestingly, Keen (1994:214) observes, in the context of Sudan, the positive relationship between markets and violence as the development of a market-oriented economy which has created winners and losers, and argues that these losers resorted to violence in order to survive the harsh realities of uneven development and the market economy. Keen's analysis is built on the insights of Rangasami (1985:1749), who argues that vulnerability to famine is a process with 'winners' and 'losers' and that its understanding necessitates looking at the strategies utilised by both victim and beneficiary, and she defines famines as a 'pressing down' or 'oppression':

Duffield (1993:134) emphasises that it is 'This political as opposed to economic construction of African famine, which has been argued to limit the usefulness of Sen's (1981) entitlement analysis. Drawing heavily on the arguments of Rangasami (1985) and on their own work in conflict zones particularly in the Horn of Africa, the 'complex emergency' theorists (David Keen, Alex de Waal, and Mark Duffield) developed an alternative framework for analysing vulnerability to starvation and famine. The main proposition of this framework is that all disasters have winners as well as losers, with famine resulting from the conscious exercise of power in pursuit of gain or advantage. According to this framework, vulnerability to famine is perceived as an outcome of a process of impoverishment, resulting from the transfer of assets from the weak to the politically strong and through sectarian and counter-insurgency warfare activities.

The 'complex emergency' approach seems to suggest that coping strategies are defective during the civil war and that social capital and safety nets collapse as a result of a conscious strategy of war. De Waal (1996, 1997) argues that social capital is one of the first casualties of civil war and that coping strategies collapse more often when associated with violence than with environmental and economic shocks, as survival strategies are systematically undermined. It is in the light of this complexity of power relations and the political dimension of famine that it cannot be attributed to natural disasters or market failure, nor can it be characterised as a temporary shock if its continuation is advantageous to the powerful (Duffield, 1993:134).

There is no doubt that the 'complex emergencies' approach has added a new and important dimension to vulnerability analysis. The drastic increase in the incidence of famine related to civil war and conflict attests to the important role that is being played by the political vulnerability, rather than economic failure or natural disasters in rural livelihoods, particularly in Africa. This approach, however, complements rather than negates the entitlement approach that has the comparative advantage of unpacking the dynamic effects of generic shocks (political, economic, natural) on the household's livelihood. The 'complex emergency' approach provides a framework for understanding the macro- or meso-political context and the dynamics of power relations.

The argument that the entitlement approach or coping strategies are defective as they overlook the issue of power relations is somewhat weak as these approaches focus on the risk-related behaviours of households exposed to shocks; they do not claim to analyse the determinants of vulnerability. In fact, the analysis of power relations, particularly the strategies adopted by the winners and those in power, will describe the characteristics, intensity and severity of political vulnerability that unfolds differentially at a household level. Clearly the 'complex emergency' approach does not claim that political shock affects all households in the same way, nor do households respond to such shock passively. This clearly indicates that a holistic understanding of vulnerability requires macro-level analysis in order to understand the context of vulnerability, as well as micro-level analysis to understand how such shocks unfold and are responded to by households.

Asset-Vulnerability Approach: The Role of All Assets

The limitations and inadequacy of the entitlement approach necessitate a more comprehensive approach that will consider all assets, particularly intangible assets. Swift (1989) presents a more comprehensive and detailed asset-vulnerability framework that is built upon the entitlement and coping strategies approaches. Unlike other approaches, Swift (1989:8) regroups the factors that determine vulnerability into two distinct categories, namely; proximate and primary factors. While primary factors refer to more general risk events, such as ecological, economic or political processes that determine the status of vulnerability at a community level, proximate factors refer to production, exchange and assets processes that classify and explain vulnerability at the household level.

Swift (1989) divides assets into investments (human capital, physical capital, natural capital), stores (liquid and non-liquid stocks) and claims (other households within the community, patrons, chiefs, other households from other communities, government and the international community). The role of assets is defined to create a buffer between production and exchange activities, which create assets when production exceeds consumption requirements. The notion of claims, as discussed by Swift (1989:11), includes a variety of redistributive processes at all levels (individual, household, community, national and international), with varying expectations of reciprocity. The inclusion of claims to the definition of assets has added a better understanding of the dynamic of vulnerability than have insights from the analysis of production and exchange failures. Another distinctive feature of this framework is that the concept of risk is introduced into the concept and definition of vulnerability. Though Swift (1989) focuses on proximate factors to elaborate the dynamics of vulnerability, he introduces the historical context, including changing trends of primary factors; to better understand the trends and changes in vulnerability over time.

The main argument of this framework is that the dynamics of rural vulnerability are largely determined by both primary and proximate factors. The reduction of assets, including intangible assets such as claims, makes households and communities more vulnerable. Having fewest assets, the poorest households reach the threshold of collapse much faster than others. Also, the low-status groups, who have fewest claims within socially stratified communities, may reach the threshold faster than other groups. A clear distinction is made between assets and poverty. While assets include claims, poverty refers only to produce tangible assets. Such a distinction makes it necessary to link vulnerability to assets, rather than to poverty. This distinction explains why poor households in rural areas are more vulnerable than poor households in urban areas, as the latter exercise more effective claims on the government than poor rural people (Lipton, 1977). Swift (1989:14) extends this argument of the role of claims to the context of civil war and attributes the cause of increasing vulnerability during the civil war to the breakdown and collapse of the moral economy and the abrogation of claims by the government.

In fact, Swift (1989) was the first to implicitly develop the asset-vulnerability framework, which has been widely adopted by various researchers to analyse vulnerability. Moser (1998) applies the asset-vulnerability framework to study household responses to the deteriorating economic situation in the context of poor urban communities. Moser (1998:5) argues that the determinants of household vulnerability include not only risk events and initial assets but also the capacity of households to manage assets. This capacity to manage and transform assets into income, food or other basic necessities greatly affects households' level of poverty and vulnerability. Moser (1998:3) identifies the critical relationship between vulnerability and asset ownership and argues that 'the more assets people have, the less vulnerable they are, and the greater the erosion of people's assets, the greater their insecurity'. The argument of linking vulnerability to assets is based on the apparent fact that assets constitute the means and tools available to households to avoid or reduce the effects of risk events.

Besides exposure to risk events, initial assets and the capacity to manage assets as determinants of vulnerability, Moser (1998:4) also recognises the important role played by social capital in risk management, not only by trust and collaboration at a community level, but also social cohesion embedded in household and intra-household level relationships. The inclusion of trust, collaboration and social cohesion at all levels (household, intra-household, community) in the definition of intangible assets, has greatly built upon and expanded Swift's (1989) definition, which focused on claims.

The asset-vulnerability framework has undoubtedly improved upon the entitlement approach, as well as incorporating the political and global perspective, by linking claims not only to households and community but also to government and the international community. In an attempt to relate the asset-vulnerability argument to the context of civil war, Swift (1989:14) argues that civil wars and civil unrest are a crucial cause of vulnerability, most obviously because of the break in the moral economy and the abrogation of claims by the government. In his later writings, Swift (1996) also emphasizes other aspects of social capital as being one of the first casualties of civil war. While the argument of attributing the increasing vulnerability to the abrogation of claims by the government is valid, as discussed in the 'complex emergency' approach, the dominant perception of the breakdown of the moral economy during civil war requires further investigation. It is most likely that social capital that is broadly defined to include claims, but also trust, networks, collaboration and cohesion, maybe strengthened or eroded during the civil war, depending on the context.

Social Risk Management Approach: Resurrection of Social Capital

While anthropologists have long recognised the crucial role played by social capital in building and sustaining the trust necessary for social cohesion, economists are beginning to recognise its importance as one of the determinants of economic growth, as well as a tool of risk management. Economists are generally comfortable with modelling the logic of household strategies as a matter of freely-made choices and decision-making, albeit subject to economic constraints without any emphasis on the social constraints that greatly influence what people do. Ellis (1998:11) argues that social and familial constraints do matter in the decision-making and choices of a household as people are concerned not only with what they do but also with their capability to change what they do, which is influenced by social context. As formal insurance and stock markets have promoted individual risk-taking and permitted a reduction in risk-bearing in developed countries, economists have started to revisit the efficacy and effectiveness of social capital in encouraging risk-taking and reducing risk-bearing in societies in developing countries.

Generally, economists reckon that, in the absence of formal insurance markets, traditional agrarian societies are able to devise informal mechanisms that function as substitutes for these missing markets (Platteau, 1997:764). This shift of focus is interesting, as these characteristics of societies in developing countries, such as reciprocity and social redistribution mechanisms that were used in the 1960s to explain the vulnerability resulting from irrational behaviours of these societies are now being resurrected as means of risk management. It is argued that despite their recognition, the traditional social support networks are now in decline not only because of conflict but also due to rise of the market and formal state systems of social security (Platteau, 1997).

This approach draws on Sen's entitlement approach, asset-vulnerability and food insecurity frameworks, and it uses assets and particularly social capital in the vulnerability analysis. While the entitlement approach focuses on poverty and the coping strategies approach focuses on consumption rationing, social risk management provides a framework for linking risk management with social capital. The concept of social risk management repositions the traditional areas of 'social protection' (labour market intervention, social insurance and social safety nets) in a risk management framework against the background of asymmetric information and different types of risk (Holzmann and Jorgensen, 2000). It has been recognised that informal arrangements, such as extended families, mutual gift-giving and egalitarian tribal, systems do play an important role in risk management in developing countries.

The main argument of this approach is that in areas in which formal insurance and credit markets are absent and coupled with problems of asymmetric information and the enforcement of contracts, informal risk-sharing arrangements may provide solutions to the problem of risk management. The work of Scott (1976) and Platteau (1997) highlighted the important role played by reciprocal exchange arrangements that are common forms of mutual support in traditional communities. A distinctive feature of informal risk-pooling mechanisms is that information is freely available and enforcement mechanisms (social pressure, punishment, or the threat of future social exclusion) can put pressure on recalcitrant participants (Hoogeveen, 2000:115).

The small size of societies in developing countries and the long and continuous type of the relations between their members allow them to overcome both the incentive problems arising from asymmetric information and the enforcement of contracts (Platteau, 1997:789). These features of informal risk pooling mechanisms make such arrangements only effective in addressing idiosyncratic risk rather than covariate risks (Rosenzweig, 1988; Rosenzweig and Stark, 1989; Lucas and Stark, 1985). Rosenzweig (1988) specifically shows how south Indian households mitigate income risks and facilitate consumption smoothing by fostering geographically dispersed kinship ties through the marriage of daughters to locationally distant households.

Despite their recognized indigenous role in risk management, these informal risk-sharing arrangements are still considered as second-best (sub-optimal) because of the constraints that prevent binding commitments. Many researchers (Coate and Ravallion, 1993; Posner, 1980; Platteau, 1997), however, show that where members of societies in developing countries have close and continuous relations, informal reciprocal arrangements may be self-enforcing, as reputation effects will dissuade individuals from re-neging on their obligations and free-riding on others' contribution. Some researchers view these informal risk-sharing arrangements as less effective during hard times and crises resulting from generic risk events (Dr`eze and Sen, 1989; Popkin, 1979; Coate and Ravallion, 1993; Davies, 1996; Kinsey et al., 1998; Devereux, 1999).

As the role of social capital is recognised in risk management, particularly with risk events, such as drought and economic shocks, there is a dearth of understanding of its status and effectiveness in the context of civil war. There is a general perception that the civil wars in Africa have greatly disrupted the social assets, which make them ineffective in providing any informal insur-ance arrangements during the civil war (Swift, 1993; de Waal, 1993a). Swift (1996) notes that social capital, as one of the bases for survival in African rural societies, is being deliberately targeted by counter-insurgency warfare and becomes one of the first casualties of civil war and its destruction or absence makes civil war even more likely.

It is an apparent perception that the relation between social capital and civil war is an inverse relationship, as the concept of social capital emphasises co-operation that downplays the positive role that civil war can play in re-ducing the socio-economic grievances that usually trigger civil wars. As the origin of civil war is less about social breakdown than the creation of new forms of political and economic relations (Duffield, 2000; Keen, 2000), such a generalisation about the inverse relationship between social capital and civil war is too simplistic as this relationship is complex and context-specific. The nature of some types of counter-insurgency warfare may strengthen the social capital of the communities exposed to such risk, as it might instead encourage the community to adopt relevant social strategies to collectively mitigate the adverse effects of such risk. Goodhand et al (2000:390), on the basis of empirical analysis of several war-affected communities in Sri Lanka, questioned the belief that violent conflict inevitably erodes social capital.

Livelihood Approach: Diversification

This approach is based on the work of Scoones (1998), Bebbington (1999) and Ellis (2000), which draws heavily from the literature on food insecurity, entitlement approach, and asset vulnerability approach. Besides recognising the asset status of households as fundamental to understanding their risk management strategies and their vulnerability, the livelihood approach expands such analysis to include households' livelihood activities and their access to these assets and activities. This livelihood approach came as a result of dissatisfaction with the income/consumption model and is basically an analytical framework for an improved holistic understanding of livelihoods and poverty. As mentioned by Farrington et al (1999:3), the livelihood approach is intended as an analytical structure to enable coming to grips with the complexity of livelihoods, understanding influences on poverty and identifying where interventions can best be made.

The main argument of this approach is that the level of a vulnerability is determined by a dynamic process that starts with the asset status of households, mediated by social factors and exogenous trends or shocks, which trigger the adoption of livelihood strategies that in turn result in a set of outcomes (Ellis, 2000:40). In other words, the framework assumes that people pursue a range of livelihood outcomes by drawing on a range of assets to pursue a variety of livelihood activities, that are shaped and influenced by risk events, trends, seasonality, structures and the processes which people face (Farrington et al, 1999:3). The main feature of this approach is the introduction of mediating processes that are classified into endogenous factors (social relations, institutions and organisations) and exogenous factors (trends and shocks, including civil war) (Ellis, 2000).

The rural livelihood strategies that result from the interrelationships between assets and mediating processes reflect the dynamic response to the changing pressures and opportunities faced by households. These livelihood strategies are categorised into various typologies. For example, Scoones (1998) identifies three types of livelihood strategy: agricultural intensification or extensification, livelihood diversification, and migration; while Ellis (2000:40) divides these strategies between natural and non-natural resource-based activities. The livelihood diversification notably cuts across most of these typologies. Generally, individuals and households may diversify on-farm, off-farm and non-farm, including migration as part of the diversification (Ellis, 2000:41). Importantly there are two distinctive types of diversification, namely livelihood activities, and asset portfolios. This makes livelihood diversification the fundamental feature of this approach in under-standing households' risk management strategies and also their vulnerability.

Generally, there is an unresolved debate on whether diversification is a transient phenomenon or a long-term livelihood strategy, or whether it is used for asset accumulation or only for risk management. The conventional view of the processes of economic change is that economic progress depends on specialisation and division of labour and that diversification is generally perceived as a transient phenomenon or one associated with the desperate struggle for survival (Saith, 1992). There is now a growing consensus that sees diversification as a proactive livelihood and risk management strategy that is adopted by both rural households and urban dwellers to improve living standards (Maxwell, 1995; Rakodi, 1995; Moser, 1998; Siegel; Alwang, 1999 and Ellis, 1998:3).

There is also an unresolved debate about the determinants and effective-ness of livelihood diversification in the rural areas of low-income econo-mies. Theoretically, the extent to which a household diversifies its livelihood largely depends on a set of factors such as location, assets, seasonality, nature of risk, culture and social relations and the opportunities to smooth consump-tion (Alderman and Paxon, 1992:3). Despite a complex set of determinants of diversification, most explanations of household diversification are attributed to assets, including social relations as they largely affect the household attitudes towards risk, as well as their effects on smoothing consumption.

The relationship between asset portfolio diversification and attitudes to-wards risk in fairly predictable risk contexts, such as drought and economic shocks, has been inconclusive in most empirical studies in low-income en-vironments (Binswanger, 1981; Binswanger and Sillers, 1983). Some studies (Rosenzweig and Binswanger, 1993), however, support the hypothesis that the composition of asset portfolios is significantly influenced by farmers' wealth and the nature of risk events. Dercon (1993:1) finds that if liquid asset holdings are large, providing a buffer for consumption shortfalls, then households will be more willing to diversify and take up high-risk activities. Moser (1998) also notes that the greater the risk and uncertainty, the more households diversify their assets to prevent asset erosion.

Dercon and Krishnan (1996:851), however, refute any argument that attributes livelihood diversification to differences in behaviour towards risk and argues that the household's livelihood diversification is better explained by differences in ability, location, and access to credit. This suggests that the effectiveness of livelihood diversification is predominantly determined by the nature of risk (both idiosyncratic and covariate risk) and by asset portfolio including social assets. There is a general consensus in the risk management literature that livelihood diversification is more effective when the household is exposed to idiosyncratic (specific) risk rather than to co-variate risk (generic).

Linking livelihood diversification to asset portfolios suggests that poor households will be less willing to bear risk, even if they have risk preferences identical to those of wealthier households. Rosenzweig (1988) and Morduch (1990) show that poor households with limited access to credit, or with less inherited wealth, tend to choose less risky livelihood strategies while non-poor households tend to diversify more and adopt riskier production strategies. Dercon (2000:18) also argues that asset-poor households tend to adopt specialised portfolios with low risk and low returns, while asset-rich households diversify more and enter into high-risk and high-return liveli-hood activities. Interestingly, Dercon (2000:19) notes that observing special-isation does not necessarily indicate that the household follows a high-risk strategy, but rather reflects the limited asset portfolio available that inhibits diversification, leaving only low-return activities free to poor households. Given the lack of empirical evidence, it is unclear whether such commonly held arguments of attributing diversification to asset ownership and the intensity of risk events are tenable and relevant in the context of civil war.

Conclusion: Vulnerability Approaches and Civil War

It is apparent from the various approaches to vulnerability analysis that there is a clear lack of understanding of vulnerability in the context of civil war. This poor understanding of vulnerability in the 'war zone' has created a ten-dency to either see civil war as a chaotic phenomenon, that will inhibit any rational behaviour to reduce vulnerability or at best to treat it like other risk events, with implicit assumptions of triggering similar responses and risk-re-lated behaviours. Such generalisations may conceal the specific and unique characteristics of each source of risk event that may explain the differential risk-related behaviours of households exposed to different types and sources of risk. In an attempt to provide an understanding of vulnerability, most approaches tend to focus exclusively on the dynamics of vulnerability at micro-level, while others such as the 'complex emergency' approach focus on the macro context. This shows that each of the approaches discussed emphasises some important aspects and elements of vulnerability, but is insufficient on its own to provide a holistic understanding of vulnerability. This clearly highlights the need to synthesise and anchor the synergies provided by these approaches into a framework that will reflect and provide an understanding of all elements of vulnerability in the context of civil war.

The other important observation across the various approaches to vulnerability with the exception of the 'complex emergency' approach is the exogeneity assumption of risk events, which tends to discourage assessing the determinants of risk events that are crucially important in understanding the level of vulnerability in rural communities. Unlike other risk events, understanding the causes and characteristics of civil war (see Chapter 4) is not only important in finding a solution for civil war, but also in understanding the differential livelihood strategies adopted by the communities exposed to various types of counterinsurgency warfare. There is also a commonly held view, and a sweeping generalisation made across various approaches, of linking the level of household vulnerability with assets, including political assets, in the case of the 'complex emergency approach'. It is questionable whether this general assertion is relevant in the context of civil war and it requires in-depth empirical validation (see chapter 6) at the household level. Other general assertions, attributing the determinants of diversification to asset ownership and intensity of risk event, as well as unwittingly juxtaposing civil war and social capital deficiency, may need to be critically assessed in the context of civil war.

CHAPTER THREE

A Framework for Household Vulnerability and Resilience Analysis

Introduction

This chapter sets out a framework for analysing household risk management and its outcomes in terms of vulnerability and resilience. The framework is primarily based on the livelihood approach and risk management literature and largely draws on work on the entitlement approach, asset-vulnerability framework, coping strategies, and social risk management framework, as discussed in Chapter 2. The common theme cutting across these approaches is the recognition of the asset status of households as fundamental to understanding the options open to them, the strategies they adopt for survival, and their vulnerability to risk events and shocks (Ellis, 2000:28). The underlying assumption of these approaches is that households are not passive when faced with adverse events and trends, but consciously take proactive actions, with whatever they have to confront the adverse effects of these risk events. In other words, these approaches look positively at what people have, rather than negatively at what they do not have and how desperate things are (Moser, 1998:1). However, despite the recognition that households do take risk events as a starting point for their livelihood strategies, these approaches have in common assumed risk events as being exogenous to their framework for the analysis of household vulnerability and resilience.

This framework for analysing household risk management will be known as the 'risk-livelihood-vulnerability framework', with the concepts of risk, livelihood and vulnerability as its main building blocks. Unlike other approaches, the framework starts with risk events and their characteristics rather than with assets, and this conception provides a holistic and comprehensive understanding of the dynamics of household vulnerability. The framework mainly focuses on a micro-level analysis of the household vulnerability, particularly in the context of civil war, as there has been a great deal of focus on meso- or macro-levels, with limited or a dearth of understanding of risk management strategies at the household level.

The chapter proceeds as follows. The next section sets out the framework in some detail. Section 3 discusses risk events and their characteristics, followed by a discussion of livelihood assets and their attributes in Section 4. The mediating processes and livelihood strategies are discussed in Section 5, while livelihood outcomes are discussed in the context of household vulnerability models in Section 6.

Household Vulnerability Analysis: Risk-Livelihood–Vulnerability Framework

The tendency to focus on a macro - or meso - analysis of livelihoods and risk management has been recognised to provide a less insightful understanding of micro-dynamics, particularly at household level. This tendency has been to gradually move away from a macro analysis towards the village, household, and individual levels but with a recognised scope for simultaneous analysis at all levels (macro, meso and micro). The framework for analysing household risk management is set out as a two-dimensional representation in Figure 3.1. The primary objective of this diagram is to synthesise and organise the various approaches discussed in Chapter 2 into a coherent framework that identifies the entry points and critical processes in risk management. It is recognised that such a framework in the form of a diagram will not be able to capture the dynamics of household risk management that, in practice, it involves a great deal of feedback and complex interactions between the components of the framework.

Though these dynamic interactions will be implied rather than stated in Figure 3.1, some key dynamic processes are identified and discussed in the course of describing the framework. The limitations of such a two-dimensional representation to capture the complex process of household risk management are recognised at the outset. Though the reference scale of the framework takes the household as unit of analysis, the same diagram can also be used to think through the risk management in larger-scale geographical zones that share important features in common, such as their exposure to risk events or shocks.

Figure 3.1:
Risk-Livelihood Strategies-Vulnerability Framework

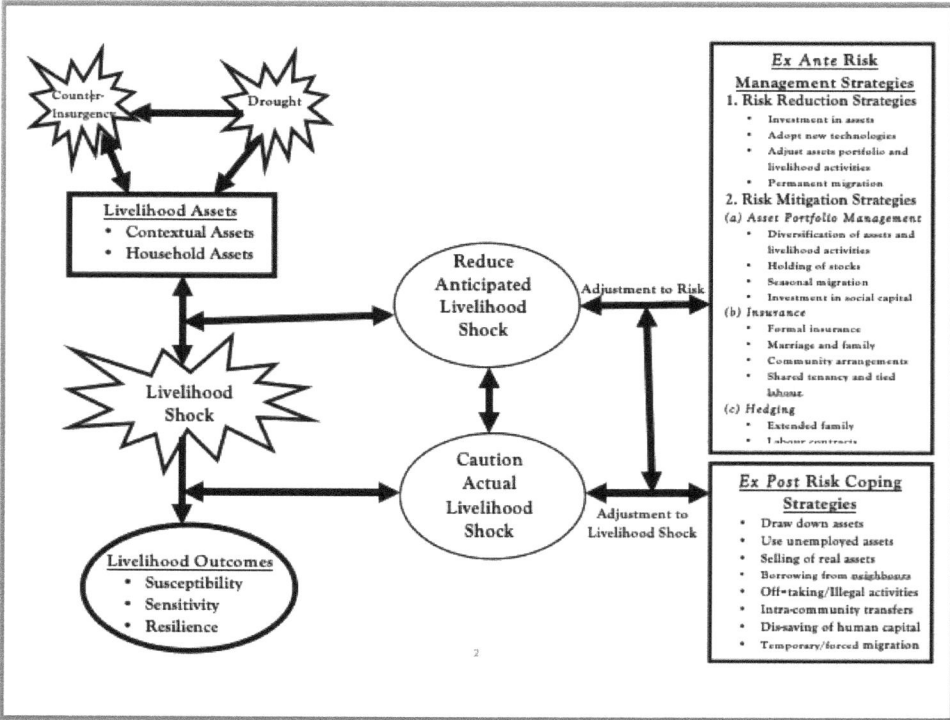

While a large-scale perspective may help to broadly identify the dynamics of livelihood strategies, it lacks sensitivity to variation between households or individual members of households. In describing the framework as shown in Figure 3.1, it is the rural household that is taken as the main social unit to which the framework is applied. This implies that at village or community level we do not expect to observe a similar pattern of livelihood strategies, as different households will adopt strategies according to their asset status and the type of risk events they are exposed to. Also, the joint livelihood strategies of individuals within the household are likely to be powerfully constrained by, and to overlap with, the livelihood strategy of the household. Ellis (2000:31) argues that the household as a unit of analysis poses a barrier to understanding the dynamics of livelihood strategies if an unnecessarily narrow, unitary, and static view of the household is taken. The meso-level perspective of the framework will help in providing comparative risk management strategies across communities exposed to different types and characteristics of risk events.

The framework has been developed to understand conceptually the dynamic process of risk events, household livelihood assets, the risk management process through livelihood strategies and the resultant livelihood outcomes. This framework regards the asset status (owned, controlled, claimed or accessed) of households as the households' basic livelihood building blocks, and consequently they are fundamental to understanding households' risk management strategies and their vulnerability as the outcome of these strategies.

The framework identifies two critical periods of risk management – the period before the occurrence of a risk event and the period after its occurrence – that constitute the basis for human reaction to risk and its management. As the household's reaction to risk and its management primarily depend on the assets available, risk management has been narrowly perceived as being synonymous with an asset-based management approach that uses a broad definition of assets. It is on the basis of this understanding that household risk management is broadly referred to as the set of mechanisms used by households to deal with the anticipated or actual losses associated with uncertain events and outcomes (Siegel and Alwang, 1999). This set of mechanisms basically draws on assets that are categorised into assets (human, natural, physical, financial) to which households have direct ownership (household assets), and assets (markets, social capital, transfers including food aid, infrastructure including public services, institutional and political) over which households have no direct ownership (contextual assets), as well as household livelihood activities.

The framework suggests that the process of risk management starts with households having perceptions about risk events. The risk events in terms of their perception and occurrence are transmitted, depending on the nature of risk, through livelihood assets, as shown in Figure 3.1. Depending on the households' perceptions of risk events, their livelihood asset base, they voluntarily and deliberately adopt ex-ante risk management strategies before the occurrence of risk events to reduce the anticipated adverse effects of these events on their livelihoods. When the risk event occurs, households take ex-post livelihood strategies to cushion the actual adverse effects of the livelihood shock on their consumption and well-being. There is, however, no common agreement about whether ex-post strategies are an aspect of risk management strategies. While some writers (Ellis, 1998; Siegel and Alwang, 1999) consider ex-post strategies as unplanned reactions to unexpected livelihood failure, others (World Bank, 1990; Alderman and Paxon, 1992; Siegel and Alwang, 1999; Devereux, 2000) consider them as an integral part of the household risk management behaviour. In this framework, ex- post strategies are considered as part of the household risk management strategies. As shown in Figure 3.1, both sets of strategies (ex-ante and ex-post) are sequentially and interdependently adopted and decided by a household, as part of the planning process in anticipation of, and in response to, risk events and outcomes.

The effectiveness of the households' risk management strategies depends not only on their initial asset ownership, but also on their ability to transform their initial assets into livelihoods as ex-ante measures (income smoothing), and their ability to transform livelihoods into consumption and well-being as ex-post measures (consumption smoothing). The way the household succeeds in managing risk events, their outcome and the pattern of occurrence of risk events will all improve the household's risk-learning curve that will greatly affect household attitudes and behaviour in subsequent periods of risk management.

The main building blocks of the framework, as set out in Figure 3.1, include risk events, livelihood assets, livelihood strategies (ex-ante risk management strategies and ex-post context-specific livelihood strategies) and livelihood outcomes in terms of vulnerability, consumption and well-being. These main components of the framework and their interdependence and interactions are elaborated and discussed below.

Characteristics of Risk Events

The starting-points of the framework are the sources and characteristics of risk events and shocks that are faced and confronted by households. The sources and characteristics of risk events play crucial roles in the management of risk and have a bearing on the selection of risk management strategies. The capacity of households or communities to confront risk events or shocks and the appropriate livelihood strategies to be adopted, largely depend on the characteristics of risk events, their source, correlation, frequency and intensity (Siegel and Alwang, 1999; Holzmann and Jorgensen, 2000:11). Dercon (2000:2) recognises that though the sources of risk are important in understanding risk management, the characteristics of the risk events and shocks are equally important in explaining the choice of risk management strategies adopted by households.

Generally, the main sources of risk that are faced by rural communities in the developing countries are categorised into natural, health, life-cycle, economic, social, political and environmental (Holzmann and Jorgensen, 2000:12, Sinha and Lipton, 1999). These sources of risk can take the form of sudden shocks, long-term trends, or seasonal cycles with differential impacts on a household's choice of risk management strategies. Interestingly, even within the main categories of the sources of risk, there are different and specific sources of risk events with unique characteristics. This clearly suggests that the generalised categorisation of the sources of risk is not sufficient in understanding and explaining the risk management strategies adopted by households.

Besides the sources of risk events, the other characteristics of risk events, such as intensity, duration, predictability, recurrence (seasonality) and geographic or social spread, are equally important in risk management analysis. Risk events with a narrow geographic or social spread are called idiosyncratic (specific) risks, while risk events with a larger geographic or social spread are called covariate (generic) risks. Devereux (1999:6) notes that vulnerability as a complex concept is determined partly by risk factors that are generic to groups of individuals or households who are linked geographically (joint 'exposure'), and partly by risk factors that are specific to each individual or household (individual 'sensitivity'). The contribution of each category of risk events (idiosyncratic and covariate) to the total variability of household livelihood plays an important role in risk management. Idiosyncratic risks are more manageable by households than covariate risks as they can be insured against with formal or informal insurance transfers, but covariate shocks cannot (Dercon, 2000:3).

The degree to which these risk events are managed is context-specific and it is largely determined by the specific characteristics of risk events. Any attempt to draw generalised statements about the magnitude of the idiosyncratic component of various sources of risk will conceal the specific characteristics of risk events that are more important in explaining household risk-related behaviours. For example, the sources of risk associated with the environment tend to be meso-covariant, while the covariance of those sources of risk, that is social, political (including civil war) and economic in nature, range from being purely idiosyncratic to meso-covariant and macro-covariant.

It is implicit in the literature of risk that civil war is generically labeled as a covariate in that it simultaneously affects many or all households in a community (World Bank, 2001:2). This implicit assumption about the generic nature of civil war grossly conceals the dynamics and characteristics of civil war. In the context of the civil war, it may be argued that the conventional warfare between rebels and government shows macro-covariance, while the counter-insurgency warfare that emanates from within the community tends to be meso-idiosyncratic, and the counterinsurgency warfare that is exogenous tends to have meso-covariance. It is generally argued in this framework that the choice and effectiveness of the household risk management strategies adopted by households is largely shaped by the specific nature and unique characteristics of each risk event.

Besides the sources and nature of risk events, other characteristics, such as the frequency of shocks and the repeated nature of risk events, play important roles in the choice and effectiveness of the risk management strategies adopted by households. Some risks can be repeated, such as annual seasonality or recurrent droughts, others are singular events. The more severe, prolonged, or repeated the shocks are, the more households are unable to manage the actual and potential effects of such shocks. Relatively small and frequent risk events are more easily confronted and managed by households than are large and infrequent shocks. However, it could equally be argued that small and frequent risk events are much worse than a single acute risk as they gradually erode the household asset base and make them vulnerable to small shocks in the long run (Watson, 2002). Also, if risk events come together (bunched), then they become difficult to manage.

Despite the general recognition that the sources and characteristics of risk events have an important bearing on the choice and effectiveness of risk management strategies, the risk literature focuses less on the determinants of the risk events. Most debates in the risk literature attach more importance to the level of risk exposure than to its determinants. What is apparently not clear in the risk literature is the causal relationship between risk exposure and household assets. It is generally implied or assumed in the risk literature that risk events are grouped together and treated as exogenous factors that are independent of household asset ownership and that they will trigger similar patterns of household responses (Siegel and Alwang, 1999; Farrington et al, 1999; Moser, 1998; Sen, 1981). This assumption of exogeneity is crucial in the risk literature as it narrowly allows treating risk management as an asset-based approach.

The relevance of this assumption of de-linking the causes of risk events from household assets to the context of civil war requires a better under-standing of the aetiology of civil wars. In an attempt to contribute to an improved understanding of the causation of civil war, various disciplines present their analysis of the civil war causation that is conceptually grounded in their monodisciplinary perspectives. The debate on the causation of civil war has boiled down to two competing theoretical perspectives on whether civil wars are caused by inner determinants (instincts, needs, impulses, and drives), or by outer determinants (socio-political environment).

Civil war is a complex phenomenon that is extremely difficult to analyse either by one discipline or to attribute to one or a few factors in isolation from other factors. Keen (1998, 2000) recognises the need to look at civil wars in a holistic way and attributes the view of portraying civil war as irra-tional behaviour to a visible rigidity in some academic disciplines, that fail to analyse civil war phenomena within their ordered and predictable orbit of analysis. It is apparent that no monocausal approach is able to capture the dynamic of human behaviour, though each approach has an important contribution towards understanding human behaviour. It is clear, however, that human behaviour is neither driven by inner forces nor buffeted help-lessly by environmental influences, but it is rather best understood in terms of a continuous reciprocal interaction between behaviour and its controlling conditions. The divergent views of the causes of civil war can be attributed mainly to three factors: level of analysis (macro, meso or micro), a period of analysis (pre-conflict and during the conflict) and subjective value attached to the desired outcome (post-conflict) for states at war with their citizens.

Most research on the causation of civil war tends to focus on meso-factors during the civil war and their analysis runs the risk of ascribing the conditions during the civil war rather than pre-war conditions as causes. The few research studies that have analysed the pre-war situation tend to unambiguously impute the causes of civil war to socio-economic and po-litical grievances, that have been generated by the unpopular policies of elite and their 'shadow states', exacerbated by macro and regional and global conditions. In the midst of the conduct of the civil war, it is not surprising to observe irrational behaviour, economic agendas, ethnicity, religion and greed as dominating this critical period, as a way of sustaining the fighting activities of the warring parties through the "privatisation of violence" and counter-insurgency and insurgency warfare. This clearly suggests that the aetiology of civil war is a complex reality that can only be understood by investigating all major structural and behavioural variables of the human situation, rather than by focusing on a single perspective or causal paradigm.

Deng (2002a) argues that a comprehensive understanding of the causation of civil wars requires considering three levels of analysis (global, national and community) in the context of three phases of civil war (pre-, during and post-conflict). The main argument is that civil wars are mul-ticausal and sustained primarily by greed and economic motives through counter-insurgency warfare. In other words, the contemporary civil wars are largely caused by various 'war production factors' at global, national and community levels and are equally sustained by various 'war reproduction factors' at macro, meso and micro levels (Cliffe and Luckham, 2000).

This suggests, unlike other risk events, that the occurrence of counterin-surgency warfare as a risk event during the civil war is not exogenous, but is triggered by the assets and wealth of communities and households. This distinctive linkage between civil war and household assets is shown as an interdependency (two-way) arrow in Figure 3.1. This unique characteristic of civil war suggests that, besides the sources and characteristics of the risk events, the determinants of the risk events also play an important role in the choice and effectiveness of household risk management strategies. Also, civil war has causal relations with other risk events such as climate change. There is now a growing body of evidence of the link between climate change or weather fluctuations and civil wars (see Figure 3.1). In the case of sub-Saharan Africa, there are cumulative research findings that show strong historical linkages between civil war and both long and short term temperature trends, with warmer years leading to significant increases in the likelihood of war (Burke et al, 2009 and Hendrix and Glaser, 2007). The causes, characteristics and comparison of the major risk events that were faced by households in the 1990s, particularly civil war and drought, are elaborately discussed in the context of Sudan in Chapter 5.

Livelihood Assets

The second component of the risk management framework is the livelihood assets and means of livelihood. Livelihood assets are the core building blocks upon which households are able to confront and manage risk and shocks through production, labour markets, and reciprocal exchanges with other households. These livelihood assets are not only a stock of wealth that is used to generate well-being but they also shape and affect in a number of ways the choice and effectiveness of risk management strategies. The main categories of livelihood assets that are used in the framework are 'household assets' and 'contextual assets', as shown in Figure 3.1. The separation of 'contextual assets' from 'household assets' is important in order to capture the contextual environment within which households access or accumulate their assets.

Siegel and Alwang (1999:11) expand the definition of assets to include political and institutional assets, such as participation, empowerment, human rights, rules and regulation and access to markets. These political and institutional assets are generally defined as the set of 'mandatory universal rights' to which all people are entitled. The existence of these well-defined 'universal rights' and their enforcement are critical not only to households' management of their assets but also in managing and confronting risk events. The absence of these assets with the exception of access to markets in the context of civil war makes some researchers to analyse household vulnerability narrowly in the context of political vulnerability. Also, access to markets is considered to be a critical "contextual asset" as it influences the availability and accessibility of goods and services. In the context of civil war markets become increasingly important as demand for liquid assets is expected to relatively increase, unlike drought where people will prefer the accumulation of physical assets and stocks.

The main features of the assets that are relevant in shaping the choice and effectiveness of risk management strategies include the level of asset ownership, types of assets, linkages between different levels of asset ownership (household, community and extra-community levels); attributes of assets and relationship between risk events and assets. Generally, the more assets are available to a household, the more the household is able to confront and manage risk event and shocks as the anticipated and actual effects of risk events are transmitted through assets, as shown in Figure 3.1. However, this argument is crucially based on the assumption that risk events are exogenous and suggests that the occurrence of risk events and shocks is not triggered by the level of household asset ownership. In the context of civil war, as discussed earlier, such argument is context-specific as a risk event, such as counter-insurgency warfare, is largely triggered by both greed and grievances that target household assets and the means of livelihood.

The types of assets available to households play equally an important role in risk management. While human and physical assets are private property resources, natural assets are often characterised as common property, particularly in the context of rural communities. These common property resources are mediated through social capital that generally determines individual and household access to, rather than ownership of these common property resources. This makes social capital crucially important in explaining and understanding household risk management strategies as well as their vulnerability over time (Siegel and Alwang, 1999:11). In the context of civil war, particularly counter-insurgency warfare, social capital becomes increasingly important, as it becomes the target as well as the source of binding people together, to adopt collective actions to confront the adverse effects of the common risk event.

Besides the level of household assets ownership, access and types of assets, the attributes of these assets play equally an important role in household risk management through income generation and as a store of wealth and savings. Importantly, the attributes of a particular portfolio of assets are household-specific, and the attributes of individual assets change over time with the changing risk events or shocks faced by households (Siegel and Alwang, 1999:12). Generally, various attributes of assets have been identified, but the most relevant attributes in the context of rural communities include the level of substitutability of assets, the store of wealth, liquidity, lumpiness, mobility and ability to satisfy basic needs. The degree to which individual assets can be used alone, or serve as substitutes or complements in generating household well-being, is important in risk management. The level and degree of interaction of the household asset portfolio determines the magnitude of asset portfolio covariance, which affects the effectiveness of the risk management strategies adopted by households. As social capital has the unique and distinctive attribute of complementing other productive assets, this attribute places social assets at the heart of the risk management strategies.

In the context of rural communities who lack access to financial intermediation services, the asset attribute of storing wealth becomes important, as households will tend to hold assets as precautionary savings. In the context of agro-pastoralist societies, livestock has a special attribute as a good store of wealth that has value as collateral and added value as a social status symbol. Equally, investment in social assets provides a similar attribute to livestock as a store of wealth, as it provides households with claims on other assets. While this attribute of livestock as a store of wealth makes it an important asset for households in confronting risk events, it is the same attribute of livestock that may make it, paradoxically, an immediate and deliberate target of counterinsurgency warfare in the context of civil war.

The degree to which assets can be liquidated constitutes an important attribute in risk management and largely depends on the lumpiness and mobility of assets and the existence of markets. This attribute is important, as it makes assets a useful means for precautionary savings and self-insurance, which constitute the crucial aspects of household risk management strategies, particularly diversification. Food stocks provide the important attributes of liquidity, divisibility and mobility that make it possible for households to self-insure and access credit. Livestock also provides these attributes, particularly mobility, and where there are operational markets, it provides attributes such as liquidity and divisibility.

But note that some assets deteriorate over time (food stocks), while others appreciate (livestock – through breeding). Some types of livestock, such as cattle and camels, are lumpier and less divisible than goats and sheep (Dercon, 1996). Also, the ability of assets to provide and meet the basic needs of households is an important attribute in risk management, particularly in the context of rural households, who are poorly integrated into markets. Assets, such as the natural resource base (land, water, forest, pastures, wildlife and fisheries), basic household assets (housing, household goods, storage and utensils) and stocks (food and livestock) are important assets in risk management as they provide the basic consumption needs of households. In the context of civil war, particularly counterinsurgency warfare, assets such as land (not privately owned and cannot be converted into cash as easily as other assets such as livestock) and its related livelihood activities are rather immobile, which may limit their effectiveness in confronting risk events and shocks.

Though almost all assets, as discussed above, are useful risk management instruments, some assets with specific attributes will be more relevant to the context of civil war than others. Some assets with distinctive and favourable attributes in managing the risk of 'normal' shocks, such as drought, may expose households to increased vulnerability and susceptibility to risk events, particularly in the context of civil war. It is generally argued in this framework that the level of households' asset ownership is not sufficient as their attributes are equally important in explaining the level of households' vulnerability to risk events.

Household Livelihood Strategies

The third component of the framework is the risk management strategies that are adopted by households in the face of risk events, as shown in Figure 3.1. As rural households are faced with the lack of market institutions and public provisions, most of the risk management strategies adopted by households to confront risk tend to be self-protection through informal and personal arrangements (Alderman and Paxson, 1992; Besley, 1995; Ellis, 1998). Household livelihood strategies are basically categorised into ex-ante risk management strategies and ex-post livelihood strategies.

Ex Ante Risk Management Strategies

As shown in Figure 3.1, ex-ante risk management strategies are adopted by households to adjust to risk before its occurrence. These ex-ante household livelihood strategies aim to reduce the probability of the risk occurring and the household's susceptibility to risk (reduction strategies), and/or to reduce the potential impact if the risk were to occur (mitigation strategies). Besides assessing how households in risky environments confront risk events, understanding the ex-ante risk management strategies sheds light on the risk-related behaviours of households, particularly those exposed to civil war and counterinsurgency warfare. While risk reduction strategies refer to government policies related to macroeconomic, public health, environment and human resource development in the context of shocks, such as drought and macroeconomic shocks, collective community action to defend themselves against raids and attacks is the relevant prevention strategy during the civil war. At household and micro-level, households pursue preventive strategies, such as the adoption of less risky production and livelihood activities and migration (Holzmann and Jorgensen, 2000:17).

The Risk Reduction Strategies include investment in assets, adjust assets portfolio and livelihood activities, adoption of new technologies and permanent migration, while the most relevant Risk Mitigation Strategies include asset portfolio management, insurance and hedging, as shown in Figure 3.1. Portfolio diversification includes reliance on a variety of assets or livelihood activities with uncorrelated returns, and investment in human, physical assets, including storing of goods for future consumption and social capital (rituals, reciprocal gift-giving). Though portfolio diversification is an important risk-mitigation strategy adopted by households to confront risk events, such as drought and economic shocks, the relevance of such argument in the context of civil war is a profound gap in the literature of vulnerability.

Insurance (formal or informal) as one of the mitigation strategies adopted by households in risky environments involves pooling together a number of participants, whose risks are less correlated. In the context of rural households, the most relevant informal insurance mechanisms include marriage, especially outside one's community, family and community arrangements, shared tenancy and tied labour (Holzmann and Jorgensen, 2000:17). Unlike formal insurance arrangements that rely on a large pool of participants with less correlated risks, informal insurance has the advantage of low information asymmetry. Another mitigation strategy available to rural households is hedging as a risk exchange strategy. The concept of hedging is borrowed from finance theory (e.g. forward exchange rate contracts) and is based on risk exchange or the payment of a risk price to somebody for assuming that risk (Holzmann and Jorgensen, 2000:14). Informal and personal hedging mechanisms in the context of rural communities are found in family arrangements, such as marriage and extended family, and some forms of labour contracts.

Ex Post Livelihood Strategies

When a risk event occurs and ex-ante risk management strategies fail either to prevent its occurrence or to mitigate its adverse effects, households adopt ex-post strategies to alleviate the impact of the risk event or shocks as shown in Figure 3.1. The ex-post livelihood strategies are adopted by households after the occurrence of a risk event, and as behavioural adjustment mechanisms aim at cushioning the actual livelihood shock in order to smooth consumption. These ex-post livelihood strategies are usually referred to as coping strategies and include a wide range of behaviours, such as forced migration, selling of assets and labour, reduction of food intake and the number of meals, dis-saving of human capital, increased reliance on wild food collection and hunting, and borrowing.

The real question is whether these informal household risk management strategies, in the context of rural Africa, are effective and able to reduce household vulnerability to risk events and whether they are declining over time? The opinion is divided about the effectiveness of these informal risk management strategies in reducing vulnerability. These strategies are often described as being not very effective because of limited and imperfect markets that are conditioned by generic risk, a low population density, high transport costs and simple technology that characterise much of rural Africa (Pingali and Binswanger, 1986).

Besides these reasons, the level of poverty and the nature of the risks faced by households in rural Africa largely explain the ineffectiveness of the informal household risk management strategies. Institutional market failures are widely manifested in Africa in terms of lack of credit and savings markets, high transaction and information costs, non-price barriers to entry into financial networks (related to a person's social standing or ethnic group), and the widespread reliance on non-financial forms of insurance (mostly livestock) (World Bank, 2001:16). As such, it is generally argued that the private and informal insurance arrangements that are adopted by households in the African rural communities do not constitute anything like full insurance for the poor and, as such, are relatively ineffective in reducing vulnerability, despite their diversity and prevalence.

Against this convincing evidence about the ineffectiveness of informal risk management strategies, there is also growing evidence that suggests that these strategies in some rural communities in Africa do perform well in reducing the vulnerability to risk events. For example, Platteau (1997) shows the role played by informal risk-sharing arrangements as an effective way through which rural communities can achieve a significant degree of protection against income fluctuations and other hazards beyond their control. Carter (1997) also shows in West Africa that diversification and reciprocity can substantially dampen and reduce risk exposure.

Reardon (1997) shows the dominant importance of non-farm wage labour as a household income diversification strategy in reducing vulnerability to risk events in Africa. In the context of rural Gambia, it was shown how community and kinship ties often play a crucial role in minimising vulnerability, especially at the onset of crop failures, depletion of food stocks, and very high food prices. In addition, Naeraa et al (1992) found that informal social security systems played a vital role in sustaining the poorest and most vulnerable rural households in Namibia (World Bank, 2001). Also, it was found that informal savings and credit associations in Nigeria were able to cope well with the risks associated with asymmetric information, transaction costs and moral hazards, through locally sustained valued mechanisms (World Bank, 2001).

Though there is an unresolved debate about the effectiveness of household risk management strategies in rural communities, it is generally recognised that households use a range of informal strategies (World Bank, 2001:xii). In the context of sub-Saharan Africa, it has been recognised that both poor and non-poor households are far from passive in confronting risk (World Bank, 2001:15). They typically try to anticipate the occurrence of different types of shocks and engage in ex-ante risk reduction and mitigation behaviour, in which they forego some income in exchange for an insurance premium against a shock that will occur in the future. They also engage in ex-post coping behaviour that involves actions that they take after a shock has occurred, with the intention of sustaining and smoothing their consumption in the face of a sudden income shock. This small but growing evidence in Africa about the performance of informal risk management strategies clearly challenges the dominant and general perception about the ineffectiveness of these strategies and suggests the context specificity of these strategies.

These arguments about the ineffectiveness of these strategies are generic and may conceal variations across countries and communities and over time, so there is a need to contextualize the performance of these strategies to provide a better understanding. As the effectiveness of these informal household livelihood strategies is doubted in the context of risk events, such as drought and economic shocks, there is a growing perception that these livelihood strategies will not be effective in the context of civil war, despite limited evidence and a dearth of information.

Livelihood Strategies Outcomes: Household Vulnerability and Resilience

The fourth component of the risk-livelihood-vulnerability framework is the outcomes of household risk management strategies that are represented by the level of vulnerability at a given point of time, and its other forms, such as the level of well-being and consumption, as shown in Figure 3.1. Risk is more associated with vulnerability as a dynamic concept that focuses on changes in socioeconomic status (Glewwe and Hall, 1998). The level of vulnerability, as shown in Figure 3.1, generally measures the outcomes of household livelihood strategies.

The level of vulnerability as the ex-ante and ex-post state is to be measured as in the framework in terms of exposure to risk (susceptibility), the intensity with which the risk event is experienced (sensitivity), and the capacity to resist downward movement in well-being as a result of the occurrence of a risk event (resilience) as suggested by Bayliss-Smith (1991:7) and Davies (1993:62). As shown in the framework, the determinants of vulnerability include types and characteristics of risk events, level of household asset ownership and, most importantly, the way households transform assets into livelihoods.

There is a common consensus in the risk literature that the poor are more susceptible to risk because they have fewer tools (assets) at their disposal to defend against risky events and thus suffer proportionally greater welfare losses for given levels of risk. Contrary to this narrative, this framework suggests that any vulnerability analysis that focuses only on the initial level of household asset ownership will not capture the other determinants of vulnerability. Although risks are transmitted to households through household assets, as shown in Figure 3.1., the outcome of such transmission may be negative or positive depending on the type of risk events. Unlike risk event such as drought, it may be argued in the context of civil war that the household assets may become a source of the susceptibility of the household to risk event such as counterinsurgency warfare.

Taking famine as the lowest downward movement in household vulnerability, many theories have been developed to understand the causes of famine. Most famine theories - demographic, entitlement and complex political emergencies - attribute the causes of famine to initial shocks or risk events, such as natural disasters, economic crisis and civil war, to which the communities or households have been exposed. The conceptualisation of famine causation in the context of risk events or shocks resulted in seeing famine initially as an 'act of God' in terms of ecological shock, or due to the 'laws of nature' in terms of excessive population growth. More recently, it is increasingly been seen as 'economic crisis' in terms of entitlement failure, and an 'act of man' in terms of government policies and civil war (Devereux, 2001b).

The famines resulting from the civil war are seen as the product of a failure of political accountability (political assets and contextual assets) and are labelled as 'political famines' or 'war famines' with people living in civil war zone seen as victims (de Waal, 1997). Devereux (2001b:121) argues that war, unlike other risk events, can be seen as a comprehensive explanation of a certain type of famine, because of its multiple effects on all elements of the food system, and he remarks without evidence that in political famines the rich are generally as vulnerable as the poor. These emerging new terms of 'political famines' or 'war famines' may rightly highlight the macro and meso level of household vulnerability but may not be sufficient to unpack the dynamics of vulnerability at the micro-level of the household.

The explanation of famine causation in terms of contextual assets and primary triggers and shocks is rather simplistic, as it fails to recognise the household proactive livelihood strategies that are aimed at reducing the anticipated and actual adverse effects of these shocks and risk events. The available famine theories have not rigorously, with the exception of the coping strategies literature (Corbett, 1988; Jodha, 1975; Watts, 1983; Devereux, 1993), linked the occurrence of famine to the failure of household risk management strategies. Attributing famine to the failure of household livelihood strategies clearly explains why some households sustain the effects of some risk events, while other households become increasingly vulnerable to famine.

According to the risk-livelihood-vulnerability framework, as shown in Figure 3.1, the level of vulnerability is the outcome of household risk management strategies that will either improve the household level of resilience or will lead to higher levels of vulnerability. Though the level of a household vulnerability is related to sources of risk, all risk events are transmitted through asset and household livelihood strategies that determine the level of vulnerability as livelihood outcomes. Even a risk event such as civil war is not entirely linked with vulnerability as a large proportion of it is transmitted through household assets. The distinctive characteristic of civil war, particularly counter-insurgency warfare, of being triggered by household assets and climate change may result in livelihood outcomes that may be different from those caused primarily by drought.

It has generally been recognised, particularly in the context of risk events such as drought and economic shocks, that household risk management strategies can increase the vulnerability of the poor over time, as some strategies tend to deplete or slow down the accumulation of productive assets (Siegel and Alwang, 1999:1). This argument is equally true in the context of civil war not only for poor households but also for non-poor households, as repetitive recurrence of counter-insurgency warfare may make non-poor households increasingly vulnerable. The level of household vulnerability in the context of civil war is likely to be relatively higher than in other risk events, not only because of the consistent erosion of assets but also because of the depletion of contextual assets including poorly functioning markets and the lack of public intervention to provide for efficiency-enhancing risk management strategies.

Although there is a growing recognition of the apparent difference be-tween vulnerability and poverty, there is still a tendency to confuse these two concepts, as is apparent in the preceding discussions and arguments. For example, the literature on poverty and vulnerability focuses on groups that are already poor and more likely to experience larger than average declines in socioeconomic status, with little attention being given to non-poor households that may also be vulnerable (Glewwe and Hall, 1998:182). It is not always true that poor households are necessarily more vulnerable than non-poor households, as vulnerability is determined not only by the level of livelihood assets ownership but also by other factors, such as type and characteristics of risk events. For example, subsistence-oriented poor farmers in remote rural areas are not directly vulnerable to national and international economic shocks, as their self-sufficient socio-economic status is relatively insensitive to and limits the impact of such shocks.

Glewwe and Hall (1998) show, on the basis of panel data from Peru, that while most households' incomes are sensitive to regional, national and international economic conditions, subsistence farmers and other relatively autarchic households are less affected by, and thus less vulnerable to, eco-nomic shocks. On the other hand, poor subsistence farmers will be more vulnerable and affected by the occurrence of drought than are non-poor households in rural areas, or poor labourers in the urban context. With the repeated, sequential and severe reoccurrence of drought, poor and non-poor households in the rural context are likely to be equally vulnerable. These arguments are even more relevant in the context of civil war.

In order to understand the dynamics of household vulnerability, the risk-livelihood-vulnerability framework borrows from the vulnerability model developed by Siegel and Alwang (1999)[1]. According to this model,

---

1   According to Siegel and Alwang (1999:65), vulnerability is generally defined in terms of the expected value of welfare $E(_{xit+1})$ output (for i^{th} household in the tth time period) in relation to poverty or the minimum level of survival ($x\star$), given the state of nature in the initial period, that includes conditioning variables (x_{it},) that are specific to households, such as assets (A_{it}) and exogenous variables or shocks (risk events), such as rainfall, prices or civil war (Z_t). Thus a household is defined as vulnerable if:
$E(_{xit+1}) \leq x\star$ (1)
Generally in an axiomatic approach the probability of being vulnerable or poor is defined as:
$Pr\{ x_{it+1} \leq x\star | x_{it}, A_{it}, Z_t \}$ (2)
Given the distribution of x_i ($f(x_i)$), then the probability of being vulnerable (poor) is defined as: $x\star$
$Pr\{.\} = \int_0^{x\star} (f(x_i) \, dx = v_{it} =$ Vulnerability index of household i.   (3)

the main determinants of vulnerability include conditioning variables (x_{it}) that are specific to households, such as assets (A_{it}) and exogenous variables or shocks (risk events), such as rainfall, prices or civil war (Z_t). In fact the household welfare output (x_{it}) represents the socio-economic status of a household at a given point of time. A household is, therefore, defined as vulnerable when its exposure to a risk event (Z_t) is likely to change its future socio-economic status $(E(x_{it+1}))$ to below the minimum level of survival $(x^\star)$.

As the socio-economic status of household is largely assumed to be determined and conditioned by the level of household asset ownership (A_{it}), the literature on vulnerability pays less attention to risk events that are assumed to be exogenous with no differential effect on the socio-economic status of households. While it might be reasonable to assume risk events, such as rainfall and price (economic shocks), are exogenous variables in household risk management, such an exogeneity assumption is questionable in the context of civil war. It is instead hypothesised in the risk-livelihood vulnerability framework that risk event (Z_t), such as counter-insurgency warfare, is not only an endogenous variable but is triggered by household asset ownership (A_{it}). In other words, while risk events such as drought and economic shock, are modelled as exogenous, it is argued in the context of civil war that asset holdings constitute a source of 'endogenous risk', such as counter-insurgency warfare.

In analysing household vulnerability in rural Africa, the World Bank developed vulnerability models that narrowly focus on the minimum poverty level and variations in income, and generally suggest that the welfare outcomes of realised risk for the poor can be a downward spiral and poverty trap, whereas, for the non-poor, welfare losses can be much less severe (World Bank, 2001:49). Though it is true that households with more assets are likely to sustain the impact of risk events, it is not always true that all households are equally exposed to the same risk events, as some risk events and shocks tend to be specific to some households rather than others. Taking into account the nature and characteristics of a risk event, it is arguable that a household that finds itself above the poverty line $(x^\star)$, but with a high exposure to risk events, should not be considered less vulnerable than a household whose consumption level is certain, but at or even below the poverty line.

It is clear from the preceding discussion that risk events (Z_t), such as rainfall and civil war, play an important role in determining the level of vulnerability. That is, depending on type, nature, characteristics, severity and probability of risky events (Z_t), households at time t=1 whose initial wellbeing (x_{it}) is either below or above the poverty line ($x\star$) might both be considered vulnerable. In the case of generic risk events, such as drought, it is most likely that households with more assets are more able to sustain its effects than those households with fewer assets in the rural context.

In the case of civil war, particularly war between government and rebels, that tends to be generic, the relevant risk event for the analysis of rural livelihoods and vulnerability is counter-insurgency warfare that is used to sustain the war efforts through greed and economic interests. As counter-insurgency warfare is specific, and its occurrence is hypothesised to be triggered largely by assets and drought, then it is likely that the non-poor households (x_{npt}) will experience a higher welfare loss, and are thus more vulnerable to the recurrent shocks of counter-insurgency warfare than the poor households (x_{pt}). With repeated occurrence of counter-insurgency warfare, the non-poor households are likely to experience a downward spiral of vulnerability and their socio-economic status may decline below the minimum level of survival and end up even lower than or at par with that of poor households. Although the poor households will experience welfare loss as a result of counter-insurgency warfare, the negative change in their socio-economic status will be less severe than or at the same level of that of non-poor households.

These hypothetical livelihood outcomes of civil war, particularly of counter-insurgency warfare, are not adequately validated by in-depth analysis in the context of civil war. The patchy and limited research assessing vulnerability in the context of civil war tends to make generic statement about the level of vulnerability at the meso-community level rather than at micro-household level. For example, this phenomenon of counter-insurgency warfare and its resultant 'asset transfer economy' in southern Sudan has been recognised by some researchers (de Waal, 1993; Duffield, 1993; Keen, 1994; Deng, 1999). Some have even generally concluded (Keen, 1994; Duffield, 1993) that in the context of 'asset transfer economy', vulnerability is associated more with wealth than poverty.

Comparing these hypothetical livelihood outcomes of civil war with those of drought, it becomes very clear that the dynamics of vulnerability are quite different and largely shaped and conditioned by the nature of risk to which households are exposed. While non-poor households exposed to counter-insurgency warfare may experience a rapid decline in their socio-economic status, falling below a minimum survival level, the non-poor households in the context of drought may experience limited welfare loss and recover quickly to the pre-drought socio-economic status. This differential level of vulnerability is primarily attributed to the fact that the intensity and recurrence of counter-insurgency warfare, unlike drought, are paradoxically conditioned and triggered by wealth and assets and make non-poor households more susceptible to counterinsurgency warfare attacks than poor households. These hypothesised differential livelihood outcomes have not been assessed before by empirical research, and this book attempts to contribute towards filling this literature gap by analysing and comparing the dynamic of vulnerability and livelihood outcomes of households exposed to drought and counter-insurgency warfare in southern Sudan.

Conclusion

The chapter has set out the theoretical and conceptual framework that will guide discussion of the main research questions in the subsequent chapters. The 'risk-livelihood-vulnerability framework' has been developed to provide the conceptual basis for analyzing and understanding the dynamic process of risk events, household livelihood assets, the risk management process and its resultant livelihood outcomes in terms of household vulnerability. The 'risk-livelihood-vulnerability framework', unlike other approaches, is based on risk events, household livelihood assets as its main building blocks, livelihood strategies and vulnerability as an outcome of livelihood strategies.

The starting point for understanding and analyzing household risk management and vulnerability is the sources and characteristics of risk events that are faced and confronted by households. Besides the sources of risk events, other characteristics, such as intensity, duration, geographical or social spread, frequency and the repeated nature of risk events, all play important roles in understanding household risk management strategies and vulnerability. As risk events are generally assumed exogenous to household livelihood activities, the relevance of this assumption has been questioned in the context of civil war.

The 'risk–livelihood–vulnerability' framework identifies two important household livelihood strategies: *ex ante risk management strategies* and *ex post livelihood strategies*. While it has been recognised in the risk literature that poor and non-poor households are far from passive in confronting risk, there is an unresolved debate about the effectiveness of household livelihood strategies, particularly the *ex ante risk management strategies*. It is even arguable in the risk literature, given the nature of civil war, whether households exposed to prolonged civil war would take any *ex ante livelihood strategies*. This poses the basic conceptual research questions whether households exposed to prolonged conflict take *ex ante risk management strategies*? This broad research question and other related research questions on asset management, particularly livelihood diversification and social capital, are discussed in chapter 5.

The last component of the 'risk–livelihood–vulnerability' framework is the outcome of household risk management strategies that is represented generally by the level of household vulnerability. There is a well-founded argument in the risk literature of associating a household's vulnerability more with the level of asset ownership than with sources of risk, because of the exogeneity assumption of risk events. This commonly held opinion of linking vulnerability to assets alone has been conceptually questioned, particularly in the context of civil war. The 'risk–livelihood–vulnerability' framework conceptually hypothesises in the context of prolonged civil war, particularly where there is counter-insurgency warfare, that non-poor households will be as vulnerable as poor households. This poses a basic research question about who is more vulnerable during civil war, poor or non-poor households? The outcomes of household risk management strategies and vulnerability are discussed in Chapter 6.

CHAPTER FOUR

Household Risk Events: Sources and Characteristics

Introduction

This chapter discusses the first component of the risk–livelihood–vulnerability framework presented in chapter 3. It generally discusses the trajectory of vulnerability in southern Sudan and main sources of risk events faced by research communities in the 1990s such as drought and counter-insurgency warfare and with less emphasis on insurgency warfare (guerrilla warfare) that is beyond the scope of this book. The main objective of this chapter is to discuss in more detail the risk events faced by the research communities in the 1990s. The chapter discusses and compares the research communities on the basis of their exposure to various risk events during the 1990s. The genesis of political vulnerability, exclusion and asset transfer from southern Sudan is discussed in Section 2. The evolution of the military doctrine of counter-insurgency warfare in Sudan is discussed and assessed in Section 3. The main risk events as perceived by the research communities and households in the 1990s, are discussed and compared in Section 4.

The ways and manner in which civil wars are conducted, prosecuted and sustained are more important than their primary causes, particularly for rural African communities. It is argued that much of the human devastation can be traced back to the criminal tactics with which the war is fought (ICG, 2002:115). What is most hurting African rural livelihoods is more related to the conduct of civil war than to other risk events, or the conventional warfare between rebels and governments. The structural transformation in the conduct of contemporary civil warfare in Africa is largely associated with the economic crisis and the end of Cold War and superpower patronage that have had a profound impact on military establishments (de Waal, 1996). As governments at war with their citizens are becoming increasingly unable to sustain and control their armies, they turn to local sources of provisioning through counter-insurgency warfare that involves intense predatory behaviour of soldiers and their militias.

The original idea of guerrilla warfare is rooted in Mao Tse Tung's ideology of waging a people's war, and he famously described a guerrilla among the people as being a fish in water. While liberation movements have adopted this doctrine of guerrilla warfare across the world as effective military tactics, the states that are at war with these liberation movements usually adopt counter-guerrilla warfare that is described as 'draining the water from the fish'. The doctrine of counter-guerrilla warfare is largely associated with the Western colonial rulers, as they discovered that conventional military engagements could not help to defeat the liberation movements with regular armies. According to de Waal (1993a: 36), the most systematic exponent of counter-insurgency theories has been French military activities in northern Africa. One of the first theoreticians was General Lyautey, commander of the French forces in Morocco, who described a guerrilla as 'a plant which grows only in certain ground...... the most efficient method is to render the ground unsuitable for him' (cited in Gottman, 1945:242). During the Algerian war, a French military advisor described this strategy of 'making the ground unsuitable for the guerrilla' as follows:

> *'Anything that could facilitate the existence of the guerrillas in any way, or which could conceivably be used by them – depots, shelters, caches, food crops, houses, etc. – must be systematically destroyed or brought in. All inhabitants and livestock must be evacuated from the (guerrillas') refuge area. When they leave, the intervention troops must not only have destroyed the (guerrilla) bands but must leave behind them an area empty of all resources and absolutely uninhabitable.'* (Trinquier, 1964:85)

Other Western colonists pursued counter-insurgency warfare campaigns against liberation movements in their colonies, which were similar and closer to the spirit of Lyautey and the French military campaigns adopted in northern Africa. Thompson (1966) showed an example of how British and American campaigns to defeat the communist insurgency in Malaya and Vietnam respectively were similar to the counter-insurgency campaigns pursued by the French in northern Africa. The post-independence African leaders who inherited political power, instead of winning political support from all their citizens, they adopted similar counter-insurgency campaigns to suppress the civil war waged by communities whose political aspirations had not been met by the independence political arrangements (e.g. excluded ethnic minorities). The ruling elite in post-independence Africa, despite amassing considerable personal wealth, has presided over states that lack the means for effective and disciplined counter-insurgency and have resorted to recruiting civilians into unpaid militias (Keen, 2000). The civilian population that is recruited into unpaid militias to wage counter-insurgency warfare on behalf of governments is primarily motivated either by fear, need or greed, or some combination of the three (Keen, 2000:24).

The common trend cutting across various counter-insurgency campaigns is that they all stress the need to engage and destroy the guerrilla forces, and have treated the local population as though they were actual enemies rather than potential allies. Rather than winning the local population over from supporting rebel forces, counter-insurgency campaigns have been more prone to inflicting punishment on the local population (de Waal, 1993a).

Genesis and Trajectory of Vulnerability and Assets Transfer

Since independence in 1956, Sudan has been at war with itself and has wasted most years of its independence in major civil wars (1955-1972, 1982-2005) that have resulted in a huge death toll and massive internal displacement and exodus to neighbouring and other foreign countries. A comprehensive understanding of the causes and origins of the civil war in Sudan is evidently crucial, as the ultimate sustainable solution will largely depend on it. Despite the fact that Sudan has been at war with itself since its independence in 1956, the debate on the genesis and causes of the recurrent civil wars is divisive and far from settled.

The characteristics of most African civil wars are directly or indirectly rooted in historical legacies, with their genesis in the colonial period. Given the prolonged duration and the depth of the conflict in Sudan, it is important to place the political vulnerability experienced by the people of southern Sudan in one united Sudan in historical perspective and to trace its roots to their sources. Winston Churchill (1940:2) described the first historical contacts of present southern Sudan with the outside world – Arabia, Turkey, Egypt and Britain – as a brutal invasion by outsiders 'destitute of wealth', in search of resources such as gold, ivory, water and slaves.

Instead of digging into the historical archives of Sudan, the most relevant historical period is the period of the early formation and establishment of contemporary Sudan. In fact, the genesis of political vulnerability in southern Sudan and the growth of militia groups can be traced back to the period of lawlessness and slavery. This period covers three important regimes that were largely shaped by the issues of the slave trade and asset transfers from southern Sudan: Turko-Egyptian Rule (1821-1885), The Mahdist State (1885-1898) and Anglo-Egyptian Condominium (1898-1955), the Post-Independence Sudan (1956-2005).

Turko-Egyptian Rule (1821-1881)

Turko-Egyptian Rule was ideologically and politically Islamic, represented by the Ottoman Empire in Egypt. The Ottoman Empire invaded Sudan with the clear objectives of pursuing their enemies, the Memeluks, who had fled from Egypt into Sudan, as well as having interests in gold, ivory, and other resources. Importantly, their most vehemently expressed objective was to recruit the black warriors of Sudan as slave soldiers for the Egyptian army.

The Turko-Egyptian invasion of northern Sudan in 1821 marked the beginning of the first form of centralised administration. Despite the fact that the people in the north revolted against the heavy taxes to be paid in cattle or in slaves, the Turko-Egyptian government developed over time the administrative structures, established schools, improved communication and security, all of which encouraged economic growth and commerce in the north (Lesch, 1998:27). For the non-Arab peoples in the south, southern Blue Nile (Funj), eastern Sudan (Beja) and the Nuba Mountains, the Turko-Egyptian rule was a period of lawlessness and slavery, as it caused disastrous destruction of livelihoods, initially due to the seizure of men to replenish the army in Egypt. Besides the Turko-Egyptian raids, private Arab armies also organised periodic ghazwas (slave hunts) in which they seized ivory, slaves, and cattle (Lesch, 1998). Ottoman, northern Sudanese, and European traders established fortified stations (zaribas) in which slaves were held until they could be transported to the north, as well as to Libya, Egypt, and Arabia.

Slave-owning increased substantially within northern Sudan, where slaves began to be used not only in the army but also in other activities, such as agriculture, construction, and housework as servants and blacksmiths. Interestingly, the slaves also came to provide one of the means of paying the Turko-Egyptian standing army (Spaulding, 1982). According to Sanderson and Sanderson (1981:10), by the early 1880s almost two-thirds of the population of Khartoum (around 50,000), the capital of Sudan, were estimated to be slaves. It has been estimated that during this period almost half of the population in the Bahr el Ghazal region escaped slavery only by emigrating to other parts of southern Sudan, while weaker community groups, such as the Jur and Bongo were threatened with extinction (Keen, 1994; Collins, 1971).

The slave hunts (ghazwas) were accompanied by exploitative processes and brutal raids on livestock and grain stocks that resulted in massive asset transfer from southern Sudan (Gray, 1961). Turko-Egyptian rule greatly benefited from this process of asset transfer as its regime in Egypt was militarily weak and was desperately seeking to establish financial and political autonomy from the Ottoman sultan. Besides the Turko-Egyptian government, these asset transfers and cattle raids also relaxed the severe economic pressures faced by Syrian and Egyptian traders in the 1860s, as well as northern petty traders (jellaba), as they managed to reach to southern Sudan by a river (Holt and Daly, 1988). According to Gray (1961), by 1870 raided cattle had become the universal and indispensable medium of exchange for traders in northern Sudan.

The Mahdiyya State (1885-1898)

The Turko-Egyptian regime was replaced by the Mahdiyya, the northern politico-religious movement, in 1881 with full support from slave-traders, whose interests were threatened by the renewed efforts of the Turko-Egyptian rule's anti-slavery campaign, in response to pressure from Europe (Daly, 1986). The period of Mahdiyya (1881-1898) was an extremely costly adventure that was characterised by the breakdown of law and order, famine, drought, war and a general Hobbesian state of affairs that prevailed throughout the country (Deng, 1995:50). It is estimated that the population of Sudan fell from around 7 million before the Mahdiyya revolt in 1881 to somewhere between 2 and 3 million after the fall of the Mahdiyya state in 1898 (Daly, 1986:18). Although the Mahdiyya state could not consolidate its control over the south, its frequent raids, particularly into the Bahr el Ghazal region, further destabilised its society and economy.

However, for the north, the Mahdiyya was seen as a period of liberation that invigorated their national image and held a positive symbolic significance as a golden age (Lesch, 1998:28). In contrast, within the south, the Mahdiyya was seen as the culmination of the depredations of Turko-Egyptian rule, but with the living scars of its brutality on the southern Sudanese that reinforced the Southerner's hatred and fear of the northern Sudanese (Collins, 1962:177). This period of Mahdiyya fixed a collective memory among the Southerners that the Northerners were the primary source of their danger and vulnerability (Lesch, 1998:29).

Anglo-Egyptian Condominium (1898-1955): Southern Policy

Britain sought control over Sudan for imperial strategic reasons that were largely related to preventing other European powers from seizing the sources of the Nile and from gaining footholds along the Red Sea from which they could threaten the sea route to India and restoration of Turko-Egyptian sovereignty (Lesch, 1998). When the Mahdiyya government was overturned by the forces of Britain and Egypt in 1898, there was a renewed commitment by the Anglo-Egyptian government to suppress slavery, at least in theory (Keen, 1994). Contemporary Sudan came into being during this period of Anglo-Egyptian Condominium with two-tier separate administrative arrangements for the north and south. Although Anglo-Egyptian troops made incursions into the south in 1898 and established outposts thereby World War I, the effective, gradual and partial integration of the south into the Sudanese state occurred between the early 1920s and the late 1950s (Keen, 1994).

In early 1900, British colonial rule, despite its success in ending slave raids, was faced with opposition from the Dinka and other southern groups because of its attempt to harness southern resources with forced labour and heavy livestock taxes (Collins, 1971; Alier, 1990). The southern opposition was quelled by large-scale destruction and devastation and this allowed the government to soften its anti-slavery campaign, by allowing domestic slavery in Kordofan, to appease the Arab nomads (Baggara). The softened position of the Angelo-Egyptian government over slavery encouraged Arab nomads (Baggara) to attack Twic Dinka in 1906 and Rizeigat Arab nomads to attack Malwal Dinka in 1908 (Keen, 1994). British officials argued that such raids were to be tolerated since the Dinka were resisting the Anglo-Egyptian government (Henderson, 1939).

While British colonial rule exerted considerable efforts to modernise the economy and infrastructures in the north, it entrusted Christian missionaries to provide moral guidance, which was perceived to be more needed in the south than was economic development (Lesch, 1998). In order to protect the south from Islamic influence and to seal it off from northern dominance, as well as to stop Arabs from seizing slaves, cattle and grain from the south and the Nuba Mountains, the Anglo-Egyptian Condominium articulated this policy through the Closed District Order of 1922. This order specifically restricted Sudanese who lived outside the south, Nuba Mountains, Southern Blue Nile (Funj), Darfur and parts of eastern Sudan (Beja) to travel or live there without a special permit.

This order was followed by the Permits to Trade Ordinance of 1925 that allowed the authorities to exclude the northern traders (jallaba), who had dominated commerce in the countryside. Egyptian officials in the south were removed after 1924 and some northern officials were replaced by British officials and Arab-style dress (jallabiyya) was prohibited, as were Arabic names (Lesch, 1998). In 1928, the British formalised a language policy that allowed vernacular languages to be taught in primary schools, and English was designated the official language, while Arabic was excluded from schools and government offices. The long-term implications of the British separate South-North policy contemplated the possibility of the south being eventually linked with East Africa (Henderson, 1965:165).

These British policies towards the south gradually won the confidence of the people in the south to the extent that the British were seen less as imperialist intruders, as their policies developed in the south a sense of identity-based on indigenous culture and Christian cultural norms (Deng, 1995). And, indeed, whatever can be said against British rule in Sudan, it brought the longest period of peace and security, at least from invasion and the use of crude force, that the south has experienced throughout its recorded history. Although these British policies towards the south did not lead to the contemplated desired outcome of linking south with East Africa, they have largely influenced contemporary southern identity, which contrary to that of the north, borrowed a great deal from Western values.

The real problem with these British policies towards the south was that they did not foster economic and social development in the south and the Nuba Mountains and thereby widened the already substantial gap with the north (Badal, 1988). The limited number of missionary schools did not meet the population's needs in the south. There were no government secondary schools in the entire south until after World War II (Lesch, 1998). As late as the 1940s, government schools in the south included several elementary schools, two intermediate schools, one teacher training centre, one commercial school, and one senior secondary school (Deng, 1995:86). Key British officials blocked government and private development efforts in the south, arguing that the indigenous population had no desire to improve their economic welfare (Lesch, 1998:32). The development of markets and trade was discouraged by poor roads and transportation in the south, and labour migration to the north and urban centres was also restricted.

The northern Sudanese resented the British policy of separating the south from the north. Under pressure from Egypt and northern Sudan, the British regime changed their policy drastically and abruptly in 1945, from the separation of the south from the north to the ultimate unity of Sudan, and recognised the need to accelerate economic and educational development in the south to catch up with the north (Deng, 1995:88). As the British brokered the independence of Sudan with the northern elite, the south overwhelmingly felt betrayed, as the British not only handed over the south to the northern colonial power but were too late to affect the acceleration of socio-economic development in the south.

One former British administrator in the south observed that 'one of the biggest 'British' errors was to have a Southern Policy, which led not only to a scandalous lack of investment and education in the south but was really incompatible with the aims of a unitary state' (quoted in Deng, 1995:96). In the process of the British handing over the south to northern troops, violent resistance, revolt and mutiny by southern troops erupted in Torit in 1955, which sparked civil discontent throughout the south and fanned the flames of the first civil war that lasted 17 years, until it was resolved in 1972 with the Addis Ababa Agreement.

By the time Sudan gained its independence in 1956, the south was well behind the north in terms of economic and social development. Not to the surprise of most southerners, successive post-independence central governments pursued policies that deliberately aimed at marginalizing southerners socially, politically and economically (Deng, 2002b). The socio-economic disparity that had been scandalously created by the lack of development and education in the south during British rule had naturally widened sharply between the north and south during post-independence.

The Post-Independence Sudan: The Evolution of Counter-insurgency Warfare

There is a web of interrelated factors that appear to be characteristically associated with the growth of militia groups and counter-insurgency warfare in the post-independence Sudan. The root causes of the recurrent civil wars, and other additional conditions that have contributed to the progressive evolution of counter-insurgency warfare in contemporary Sudan, are discussed under two basic kinds of counterinsurgency warfare, namely; exogenous counter-insurgency warfare and endogenous counter-insurgency warfare. The distinctive difference between the two kinds of counterinsurgency warfare is that exogenous counter-insurgency refers to an externally instigated counterinsurgency while; endogenous counter-insurgency refers to an internally instigated counter-insurgency that emanates from within the targeted communities.

This distinction is important, not only in understanding the growth of militia groups but also in understanding better the livelihood strategies adopted by the communities exposed to these two types of counter-insurgency warfare. In the context of the Dinka research communities in the Bahr el Ghazal region, exogenous counter-insurgency warfare covers the murahalin militias (mainly Arab nomads in southern Kordofan (Misseria

Baggara) and southern Darfur (Rizaygat)) in western Sudan and the Nuer militia groups that were found in southern Sudan and hostile to the main rebels group (SPLA). Endogenous counter-insurgency warfare, on the other hand, covers mainly the Bahr el Ghazal Dinka militias that emerged from within the Dinka community in the 1990s.

Exogenous Counter-insurgency Warfare

The evolution of counter-insurgency warfare in contemporary Sudan can be traced back to the early years of the post-independence period when civil war erupted in southern Sudan in 1955 and progressively intensified in the 1980s and 1990s with new actors and dimensions. The subsequent intensification of counter-insurgency warfare in post-independent Sudan is discussed in three main periods: the 1950s-70s, the 1980s and the 1990s.

First Civil War and Inter-War Periods, the 1950s-1970s

Generally from the 1940s to the early 1960s, the movement of Arab nomads into Bahr el Ghazal was carefully controlled through annual intertribal conferences under the 'Native Administration' system (Saeed, 1982:217). By the mid-1960s, however, peaceful relations between Arab nomads and the Dinka of Bahr el Ghazal began to deteriorate, primarily because of the out-break of the first civil war between southern rebels and central government, but importantly also because of increasing economic pressures on the Arab nomads (Keen, 1990:154). Grazing land came under growing pressure as improved veterinary services from the 1950s increased the numbers of the Arab nomads' cattle (Karam, 1980), while mechanised farming and small-holder cultivation for export took increasing amounts of land in western Sudan (Saeed, 1982:252).

The first civil war and the 'southern' resistance started in the Equatoria region of southern Sudan in 1955, even before the formal independence of Sudan in 1956, because of dissatisfaction in southern Sudan about the in-dependence arrangements made by the British colonial authorities. Though southern resistance started with the Equatoria region as its epicentre, the people of Bahr el Ghazal region, in spite of the distance, immediately joined and identified themselves with the southern rebels, mainly because of their local grievances, particularly the consistent raids by Arab nomads. By the mid–1960s the close identification of the Dinka of Bahr el Ghazal region with the rebels eroded their rights to state protection, as Misseriyia Arab no-mads raids on their villages became commonplace. Little action to prevent these raids was taken by the police and army, who instead became involved as perpetrators themselves (Deng, 1986).

These Misseriyia Arab raids resulted in the displacement of the Ngok Dinka from most of their northern fertile highlands (Ngol), the border area that constituted about two-thirds of the total area, and their settlement in the southern lowlands (Pandit) in 1966. The few Ngok Dinka who were dis-placed from Ngol and migrated to the Misseriyia Arab nomads' homelands in western Sudan were even denied protection by the state. For example, in 1965 more than 200 Ngok Dinka were shot and burned to death by local residents in the presence of armed police in the major towns (al-Muglad and Babanousa) of the Misseriyia Arabs (Saeed, 1982). Similar raids and abuses by the Arab nomads without the victims being protected by the state were common in the border areas of Nuer and the Ruweng Dinka in the Upper Nile region. According to Johnson (1989:482) these Arab nomads raids as-sisted by the army, combined with declining veterinary services during the first civil war, drastically reduced the cattle population in southern Sudan, particularly Bahr el Ghazal and Upper Nile regions.

Despite large-scale cattle raiding and abuses of the southerners by both Arab nomad raids and the army, the central government did not explicitly encourage these raids during the first civil war. These raids were marked by a relatively low level of military technology (spears and a few rifles). Also, the Native Administration still used to provide mechanisms for settling the conflict until 1969, when a military regime took power. The new military regime abolished the Native Administration in 1971 and a new form of local government known as 'People's Councils' was established, consisting of members drawn from 'progressive' and 'modern' forces allied with the new regime rather than traditional leaders (Karam, 1980). The abolition of 'native administration' made the new local government ineffectual, which subsequently resulted in weakening the mechanisms of conflict resolution in the north (de Waal, 1993b:145). On the other hand, the Addis Ababa Peace Agreement signed between the southern rebels and the new military regime in 1972 restored a form of 'native administration' in the south, in the form of chiefs' court. Subsequently during the 1970s, the traditional chiefs of Bahr el Ghazal found themselves without comparable or with even weak local authorities north of the regional boundary with whom they could negotiate or settle tribal disputes and conflicts.

The situation of the Ngok Dinka of Abyei was somewhat precarious, as the area was part of the administration of Kordofan in the north and subsequently was not covered by the Addis Ababa Agreement that restored a form of native administration. As a result, the Dinka Ngok became extremely vulnerable during the 1970s. Misseriyia Arab raids and abuses intensified with explicit support from the local government officials. As Misseriyia Arabs now used modern automatic weapons that they had steadily acquired during the 1970s and early 1980s from the arms markets created by wars in Uganda and Chad and distribution from Libya (de Waal, 1993b), their raids on Ngokland resulted in the massive destruction of rural lives and livelihoods.

The Second Civil War: The Murahaleen Phenomenon

With the abrogation of the Addis Ababa Peace Agreement with the division of southern Sudan into three regions in 1981, the people of southern Sudan waged a second civil war that initially started in the northern Bahr el Ghazal region in 1981 and became organised in 1983 under the Sudan People's Liberation Movement/Army (SPLM). The people of Northern Bahr el Ghazal started organising resistance in 1981 in response to their local grievances, and in particular, to the failure of the central government to provide the necessary protection against the waves of Arab raid. When the SPLA was formed in 1983 in the Upper Nile region near the border with Ethiopia, the people of Northern Bahr el Ghazal were the first to join, with the unambiguous motive of obtaining arms and military training to protect their people and land from Arab nomad raids.

This attempt was counterproductive as most of the male adults, particularly the youth, had joined the SPLA at the Ethiopian-Sudan border, taking with them all their locally acquired light weapons, and the area was left increasingly vulnerable to the raids of the government-supported Arab nomads' armed bands known as Murahaleen (mobile militias). The Murahaleen militias were used by successive Sudanese governments as proxy forces and as an integral part of their war against the rebels in southern Sudan (Mawson, 1991). The SPLA being occupied with other pressing priorities, particularly with establishing itself as a formidable military force, by asserting and consolidating its military success in Upper Nile and Eastern Equatoria, the first SPLA forces only arrived in the northern Bahr el Ghazal area in 1987 (Deng, 1999).

During the 1980s, the Dinka communities of northern Bahr el Ghazal experienced intensified raids with considerable savagery from Arab nomads, raids that were unprecedented in the history of intertribal conflict in Sudan (Mawson, 1990). Since the mid-1980s, successive central governments have employed the classic counter-insurgency tactic of attempting to 'drain the water to catch fish', by putting military pressure on the SPLA base of support in northern Bahr el Ghazal. In the 1980s, senior army officers at the Khartoum Military College developed plans that focused on the destabilisation of the Dinka as a people as a key strategy to win the war and to deprive the south of its leadership.

According to ICG (2002:121), the objective of this counter-insurgency warfare was threefold: capturing valuable farm and grazing land for Arab communities expanding south; destroying the popular base of the SPLA and creating a larger buffer zone between north and south, and decimating the socio-economic fabric of Dinka communities. Thus, Dinka civilians, cattle, harvest and all forms of assets were considered appropriate targets for indiscriminate attacks, as part of a broader effort to break the backbone of the SPLA (ICG, 2002). By condoning and underwriting such conduct, successive central governments have created rich financial incentives for raiders, militias and slave traders to plunder southern communities, particularly Dinka, from looting livestock to exploiting slave labour on commercial farms.

Although the people of Northern Bahr el Ghazal experienced Arab cattle raids through the 1980s, people consider that the raiding intensified and reached a peak in 1985. By October 1985 the Dinka from the rural areas of Abyei had moved with their cattle closer to their main town in Abyei for protection. However, the army garrison in Abyei town did not provide protection and failed to deter the Arab raiders, as the military forces were themselves responsible for destroying the rural villages in September 1985 (Mawson, 1990:141). By the end of October 1985, the pasture around

Abyei town was all but exhausted and for this reason, coupled with the fear of imminent Arab raids, many Ngok Dinka abandoned their rural livelihoods and moved to towns and cities in northern Sudan for labouring work and protection.

According to a community survey, the population of Ngok Dinka that migrated to northern cities and towns in 1985 was estimated to be more than 80 per cent. The rest of the population began the journey south and some settled in the southern part of the Kiir River area, while those with cattle moved further south to Twic land. In December 1985, the Arab nomads with support from the army from Abyei garrison followed those who moved with cattle southward and attacked their cattle camps in the Twic area (Mawson, 1990). Similar waves of Arab raids were also experienced in the 1980s by Malual and Abiem Dinka of the Awiel area in northern Bahr el Ghazal. These Arab raids in the 1980s were largely responsible for causing famine in northern Bahr el Ghazal in 1988 (Keen, 1994).

The phenomenon of the Murahaleen militia emerged from the 1980s through to the beginning of the 21st century, and progressively became one of the most formidable armed groups and fighting forces in Sudan. In some places, the Murahaleen militias had become more powerful than the armed forces, with the result that they were effectively above the law (de Waal, 1993b). The growing power of the Murahaleen militias would have not happened if there had been no conducive conditions that encouraged the Arab nomads to join the Murahaleen militias. These conditions included among other factors economic incentives, political agenda and a deliberate military strategy. These factors are not only important in explaining the growth of the Murahaleen militia, but also shed light on the intensity, severity and persistence of this Murahaleen phenomenon in the 1980s and the 1990s.

Economic Drive: Need and Greed

The rural subsistence and economic crisis in the north and the drought that gripped western Sudan particularly affected Arab nomads from 1982 to 1984. This was followed by famine that reached its most critical point in the middle of 1985 and created the economic drive for the Arab nomads to join the Murahaleen. During the prolonged drought in the early 1980s in western Sudan, the Arab nomads, particularly the middle-aged, saw their animals die or were forced to sell them, and young men saw their fathers' herds dwindle. Livestock prices and pastoralist terms of trade in western Sudan reached their lowest point in July 1985, with cattle worth only a tenth of their pre-famine values in terms of grain (Mawson, 1990). The Arab nomads in western Sudan suffered during the drought in 1984-85 a severe loss of stock, destitution and famine, which resulted in excess mortality of 250,000 (de Waal, 1989). For young Arab nomads in western Sudan, particularly those severely affected by drought, raiding Dinka cattle was an ideal opportunity to obtain and increase their meagre capital stock (de Waal, 1993b; Keen, 1990). The transfer of stolen and raided livestock resources from northern Bahr el Ghazal to the north was estimated to be around 340,000 head of cattle between 1984 and 1986, and progressively reached more than one million rustled Dinka cattle in 1988 alone (Keen, 1990:155).

Besides raiding cattle, the Arabs in western Sudan relied on Dinka labour for cultivation and herding, and their raiding led to a resumption in the flows of labour from northern Bahr el Ghazal, that had begun to dry up with the eruption of the second civil war (Keen, 1994). This economic drive for a cheap and regular supply of labour from northern Bahr el Ghazal explained the apparent resurgence of slavery and forced labour in western Sudan in the 1980s (Africa Watch, 1990:139), and this continued through the 1990s. In addition to their function in securing livestock and labour, the Arab raids in the 1980s offered the prospect of driving the Dinka away from the often-contested pastures and grazing lands in northern Bahr el Ghazal (Johnson, 1988).

The progressive raids of the Murahaleen militias on Dinka cattle were triggered not only by the economic drive of acquiring stock but also by the complex fortunes of the livestock trade in western Sudan, which was driven by the famine and the activities of local merchants (Mawson, 1990). In actual fact, Dinka cattle are not hardy enough for the semi-desert conditions of western Sudan, which makes the rustled cattle more appropriate for sale rather than for restocking. The local traders in western Sudan faced increasing difficulties in the early 1980s, as they were being gradually squeezed out from the booming cattle trade in Abyei that attracted larger northern traders from the major cities. For example, in 1987 one head of Dinka cattle was exchanged in Abyei market for not more than a single 90-kilogram bag of sorghum, while it fetched some 27 times the value of a 90-kilogram bag of sorghum in el Obeid, a major market in western Sudan (Keen, 1990:155).

The terms of trade in livestock (supplied by the Dinka) and grain (supplied by Arab traders and the army) markets were favourable for those buying cattle and selling grain in the 1980s. The army often co-operated and colluded with merchants and became involved in the grain trade in all garrisons towns in the south, including Abyei (Africa Watch, 1990). The deterioration of pastoralist terms of trade was largely due to the threat of the Arab raids of Dinka cattle, which forced many people to sell their live-stock and move to the north for labour work rather than engaging in risky agro-pastoralist livelihoods. This huge cattle price margin and 'bonanza' to be made from purchasing cattle in Abyei market had created a powerful interest among traders and the army in maintaining and expanding it (Keen, 1990). Apparently, this booming trade was threatened by the drying up of livestock as a result of the second civil war. In order to maintain the flow of cattle from Bahr el Ghazal to the north and to maximise their profits, the traders and army personnel were keen to finance and support Murahaleen activities, as well as planning the raiding of Dinka cattle (Mahmud and Baldo, 1987; Africa Watch, 1990). There was, therefore, an economic imperative to the Murahaleen militias raiding of Dinka cattle, both for the raiders themselves and the army and the merchants who bought from them.

Political Agenda: Deflecting Northern Grievances:

The combination of political, strategic and economic pressures on central governments in the 1980s, and on subsequent governments in the 1990s, caused them to enlist the Misseriya Arab militias in organised attacks on the Dinka, by providing arms, ammunition, intelligence and effective im-munity from prosecution (Africa Watch, 1990). While economic depression, drought, and famine encouraged self-enrichment through cattle raiding, most importantly the army and northern politicians recognised the military and a political opportunity presented by the Murahaleen militias. These mi-litias offered an effective military and political means of debilitating Dinka livelihoods, the main source of support for the SPLA (Mahmud and Baldo, 1987:17), offering the prospect of gaining access to oil (Johnson, 1988), and at the same time channelling Arab nomad frustrations against the south (Saeed, 1982; Keen, 1990).

The Murahaleen militias were initially formed in the late 1970s in response to local conflicts. When the military and economic success of the Murahaleen was evident in the early 1980s, the main northern political parties (Umma Party and National Islamic Front (NIF)) began to attach increasing importance to them as an alternative armed force that was more loyal in serving their interests than the national army. When the Nimeri military regime that took power through a military coup in 1969 was overthrown by a popular uprising in the north in 1985, successive central governments relied on the Murahaleen militias to contain through counter-insurgency warfare the military success of the rebels (SPLA) in the south, which became evident in 1985 and in subsequent years. The Transitional Military Council, which replaced the ousted Nimeri regime, with the influence of some of its members, who had close business and political links with merchants in western Sudan, formalised the military role of the Murahaleen as a suitable proxy force to fight cheap counter-insurgency warfare against the SPLA (de Waal, 1993b).

When the new government was elected in 1986 and headed by the Umma party, which derived much of its political and financial support from western Sudan, particularly from the merchants who supported raiding the Dinka, it was natural that the newly elected government was keen to support the Murahaleen. According to Mawson (1990:145), most of the devastating raids of the Murahaleen on Bahr el Ghazal occurred during 1986-87, and a massacre of over 1,000 displaced Dinka occurred at Ad-Daien in western Sudan in 1987, only one year after the formation of the elected government in 1986. The report into the massacre unequivocally declared that the government was 'at the root' of the massacre and accused it of having directly introduced the Arab nomad ethnic groups into war with the SPLA in the south (Mahmud and Baldo, 1987). Despite these criticisms, the elected government of the Umma party publicly declared its commitment to arm and support Murahaleen activities against the rebels in the south, and its plan to incorporate them into the Popular Defence Force (Mawson, 1990).

While the Umma government was planning to legitimise the Murahaleen, the opposition political party (National Islamic Front (NIF)) formed a 'Committee for the Defence of Islam and Nation' in 1988, with one of its aims being to promote the cause of expanding and legitimising the Murahaleen militias (de Waal, 1993b). The formation of the committee was a clear attempt by the NIF to coax the Murahaleen out of their Umma party political aspirations into their own alliance and political sphere. When the NIF took power through a military coup in 1989, it was swift to indicate its continuing support for the general policy of using Murahaleen militias against the rebels in the south (Mawson, 1990:146). This was not surprising, as the leader of the new military regime and the then president of Sudan was well known to the Murahaleen from his 1988-1989 military position in western Sudan and Bentiu garrison in southern Sudan.

As the SPLA military activities in 1989 reached and effectively covered most rural areas of Northern Bahr el Ghazal, Upper Nile and Nuba Mountains, where Arab nomads accessed pastures and water, the raiding activities of the Arab nomads were scaled down and their access to pastures was also eroded. This expansion of SPLA military activities provided the right moment for the military regime to quickly legitimise the Murahaleen into a political and military force by promulgating the Popular Defence Act in November 1989 (Mawson, 1990:146). This Act allowed the military regime to officially co-opt the Murahaleen militias in the Popular Defence Forces, and it used them effectively during the 1990s in one of its most important counter-insurgency warfare campaigns, and using a 'scorched earth' strategy against the rebels and communities in the south. Because the regular army considered the Popular Defence Forces as a potential rival, separate command, training, funding and supply structures were set up, that made it a parallel army that became self-financed through looting and the slave-trade (ICG, 2002:122).

Besides the promulgation of the Popular Defence Act in 1989, the NIF military regime organised a religious conference in El-Obeid in western Sudan in 1993 and issued a Fatwa (an Islamic legal decree) that religiously affirmed the activities of the Murahaleen in northern Bahr el Ghazal as part of a jihad (holy war). The Fatwa specifically announced that: '….the rebels who are Muslims….are hereby declared apostates (Murtadeen) from Islam, and non-Muslims are hereby declared infidels (kuffar), who have been standing against the efforts of preaching, proselytization, and spreading of Islam. Islam has justified the fighting and killing of both categories…..with Qur'anic evidence.' With legal and religious justification, the NIF government rigorously pursed counter-insurgency and a scorched earth strategy to depopulate Northern Bahr el Ghazal and Upper Nile regions, including the resumption of institutionalised slavery with a devastating toll on and a displacement of Dinka and Nuer in the 1990s (ICG, 2002).

The exact number of Dinka held in slavery is unknown, and estimates differ widely. While the Sudanese government claimed that as few as 5,000 people have suffered from intertribal abductions (Amnesty International, 2001), some NGOs suggested that up to 200,000 have been enslaved (ICG, 2002:122). Christian Solidarity International claimed that it has purchased the freedom of 45,000 southern Sudanese since 1995, while 100,000 remain enslaved in northern Sudan (Eibner, 2001). What is certain is that slave-raiding and the practice of slavery do exist in Sudan, as corroborated and documented by numerous sources (ICG, 2002).

Endogenous Counter-insurgency: The Dinka Militia

The first civil war in the 1960s was conducted mainly through exogenous counter-insurgency, conventional warfare and guerrilla warfare. The civilian population in southern Sudan were not directly involved in the conduct of the war, except for a few individuals who were used by the government as informants to provide intelligence and security information about the movements of the southern rebels. However, some northern historians argued that during Turko-Egyptian and Mahdiyya rule slavery was practised even within the south, and southerners had captured other southerners to sell to northern merchants in the fortified stations (zaribas) (Lesch, 1998:27).

Deflecting Southern Grievances

In the early years of the formation of the SPLA, central governments capitalised on the tribal conflicts that exist among and between different ethnic groups in the south to sponsor and support southern militias against the SPLA military threat. The main southern militias sponsored by the central governments included Anya-Nya II (predominantly Nuer), Mundari militia in Equatoria, Fertit militia in Bahr el Ghazal and Murle militia in Upper Nile region. The common feature of these militias is that they all have tribal conflict and grudges with Dinka, the principal supporters of the SPLA in Bahr el Ghazal and Upper Nile regions, which made them ideal for counter-insurgency warfare against the SPLA. Unlike the Murahaleen militias who were driven by economic interest and marginalisation in the north, the southern militias arose out of local and tribal grievances and cattle-rustling in the case of the Murle and Nuer militias. Like the Murahaleen militias, the southern militias were in actual fact 'exogenous', as they were externally in-stigated and did not emanate from within the targeted Dinka communities. It may be argued that the cost of the civil war on rural livelihoods in the south that is attributed to the activities of southern militias or south-south conflict may be significantly higher than the cost directly inflicted by the central government army. Southerners killed themselves more than been killed by the central government.

Despite the growth of southern militias in other regions of the south, the Dinka of Bahr el Ghazal region were only exposed to raids from the Murahaleen militias and the Nuer militias (Anya-Nya II) until 1991, when a split occurred within the SPLA. In the early 1990s, the SPLA intensified its military operations, captured most strategic garrisons in western Equatoria and threatened to capture the remaining government garrisons in Bahr el Ghazal and Equatoria, including Juba town, the capital of the south. The Nuer militias, the most formidable militias in the south, started defecting to the SPLA by the late 1980s and early 1990s. By the end of the 1980s, the SPLA was also in control of some rural areas of northern Sudan such as Nuba Mountains in Southern Kordofan and penetrated even into Southern Blue Nile where they captured the strategic garrison town of Kurmuk in the southern Blue Nile region. The SPLA forces even penetrated the Darfur areas in western Sudan in 1991, with the objective of mobilising the indigenous and marginalised communities, particularly the non-Arab tribes, to wage their own insurgency warfare. These military achievements of the SPLA and its military expansion in the north, particularly into Nuba Mountains, Blue Nile and Darfur, posed a real political threat to the military regime in Khartoum and forced it to step up its military operations in the 1990s.

Given these military achievements by the SPLA and coupled with the ineffectiveness of conventional warfare, the central government resorted to sowing division within the SPLA by stoking Nuer-Dinka tensions, the two largest ethnic groups. This strategy of divide-and-rule was meant to deflect and turn the grievances of southerners from being against the cen-tral government to against each other, as an effective way of weakening the south and the rebel movement (SPLA). With encouragement from the central government, coupled with war fatigue and the collapse of Mengistu regime in Ethiopia, a number of key commanders of SPLA, mostly Nuer, commanders broke away from the SPLA in 1991.

The split in the SPLA resulted in the formation of the Southern Sudan Independence Army (SSIA), predominantly from the Nuer, the second-largest tribe in the SPLA after the Dinka as another feature of Nuer militias. Later another military faction, called SPLA–United, under the command of Kerubino Kuanyin (a Dinka from northern Bahr el Ghazal), separated from the SSIA in 1994. All these southern military groups did not have significant implications for the balance of power in Khartoum, as they were simply "war on the cheap" and a way of weakening the SPLA without undue expenditure on the northern Sudanese army and government money. The primary military agenda of the central government during the 1990s was to weaken the SPLA by debilitating and destroying the livelihoods of Dinka, the main supporters of the SPLA, through the Murahaleen and Nuer militias, but more importantly through endogenous counterinsurgency warfare, using Dinka militias.

The SSIA, which was predominantly made up of Nuer tribes, was incited by the central government to raise ethnic and tribal agendas and to wage vigorous tribal war against the Dinka community in Upper Nile region (Deng, 1999). In the last months of 1991, the forces of the SSIA and Nuer civilian militias launched waves of attacks on entire Dinka communities in Upper Nile, which resulted in horrific devastation of lives and livelihoods, never before experienced in the history of tribal conflict in southern Sudan (Deng, 1999:31). It has been estimated that more than five thousand people in the Bor area (the home area of the SPLA leader, Dr John Garang), mainly children and women, were massacred in a horrific manner, comparable to the Al-Dien massacre of Dinka in western Sudan in 1987. Besides this massive loss of human lives, all the livestock, the mainstay of Dinka livelihood, were looted or slaughtered. People who survived the massacre were displaced into Bahr el Ghazal and Equatoria regions and were organised into displaced persons' camps, the largest camps in the history of southern Sudan. Other Dinka communities (Ruweng, Ngok and Padang) in the Upper Nile region experienced similar attacks by the SSIA forces, which also resulted in a massive loss of life and livelihoods, and also in displacement. The UN reported in December 1991 that 'more than 200,000 residents of (the Dinka areas of Upper Nile), in an exodus unlike anything seen before in Sudan, fled south in search of food, shelter and security' (Burr, 1993:23).

The SPLA counter-attack led to war within a war between the SPLA and the splinter faction backed by the central government, caused famine in 1992-3 and furthered the divide between Dinka and Nuer communities. Soon the same social disruption felt in Dinka communities in Upper Nile region was replicated in the Nuer territory, with an added twist, as Nuer turned to fight among themselves, as well as fighting the Dinka, and being hired as a militia by the government (ICG, 2002:134). The government's strategy of divide-and-conquer was effective in achieving its aims of weakening southern resistance and dividing the SPLA, promoting the emergence of local warlords, splitting the south along ethnic lines and leading to the eventual resumption of oilfield exploration and development in the south.

By 1997 the government secured a peace agreement with the splinter factions (SSIA and SPLA-United), which allowed oil exploration and development consortia to move into oilfield areas with Nuer militia protection. Ironically, the very strategy of using Nuer militias to protect oil installations was also inherently destabilising, as much of the fighting in the Upper Nile region after the 1997 peace accord resulted from clashes between militias over who would defend the oil areas (ICG, 2002). By 1999, a consortium of Chinese, Malaysian and Canadian companies had completed a 1,600-kilometre pipeline from the Upper Nile to Port Sudan and commenced pumping oil.

The peace agreement between the central government and southern splinter factions collapsed in 1999, largely because the Nuer received none of the benefits promised, including an autonomous regional government, major development initiatives and a referendum on the independence of southern Sudan. This unleashed further confusion and conflict in the Upper Nile, as some Nuer commanders remained allied with the government, some allied themselves with the SPLA and others hedged their bets (ICG, 2002:135). Facing resistance from both the SPLA and a growing number of government-allied Nuer commanders, the government was forced to change tactics and become more directly involved in defending oilfields through the ruthless implementation of a scorched earth strategy of depopulating the areas surrounding the oilfield (Christian Aid, 2001; Gagnon and Ryle,

2001). Even the international security firm consisting of Vietnam veterans hired by the Chevron Oil Company to protect its assets in the south in the early 1980s never considered driving the indigenous people from the oilfield areas for the security of the wells (Collins, 2001:4).

Dinka Militia: Psychological Pay-offs, Fear and Greed

In the Bahr el Ghazal region, SPLA-United under the leadership of Kerubino who hailed from Gogrial county (one of the research communities) of Bahr el Ghazal region started recruiting from among his own Dinka of the northern Bahr el Ghazal region and formed in 1994 separate Dinka militias, based close to the government garrison town of Gogrial, which became the epicentre of endogenous counter-insurgency warfare in the 1990s. Unlike other southern militias, which were formed to target and weaken Dinka livelihoods rather than their own communities, the formation of Dinka militias was the beginning of new forms of counter-insurgency warfare that used the Dinka themselves to target their own communities. Given his overwhelming hatred of the SPLA for the years he had spent in detention, Kerubino became a real warlord and stripped his own people of northern Bahr el Ghazal not only of cattle and grain but also of viable livelihoods, by causing massive civilian displacement and deprivation (Human Rights Watch, 1998).

The arrival of Dinka militia on the scene in 1994 created a deleterious impact on the livelihoods of communities in Northern Bahr el Ghazal. Since 1994 the Dinka militia forces had been marauding northern Bahr el Ghazal from their base in the government enclave of Gogrial town. During the 1990s Dinka militia had been targeting most areas that produced food or held stocks, livestock and relief deliveries, stealing and looting what they could and destroying much of what remained (Human Rights Watch, 1999). These attacks on the people of Northern Bahr el Ghazal received full military and logistical support from the government military garrison in Gogrial town (Deng, 1999:31). Besides raiding and providing detailed information about their own communities, the Dinka militia made also joint and co-ordinated raids with Nuer and Murahaleen militias, who lacked local knowledge about the people and terrain of Bahr el Ghazal. While the Murahaleen militias attacked Dinka communities during the dry season, the Dinka militias were there all year round, particularly in the Gogrial area.

With weak, demoralised and unorganised SPLA forces unable to provide protection to civil populations in northern Bahr el Ghazal, the civilian population became systematically displaced internally and by 1997 almost 60 per cent of their livestock had been looted by Dinka militias (SRRA, 1998). The abduction of children and women for forced labour and slavery became commonplace in northern Bahr el Ghazal in the 1990s. While the Murahaleen militias used the abducted children and women for forced labour (farming, housework and rearing cattle) and slavery, the Dinka militias abducted adults, particularly women and girls, and used them for forced labour, such as carrying their booty, and forced marriage. The Dinka militias also developed a lucrative culture of looting, greed and anarchy in northern Bahr el Ghazal, which lured some dissatisfied and neglected SPLA soldiers to join the Dinka militias for their own security and economic agenda of acquiring wealth quickly. Deng (1999:30) compares the pattern of devastation, destruction and asset transfer in Northern Bahr el Ghazal in the 1990s with that in the era of Turko-Egyptian rule and Mahdyyia.

The need, fear, greed and a deliberate political and military agenda were the main factors behind the rapid growth, occurrence and intensity of counter-insurgency warfare waged by Dinka militia in northern Bahr el Ghazal. The economic crisis that had weakened the central governments in Sudan in the 1980s made it difficult for successive northern ruling elites to sustain and control armies. Subsequently, the northern ruling elite resorted to local sources of provisioning by harnessing the economic agenda within Arab nomads, Nuer and Dinka militias to wage counter-insurgency warfare against the SPLA cheaply, and to serve as a substitute for supplies from central government.

While the Arab militias were mainly motivated by need (drought and famine) and greed (restocking and cattle trade), the Dinka militias were mainly motivated by psychological pay-offs (revenge and vengeance), fear (SPLA soldiers joining for security) and greed (quick acquisition of wealth). This clearly suggests that the conduct of the civil war in Sudan was not only profitable for a range of groups, but people also joined the militias for reasons of security, as well as being a means of revenge and reversal of humiliation (Keen, 2000). Importantly, the link between greed and grievances has been made very clear by the gradual expansion and growth of counter-insurgency warfare in Sudan in the 1980s and 1990s. While the need and greed of

Arab nomads at the end of the 1970s and the early 1980s caused grievances among the Dinka in northern Bahr el Ghazal, such grievances triggered the early eruption of civil war in 1982, which in turn legitimised greed through counter-insurgency warfare in the 1980s and 1990s. Counter-insurgency warfare intensified in the 1990s, with profound and significant forcible asset transfers, particularly Dinka livestock in northern Bahr el Ghazal, not only to the Arab militias but also to the Dinka and Nuer militias.

The Risk Events in the 1990s:
The Households' Perceptions

Knowing the sources of risk faced by the research communities in Bahr el Ghazal region is crucially important for the understanding of the livelihood strategies adopted by households in the 1990s. Although the previous section shed light on the growth and evolution of counter-insurgency warfare, the households and communities in Bahr el Ghazal were differentially exposed to various types of counter-insurgency warfare and other risk events. Besides the historical account of counter-insurgency warfare, community percep-tions, attitudes and the importance they attached to counter-insurgency and other risk events are important in a household vulnerability analysis and for an understanding of household livelihood strategies. Since community perceptions have been discussed in the introductory chapter, the focus here will be on the households' perceptions about the sources of risk events faced in the 1990s.

On the basis of the household survey, the responses of households about main sources of risk that they faced in the 1990s are presented in Table 4.1. The Dinka militias, Arab militias and drought were identified as the main sources of risk in the 1990s. The conventional warfare between the govern-ment army and the rebels did not feature at the household level as one of the most important sources of risk that they faced during the 1990s. The households in Gogrial area, besides attaching unambiguous importance to endogenous counter-insurgency warfare (Dinka militias), they also assigned considerable importance (28%) to exogenous counter-insurgency (Arab mi-litias). This clearly suggests that the households in Gogrial area were more exposed to both exogenous and endogenous counter-insurgency warfare.

Table 4.1: Household Perceptions of the Most Important Sources of Risk in the 1990s

--Research Communities in Bahr el Ghazal--

Main Risk Events	Abyei	Gogrial	Cuiebet
Dinka Militias	38 (18%)	141 (69%)	0
Arab Militias	170 (80.6%)	57 (28%)	0
Drought	3 (1.4%)	7 (3%)	99 (100%)
Total	211 (100%)	205 (100%)	99 (100%)

Source: Household Survey

The households in the Abyei area were mainly exposed to exogenous counter-insurgency warfare (Arab militias) and to a lesser degree to Dinka militia. The simultaneous exposure to both types of counter-insurgency warfare in the Gogrial area, and to a lesser degree in the Abyei area, is associated with the distinctive characteristics and nature of endogenous counter-insurgency warfare (Dinka militias). The households in Cuiebet were primarily exposed to drought with minimal effect of counter-insurgency warfare.

In assessing the variation in the perceptions of households exposed to counter-insurgency warfare, the non-poor households (middle and rich) attach relatively more importantance to both types of counter-insurgency warfare (Dinka and Arab militias) than do poor households. Although the importance attached to drought is relatively small, the variation across households is significant, as its importance consistently and significantly declines with the level of wealth, with poor households attaching more importance to it than do non-poor households. This implicitly suggests that non-poor households were more concerned about counter-insurgency warfare than were poor households, who were relatively more concerned about the drought than non-poor households. Also, the data from the household survey found no difference in the perceptions of households headed by males and females. These findings are crucially important for understanding the rationale behind the choice of livelihood strategies adopted by various households in the 1990s.

Characteristics of Risk Events in the 1990s

Although community and household perceptions clearly identify their main sources of risk in the 1990s, understanding the characteristics of each source of risk, as shown in Table 4.2, is important in assessing household risk management strategies and vulnerability. The main characteristics of risk events, as discussed in Chapter 3, are used to compare the most important risk events faced by the communities in Bahr el Ghazal in the 1990s. These characteristics include geographical spread, frequency, occurrence, duration, interaction with other risk events, information, and learning from past experiences. These characteristics are discussed under each source of a risk event and compared with other risk events in the context of Bahr el Ghazal region in the 1990s. It is worth noting that comparing characteristics of drought with counter-insurgency is difficult because one is largely dealing in the realm of perceptions, not objective indicators.

Table 4.2: Comparison of the Characteristics[2] of the Main Risk Events in the 1990s

--Main Sources of Risk Events in the 1990s--

Main Features	Drought	Exogenous Counterinsurgency	Endogenous Counterinsurgency
Source	Environmental	Man-made	Man-made
Geographical Spread[3]	Generic	Quasi-Generic	Quasi-Specific
Frequency	Seasonal/ Occasional	Seasonal	Regular
Occurrence	Slow-onset	Rapid-onset	Rapid-onset
Intensity	Mild-High	High	High
Duration	Seasonal	Seasonal	Year round

---

2   These characteristics are based on the community survey and my personal experience during livelihood monitoring activities in southern Sudan in the 1990s.

3   The social spread of risk event is either generic (covers the entire community) or specific (affects specific households). The quasi-generic or quasi-specific refers to social coverage that is partially but predominately generic or specific respectively.

Main Features	Drought	Exogenous Counterinsurgency	Endogenous Counterinsurgency
Correlation	Exogenous and Endogenous Counterinsurgency	Drought and Endogenous Counterinsurgency	Drought and Exogenous Counterinsurgency
Information[4]	Asymmetric	Asymmetric	Symmetric
Likely Victims	Everyone More Poor	Everyone More Non-Poor	Everyone More Non-Poor
Past Experience	High	High	Low
Post-Period	Normal	Normal	Constant Threats
Level of Adaptation	Good	Limited	Weak

There is a difference between the perceived and actual threats posed by risk events and such perceptions, rather than the actual impact of risk events, have more impact on the choice of livelihood strategies adopted by households. In fact, there is an interesting relationship between the (perceived) level of risk and level of actual impact and risk-averse behaviour. For example, a high-impact risk (perceived threat) with low probability (actual threat) might cause more risk-averse behaviour than a risk event with low perceived threat and high actual threat. This is relevant to the context of drought and counter-insurgency warfare as households might be more risk-averse against counter-insurgency warfare than a drought.

Rainfall Pattern: Bahr el Ghazal Region in the 1990s

Drought is generally an intrinsic feature of the rural environments in Sudan, particularly in Bahr el Ghazal, and has become one of the few risk events to which households are well adapted. The characteristic of a drought of being slower onset, as its threat materialising slowly, usually allows rural households to adjust their perception of the threat it poses to their livelihoods and to plan accordingly. This slow onset occurrence of drought makes possible a balance

---

4   Asymmetric information refers to availability of knowledge to one side (victims) than the other (raiders), while symmetric information refers to availability of knowledge to both sides (raiders and their victims).

between the way its threat is perceived and its actual impact and subsequently allows households to proactively adopt appropriate livelihood strategies.

Besides the nature of the occurrence of drought, its geographical and social spread is generic and covers a wide range of areas and communities. However, the generic nature of drought has been questioned in recent years as climatic conditions have changed drastically and resulted in a quasi-generic pattern in rainfall. The phenomena of El-Nino and La-Nina created climatic anomalies across Africa during the 1990s (FEWS, 1999). In Bahr el Ghazal region, the pattern of rainfall in the 1990s varied drastically, not across various counties, but even within counties and communities. The monthly variation in the Normalised Deviation Vegetation Index (NDVI) during the 1990s shows a general downward trend, reaching as low as 40 percent in northern Bahr el Ghazal, particularly during critical cultivation months (May-October).

Although the rainfall volume pattern deteriorated generally in Bahr el Ghazal during the 1990s, the areas in northern Bahr el Ghazal (Abyei and Gogrial) experienced more of a downward trend than did areas in southern Bahr el Ghazal (Cuiebet). Unlike the situation in northern Bahr el Ghazal in the 1980s when drought was no more than a secondary factor in causing livelihood vulnerability (Keen, 1994:84), it became one of the main factors in the 1990s. This suggests that the intensity of drought was relatively more severe in Bahr el Ghazal region during the 1990s, as compared to the rainfall in the 1980s.

Despite the fact that the volume of rainfall in Bahr el Ghazal deteriorated in the 1990s, there were periods of normal rainfall in 1995 and 1996. Importantly, people in Bahr el Ghazal have amplified their perceptions over the years about the threat of drought according to past experiences. For example, some communities in Bahr el Ghazal region use traditional and local indicators, such as the movement and nesting of some birds, the flowering of some wild plants, and the appearance of some stars, as ways of predicting the pattern of rainfall (Deng, 1999). Though these traditional indicators of rainfall pattern may not precisely predict when drought will strike, they generally help the rural communities in forming their perceptions about the threat of drought.

One of the important characteristics of drought is its interaction with other risk events such as counter-insurgency warfare. The rainfall pattern in northern Bahr el Ghazal was undoubtedly associated with the occurrence, duration, geographic spread, intensity, and frequency of exogenous counter-insurgency warfare (Arab militias). Arab nomads rely heavily on pastures and water sources in northern Bahr el Ghazal during the dry season (December-April).

Besides the fact that drought makes Arab nomads more desperate to access water and the pastures in Bahr el Ghazal region, it allows the easy mobility of Arab militia, who use horses for their movement. The rural community's perception of the threat of drought in northern Bahr el Ghazal is greatly influenced by the fact that the occurrence, duration, and intensity of exogenous counter-insurgency warfare are known to increase when drought occurs. This close association between drought and exogenous counter-insurgency warfare makes it difficult to dissociate the actual occurrence and perceived threat of exogenous counter-insurgency warfare from the effects of drought and their subsequent impact on the choice of livelihood strategies adopted by households. This close correlation and high-expected welfare loss clearly explain why non-poor households in Abyei and Gogrial perceive the threat of exogenous counterinsurgency warfare as more important than the perceived threat of drought (see Table 4.2). On the other hand the rural communities in Cuiebet, which did not experience the Arab militias raids in the 1990s but experienced similar rainfall patterns, perceived the threat of drought as the most important source of their risk.

Exogenous Counter-insurgency: Arab Militias in the 1990s:

Generally, the nature of Arab militia counter-insurgency is that it is quasi-generic (less specific with a semi-random pattern), seasonal (as it mainly occurs during dry season) and with sudden and swift effects for a short period of time. The geographic and social spread of exogenous counter-insurgency warfare (Arab militias) in the 1980s had generally targeted the communities in the extreme northern Bahr el Ghazal areas (Abyei) that border the Arab nomads' homeland in western Sudan (Southern Kordofan). With the devastation and massive displacement of the rural communities in these areas in the 1980s, the activities of the Arab militias expanded and extended southward in the 1990s into new areas in Gogrial. In fact, the massive displacement and protracted insecurity in the extreme northern areas of

Abyei resulted in a drastic change in vegetation cover which was gradually replaced by thorny shrubs that make the area less suitable for grazing. This change in vegetation and the withdrawal of Dinka cattle to safe areas in the southern and central areas of Bahr el Ghazal provided the necessary incentive for Arab militias to extend their activities southwards into the new areas in the 1990s.

Besides its increased geographical spread, exogenous counter-insurgency warfare (Arab militias) is correlated to both drought and, most importantly, to endogenous counterinsurgency (Dinka militias) warfare, particularly in the 1990s. The most distinctive feature of exogenous counter-insurgency warfare is that it was carried out by militias (Arab or Nuer) who were not from within the targeted communities. The main difference between the communities exposed to exogenous counter-insurgency and those exposed to endogenous counterinsurgency is that the rural communities who are adjacent (Abyei) to Arab nomads' homeland have been able to learn from their past experience with the raids from Arab militias in the 1980s. On the other hand, the communities in central Bahr el Ghazal (Gogrial) had limited experience in dealing with Arab militia attacks in the 1990s.

Unlike drought, there is more of an imbalance between the perceived threat of counter-insurgency warfare and its actual impact, because of its high specificity, unpredictability, and its potentially devastating consequences, particularly among communities with limited past experience (e.g. Gogrial). The threat of counter-insurgency warfare may be very real, but by the same token, it may not be. Owing to the potentially immediate consequences of counter-insurgency warfare, rural households were likely to perceive it as having a higher probability of materialising, and subsequently, such perceptions affect the choice of livelihood strategies. There is sometimes an overestimation of the welfare loss (Hendrickson et al, 1996) associated with counter-insurgency, particularly with exogenous counter-insurgency (Arab militias), as other factors, such as the communal collective action to protect their land (social capital) and past experiences, are likely to discount such perceived welfare loss.

Exogenous counter-insurgency warfare (Arab militias) has some characteristics that are more or less similar to that of drought, such as asymmetric information and the normal threat after the occurrence of risk events (post-period threat). Information about the livelihood strategies adopted by

households to confront exogenous counter-insurgency warfare was not easily available with Arab militias. Despite the fact that exogenous counter-insurgency has a rapid onset, its seasonal occurrence during the dry season
reduces the threat of raids during the rainy season. As shown in Table 4.2,
drought seems to have more similar characteristics with exogenous counter-insurgency warfare than it does with endogenous counter-insurgency.

Endogenous Counter-insurgency: Dinka Militias in the 1990s:

The distinctive characteristics associated with endogenous counter-insurgency warfare make it the most important and dangerous source of risk
faced for the first time by the rural communities in Bahr el Ghazal region
in the 1990s. The activities of the Dinka militia in the 1990s had a profound
negative impact on the livelihoods of the Dinka communities in northern
Bahr el Ghazal and that contributed to the famine in 1998. The devastation
caused by Dinka militia on their communities during the 1990w is summarised by one key informant during the community survey in the Gogrial
area who said:

> 'Crisis caused by God such as drought (riak Nhialec) is better than
> crises caused by human beings (riak raan), but the crisis caused by your
> own person (riak raan dou) is the worst of all.'

The most unique and distinctive characteristics of endogenous counter-insurgency warfare (Dinka militias) include specificity, symmetric information,
year-round duration, high correlation with other risk events, limited past
experience, and post-period threat. These distinctive characteristics made
endogenous counter-insurgency warfare exceptionally more threatening to
livelihoods than other risk events such as drought and exogenous counter-insurgency warfare. Unlike exogenous counter-insurgency warfare and
drought, endogenous counter-insurgency warfare is more specific as it targets households more than communities. The members of the Dinka militia
were from within their Dinka communities in northern and central Bahr
el Ghazal and, most importantly, from some of the dissatisfied SPLA Dinka
soldiers, who had the knowledge and detailed information about their communities. The duration of the endogenous counter-insurgency warfare in

the 1990s was year-round, unlike the seasonal or occasional occurrence of exogenous counter-insurgency warfare and drought.

The Dinka militia used to co-ordinate their counterinsurgency activities in Bahr el Ghazal in the 1990s with the Arab militias during the dry season and with Nuer militias all year round by providing the local knowledge and information. This suggests that although endogenous counter-insurgency warfare was not directly related to drought, its apparent correlation with exogenous counter-insurgency (Arab militias) made it indirectly associated with drought in the 1990s. Unlike drought and exogenous counter-insurgency warfare, the rural communities in Bahr el Ghazal had limited experience of the endogenous counter-insurgency warfare that erupted in the 1990s. These characteristics of specificity, unpredictability, and year-round presence made rural communities in Bahr el Ghazal attach a relatively higher welfare loss to endogenous counterinsurgency warfare than to any other risk events during the 1990s. Also, the year-round presence of endogenous counter-insurgency warfare made the threat of its occurrence continuous and constant, unlike the occurrences of drought and exogenous counter-insurgency that are followed by normal periods of calm. Generally, the characteristics of endogenous counter-insurgency are unique and less comparable to the characteristics of other risk events such as drought and exogenous counter-insurgency.

Conclusion

The genesis of political vulnerability in southern Sudan and the rapid growth of militia groups in contemporary Sudan can be traced back to the period of lawlessness, slavery, and excessive asset transfer from southern Sudan. This chapter has clearly shown the supremacy of the characteristics of civil war over its causes, in contextualising and understanding the level of exposure of rural communities to various risk events in the 1990s. Equally, the chapter has provided evidence that suggests that any generalisation in the context of 'war zone' will provide only a limited understanding of context-specificity that is crucial in understanding rural livelihoods. It has been shown that besides variation in the level of exposure to generic conventional warfare, communities in the 'war zone' differ in their level of exposure to different types of counter-insurgency warfare. Even within intra-communities, households differ in their perception of different types of counter-insurgency warfare. Understanding the dynamics, variation and perception across and within communities in the 'war zone' provides a better analysis and a nuanced understanding of rural livelihoods.

The account of counter-insurgency warfare in contemporary Sudan shows that need, greed, fear, psychological pay-offs, economic crisis and a deliberate political and military agenda largely explain the rapid growth and intensity of counter-insurgency warfare in Bahr el Ghazal in the 1990s. During that period, two types of counter-insurgency warfare have been identified, namely: exogenous (Arab and Nuer militias) and endogenous (Dinka militias). While both types of counter-insurgency warfare were used by the central government to deflect the grievances against the government and to wage war against the rebels cheaply, greed and economic interests mainly sustained both types of counter-insurgency warfare in the 1990s.

The communities of the Bahr el Ghazal region were exposed to composite and multiple risk events, including conventional warfare between rebels and government, counter-insurgency warfare, drought, floods and diseases during the 1990s. The most important sources of risk identified by households during the 1990s were counter-insurgency warfare and drought, with conventional warfare ranked the lowest, particularly in northern Bahr el Ghazal. Despite their exposure to composite risk events, the degree and level of exposure to different types of risk events varied significantly across and within the communities of Bahr el Ghazal in the 1990s. While communities in far northern Bahr el Ghazal (Abyei) were more exposed to exogenous counter-insurgency (Arab militias), the communities in central Bahr el Ghazal (Gogrial) were particularly exposed to endogenous counterinsurgency (Dinka militias) while drought was prevalent in most parts of Bahr el Ghazal region.

The comparison of the main sources of risk (exogenous and endogenous counter-insurgency and drought) faced by households in Bahr el Ghazal in the 1990s clearly suggests that endogenous counter-insurgency warfare has distinctive characteristics, with more profound impact on rural livelihoods than any other sources of risk. Unlike other sources of risk (drought and exogenous counter-insurgency), endogenous counter-insurgency is more specific with year-round occurrence, coupled with limited past experience and having a high correlation with other sources of risk, particularly exogenous counter-insurgency warfare. In the comparison of the research communities in terms of the level of exposure to various sources and characteristics of risk events during the 1990s, households in the Gogrial area were exceptionally and distinctively exposed to repeated and 'bunched' sources of risk events (endogenous counterinsurgency, exogenous counterinsurgency and drought).

At the intra-community level, non-poor households (rich and middle-income) attach relatively more importance to both types of counter-insurgency warfare than do poor households, who in turn significantly attach more importance to drought than do non-poor households. This finding implicitly suggests that non-poor households were more concerned about counter-insurgency warfare than were poor households, who were in turn more concerned about drought than were non-poor households during the 1990s.

CHAPTER FIVE

Confronting Civil War:
The Household Livelihood Strategies

Introduction

I t is generally recognised that rural households are proactive in confronting risk events, particularly drought and economic shocks. Despite such recognition and as discussed in the previous chapters, households during civil war are perceived as unable or passive - given the nature and characteristics of civil war - to confront the consequences and effects of civil war on their livelihoods. The main aim of this chapter is to assess, using the data generated from fieldwork study, the livelihood strategies - particularly the risk reduction and mitigation strategies - adopted by households to confront counter-insurgency warfare in Bahr el Ghazal region during the 1990s. Specifically, the chapter attempts to test the "risk-livelihood-vulnerability framework" to assess the main research question on whether households exposed to protracted civil war do take *ex ante* risk management strategies. Assessing and understanding the *ex ante* risk management strategies adopted by households exposed to protracted civil war and counter-insurgency warfare will undoubtedly shed light on their risk-related behaviours, which are at present inadequately and poorly understood.

It is important to recognise from the outset of this chapter that the main focus is on the effects of counter-insurgency warfare on rural livelihoods, particularly household asset management and livelihood strategies. Although insurgency warfare, including the proliferation of small arms, warlord behaviour and combatant survival strategies, does have profound effects on rural livelihoods, assessing its effects on rural livelihoods is beyond the scope of this chapter. However, the most relevant effects of insurgency warfare on the choice of household livelihood strategies will be highlighted and emphasised. Deng (1999) has discussed and highlighted the effects of some characteristics of insurgency warfare on the Dinka livelihood. The proliferation of small arms in Dinka society, particularly in the hands of the youth, has produced undesirable changes in the relationship between age groups, as it has shifted the centre of traditional authority away from the older age group (Deng, 1999:59).

The strong traditional aspiration of youths to become elders and to enjoy the fruits of older age groups as figures of respect, wisdom and knowledge has gradually been fading with the emerging militaristic culture that has had profound effects on traditional social mechanisms and social capital. The high level of youth recruitment into the rebel forces has brought a drastic demographic change, as older age groups, particularly women, are becoming increasingly responsible for providing livelihoods not only for their households but also for sustenance of the combatant rebel soldiers. Ironically, it is difficult to separate the effects of insurgency warfare on rural livelihoods from those related to counter-insurgency warfare. Subsequently, any general conclusion about the effects of counter-insurgency warfare on rural livelihoods may reflect the multiple and compounded effects of both types of warfare. As the research communities have all been exposed to insurgency warfare and drought, it is safe to argue that the observed variations in their livelihood strategies adopted in the 1990s could be largely explained by the variations in their level of exposure to different types of counter-insurgency warfare.

This chapter analyses the second component of the risk-livelihood-vulnerability framework discussed in chapter 3. It is organised as follows: the *ex ante risk management strategies*, particularly the *risk reduction livelihood strategies*, are discussed, analysed and compared across and within the research communities in Section 2. The comparative *risk mitigation livelihood strategies* are analysed in detail in Section 3. Investment in *social capital* and informal insurance arrangements as part of risk mitigation livelihood strategies are then discussed separately in Section 4. The general conclusions and main findings of the chapter are summarised in Section 5.

Given the level of exposure to counter-insurgency warfare in Bahr el Ghazal in the 1990s, as discussed in Chapter 4, the question is what livelihood strategies were adopted by households to confront the adverse effects of counter-insurgency warfare in the 1990s? It is generally perceived in the risk literature that the very nature of civil war, in terms of its unpredictable and sudden characteristics, makes it extremely difficult for households exposed to risk events such as counter-insurgency to take any *ex ante* measures to reduce the anticipated adverse effects. It is argued in the risk literature, as discussed in Chapter 3, that the higher the risk the more households will diversify in order to reduce the adverse effects of risk events. It is observed that risk aversion declines with wealth and poor households will be less willing to bear risk, even if they have risk preferences identical to those of wealthier households. It is also argued that non-poor households tend to diversify more than poor households do. These observations and findings in the risk literature, as discussed in Chapter 3, are revisited in the context of the household livelihood strategies adopted in the context of risk events, such as counterinsurgency warfare.

Risk Reduction Livelihood Strategies: Reducing Susceptibility

Generally, risk reduction strategies, as discussed in Chapter 3, refer to the livelihood strategies adopted by households before the occurrence of a risk event, with the aim of adjusting to risk and reducing the anticipated livelihood shock and the household's susceptibility to risk. Although these risk prevention strategies have more bearing at the national and community levels, households at micro level do adopt some prevention strategies, such as adjusting livelihood activities and the reallocation of household members. The methods[5] used in this section comprise an analysis of the sources of livelihoods, primary livelihood activities and the construction of typologies of livelihood

---

5   In applying approaches such as income portfolios, diversity indices and typology of livelihood activities to capture the degree of diversification or specialisation in rural Tanzania, Ellis (2000:214) finds that the typology of livelihood activities approach gives a more accurate picture of the degrees of specialisation than do the mean diversity indices.

strategy, across research communities and across wealth groups, the roles of the members of households and investment in human asset including permanent migration.

Adjusting Sources of Livelihoods in the 1990s:

Given the lack of household income portfolio data to determine the proportional contribution of each source of income[6] , we used participatory rural appraisal methods (proportional piling) to gauge the proportional contribution of each livelihood activity to the overall household livelihood at the community level. In order to assess the level at which households adjusted their sources of livelihoods to confront counter-insurgency warfare, their current sources of livelihoods are compared with the pre-war period. In order to reveal visually the change and adjustments in the sources of livelihoods in the 1990s within each research community, radial graphs[7] are used to present the data from the community perception as shown in Figure 5.1-5.3. Before the civil war, the Dinka economy in Bahr el Ghazal was based on transhumant animal husbandry, agriculture, fishing, trade and a limited dependence on gathering (Deng, 1999). It is clear from Figure 5.1-3 that agriculture and animal husbandry contributed more than 60 per cent of the overall livelihood in the pre-war periods across the Dinka communities in Bahr el Ghazal region.

Generally, the critical feature in Figure 5.1-3 is the remarkably low contribution of livestock, one of the principal livelihood activities in the pre-war periods, to overall household livelihood in the 1990s, particularly among the communities (Abyei and Gogrial) exposed to counter-insurgency warfare. This clearly shows the rapid depletion of livestock in the 1990s as a result of the counter-insurgency warfare in the 1990s (as will discussed and analysed in Chapter 6). Interestingly, the broad differences in the share of crops across

---

6   Ellis (2000:210) shows in the case of rural Tanzania that income portfolios are more useful for describing broad village activity profiles than they are for distinguishing the livelihood strategies of sub-groups within a larger population.

7   Plotting sources of livelihood is equivalent to plotting asset pentagons (Carney, 1998:6) and a means of using qualitative impressions to illustrate adjustments and changes in sources of livelihoods. Since the axes of radial graphs have true scales, comparisons of changes and adjustments in sources of livelihood can be made between pre-war periods and the 1990s (Ellis, 2000:220).

research communities are notable, as the proportion of livelihood obtained from agriculture in the 1990s declined in Gogrial and Cuiebet to less than 50 per cent of the level in the pre-war periods and slightly increased in Abyei area.

The share of gathering and wild foods increased remarkably in the 1990s across the research communities, particularly among households exposed to endogenous counter-insurgency warfare (Gogrial), and to a lesser extent in the Abyei area. Of great interest is the share of kinship support, although it is a small share, it declines drastically among households exposed to endogenous counter-insurgency warfare (Gogrial), while it remains almost the same among households exposed to drought (Cuiebt) and slightly increases among households exposed to exogenous counter-insurgency warfare (Abyei).

In spite of the fact that generic data collected at community level may lack precision and make it difficult to draw firm conclusions, such data provide general but important trends in comparing communities, rather than groups or individual households. It is visually clear from these radial graphs that the research communities adjusted differently in their sources of livelihoods to confront various sources of risk events in the 1990s. While the Abyei area results display a great amount of homogeneity in their sources of livelihoods, the Gogrial and Cuiebet results reveal a great amount of changes in their sources of livelihoods in the 1990s, as compared with the pre-war periods.

While in Abyei all sources of livelihoods increased slightly to compensate for the decline in the share of livestock, those households in Gogrial adjusted their livelihoods towards gathering of wild foods and those facing drought became more dependent on livestock and the gathering of wild foods. Another interesting observation is that the adjustments of the sources of livelihood during the 1990s by households exposed to exogenous counter-insurgency (Abyei) were relatively less dramatic than the adjustments experienced by the other communities.

Adjusting Primary Livelihood Activities in the 1990s

It is apparent from the foregoing discussion that utilising adjustments and changes in the contribution of the sources of livelihood in order to evaluate the livelihood strategies in the 1990s is compromised by the inability to capture the relative level of participation in each activity. Specifically, the

Figure 5.1-5.3: Livelihood Activities Before and During Civil War

Figure 5.1 Abyei Livelihood Activities

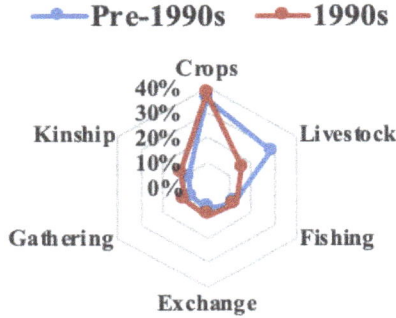

Figure 5.2 Gogrial Livelihood Activities

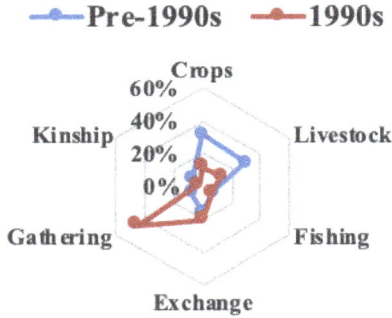

Figure 5.3 Cuiebet Livelihood Activities

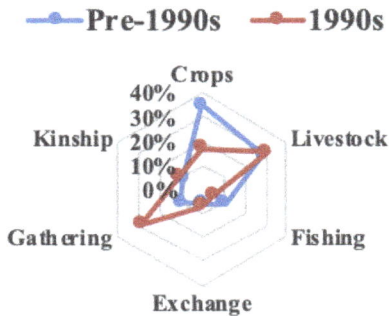

community survey data presented in Figure 5.1-5.3 do not provide any information about the proportion of households engaged in each livelihood activity, which can be compared across research areas and sample households. Alternatively, we should have used the *livelihood diversity index*[8] measure (Chang, 1997) to provide a summary statistic that captures both income shares and participation shares in a single figure that can be compared across research communities and sample households (Ellis, 2000:213).

Given the convincing and critical observations provided by Ellis, (2000)[9] about the utility of diversity indices and lack of detailed data, we used the '*typologies of livelihood strategies*' approach that was developed by Ellis (2000:214) to analyse livelihood diversity in rural Tanzania. This approach classifies each sample household according to a typology of livelihood strategies, and replaces mean income portfolios with a proportional measure of the distribution of households between different livelihood activities. In the context of the research communities, we constructed from household survey[10] data four typical livelihood activities (farming, pastoralism, trading and agro-pastoralism)[11] that lie along a specialisation-diversification continuum as effective way of assessing the adjustment in livelihood activities. The aim of constructing a typology of livelihood strategies is to reveal within which category of activities (farming, pastoralism, trading) specialisation occurs, and to explore the combination of activities (primarily agro-pastoralism) that represent diversified livelihood strategies and adjustment in livelihood activities. Asking households about their main livelihood activities before and during the 1990s, the summary of their responses is shown in Table 5.1.

---

8   The livelihood diversity index is commonly used in studies of biodiversity and also found in portfolio analysis in financial economics and is applied in development studies to describe diversity best in terms of both the number of activities and the distribution of total income between them (Ellis, 2000).

9   Ellis (2000) observes that the diversity index provides surprisingly little insight into the comparison of livelihood strategies across location or income-wealth category and it adds little to the information obtained from the breakdown of total income that income portfolios offer.

10   In the household survey there was a question asking specifically the principal livelihood activity or combination of activities adopted by household in the 1990s and in the pre-war periods.

11   In the household survey there was a question asking specifically the principal livelihood activity or combination of activities adopted by household in the 1990s and in the pre-war periods. In constructing typologies of livelihood strategies, Ellis (2000) identifies six categories (crops, livestock, non-farm, crop/livestock, livestock/non-farm, crop/non-farm) to classify sample households in rural Tanzania.

Table 5.1: Classification of Household
Livelihood Activities in the 1990s

--Typologies of Household Livelihood Strategies--

Research Communities	Periods	Agro-Pastoralist	Farming	Pastoralist	Trading	Total
Abyei	Pre-War	185 (88%)	13 (6%)	0 (0%)	13 (6%)	211
	1990s	166 (79%)	13 (6%)	32 (15%)	0 (0%)	211
Gogrial	Pre-War	205 (100%)	0 (0%)	0 (0%)	0 (0%)	205
	1990s	120 (59%)	85 (41%)	0 (0%)	0 (0%)	205
Cuiebet	Pre-War	147 (100%)	0 (0%)	0 (0%)	0 (0%)	147
	1990s	143 (97%)	4 (3%)	0 (0%)	0 (0%)	147

Abyei Community: Reverting to Pastoralism

It is clear from Table 5.1 that while trading existed as a livelihood activity in the pre-war period in Abyei area, it vanished in the 1990s and pastoralism emerged as a new livelihood strategy in the 1990s. Interestingly, while about 88 per cent of sample households were relying on agro-pastoralist livelihood activity during the pre-war period, the proportion of households that earns its living from agro-pastoralist activity declined to 79 per cent in the 1990s. While the proportion of households depending on farming did not change in the 1990s, pastoralism emerged as a significant new phenomenon during the 1990s, with almost 15 per cent of the sample households adopting it as their main livelihood activity. Interestingly, the households that adopted pastoralism in the 1990s were previously agro-pastoralists (94 per cent) during the pre-war periods, meaning that specialisation was preferred to diversified-livelihood strategies. The disappearance of trading as a special-ised livelihood strategy in the 1990s also indicates that not all specialised livelihood strategies are appropriate, and suggests instead the preference for pastoralism as the most appropriate specialised livelihood strategy during the 1990s.

The decline in the number of sample households who adopted diver-sified agro-pastoralist livelihoods and the increased adoption of pastoralism by households who were previously agro-pastoralists both indicate that diversification of livelihood activities is not the best option in the context of counter-insurgency warfare. Using chi-square statistical test to assess the difference between the livelihood strategies in the 1990s and pre-war periods, the *chi-square* value (39.334) is significant ($P = 0.000$) and clearly suggests the significant difference between the household livelihood strategies in the 1990s and the pre-war periods. Conversely, the statistical association between the livelihood strategies in the 1990s and the pre-war periods is not only negative (*Pearson's R* = -0.017), but insignificant ($P = 0.804$), and so we must accept the null hypothesis that there is no significant correlation between the livelihood strategies adopted during the two periods.

In order to unravel and to know the type of households that adopted specialised livelihood strategies (pastoralism or farming), or a diversified livelihood strategy (agro-pastoralism), in the 1990s in Abyei area, the sample households are classified according to their wealth status and typologies of livelihood activities, as shown in Table 5.2. It is clear that while most households still maintained an agro-pastoralist livelihood, the middle and non-poor households adopted pastoralism more than poor households, who increasingly adopted agro-pastoralism in the 1990s. Interestingly, while the proportion of poor households who adopted a diversified agro-pastoralist livelihood increased from 69 per cent in the pre-war period to 80 per cent in the 1990s, the proportion of non-poor households who did the same declined to 71 per cent in the 1990s compared with 91 per cent in the pre-war periods.

Apparently, this finding clearly suggests that the poor households tend to diversify more than non-poor households, particularly in the context of households exposed to exogenous counter-insurgency warfare. This finding is not consistent with Ellis' (2000:216) findings in rural Tanzania, which show that poor households are more likely to specialise in crop production than either middle– or high-income households, who are more likely to specialise in non-farm activities or to follow a mixed crop-livestock strategy. Although we cannot draw firm conclusions, this finding challenges, at least in the context of exogenous counter-insurgency warfare, the posited argument that links diversification positively with the level of income (Fafchamps, 1992; Alwang et al., 1996; Moser, 1998; Alwang and Siegel, 1999).

The statistical test (chi-square value = 31.8; $P = 0.000$) shows a statistically significant difference between the livelihood activities adopted in the

1990s and wealth status in Abyei area. The adoption of pure pastoralism by middle-income and non-poor households as their main livelihood activity in the 1990s, rather than the diversifying of their livelihood activities, clearly suggests relatively high risk-aversion behaviour of the non-poor households. Such behaviour of middle-income and non-poor households challenges, at least in the context of civil war, the proposition that risk aversion declines with wealth.

Table 5.2: Wealth and Adjustment in Livelihood Activities in Abyei, 1990s

Wealth Status	Periods	*--Typologies of Household Livelihood Strategies in the 1990s--*				
		Agro-Pastoralist	Agri-culturalist	Pastoralist	Trading	Total
Poor	Pre–War	20 (69%)	9 (31%)	0 (0%)	0 (0%)	29
	1990s	55 (80%)	12 (17%)	2 (3%)	0 (0%)	69
Middle	Pre–War	102 (90%)	3 (3%)	0 (0%)	8 (7%)	113
	1990s	101 (79%)	1 (1%)	26 (20%)	0 (0%)	128
Non-poor	Pre–War	63 (91%)	1 (1%)	0 (0%)	5 (7%)	69
	1990s	10 (71%)	0 (3%)	4 (29%)	0 (0%)	14

Source: Household Survey/SPSS Output

The rationale and reasons for the adoption of pastoralism during the 1990s will be elaborated in the next section, where the management of each constituent of the livelihood portfolio of activities is discussed. However, from the community focus group discussion, the adoption of pastoralism in the 1990s is a clear case of an *ex ante* livelihood strategy, aimed at reducing exposure to risk events, such as counter-insurgency warfare. Farming in the context of counter-insurgency warfare tends to be riskier than pastoralism, as it necessitates households to be in stationary and permanent settlements, which make them more susceptible to counter-insurgency raids.

Gogrial Community: Pushed to Pure Farming as Necessity

It is clear from Table 5.1 that while all sample households (100 per cent) in Gogrial area were agro-pastoralists in the pre-war period, nearly half of them

(41 per cent) resorted to pure farming as their core traditional livelihood activity in the 1990s. Despite the fact that crop farming is a risky livelihood activity in the context of civil war, more households in Gogrial area were forced to adopt it in the 1990s, primarily because of necessity and lack of other livelihood options. This apparent increased adoption of pure farming in the 1990s across all wealth groups (poor, middle and non-poor) that were previously agro-pastoralists, reaffirms the earlier observation in the case of Abyei, that diversification of livelihood activities is not the best livelihood strategy option in the context of counter-insurgency warfare.

The activities of the Dinka militias in the Gogrial area in the 1990s stifled any attempt to possess or acquire livestock or any other valuable assets, which left households with no other choice except farming and gathering of wild foods, as shown in Figure 5.2. In spite of a shift towards farming as the main livelihood activity in Gogrial area, the contribution of crops to the overall household livelihood declined considerably, as seen in Figure 5.2. In order to trace whether this shift from agro-pastoralism to pure farming had been experienced by specific groups of households, the newly adopted livelihood portfolio of activities in the 1990s was cross-tabulated with the wealth status of households. The chi-square test ($X^2 = 3.2$; $P = 0.073$) shows no statistical difference between the newly adopted livelihood activities across various categories of households (poor, middle and non-poor). This shows that the households in Gogrial experienced a structural wealth status change that makes it less sensitive to explain the variation in the portfolio of livelihood activities adopted in the 1990s.

In comparison to other areas, the households in Gogrial area experienced a drastic change in their portfolio of livelihood activities in the 1990s, with almost 41 per cent of households shifting away from a diversified agro-pastoralist livelihood activity and adopting pure farming. Gogrial area is followed by Abyei area, where about 10 per cent of sample households shifted away from diversified agro-pastoralism livelihood activity and adopted pure farming or pure pastoralism instead in the 1990s. The households that were exposed to drought (Cuiebet) retained their diversified agro-pastoralist livelihood (97 per cent) in the 1990s, with an insignificant percentage (3 per cent) of households moving to a mono-portfolio of livelihood activity (pure farming) in the 1990s, as shown in Figure 5.3. This clearly suggests that households exposed to drought are more likely to diversify their portfolio

of livelihood activities than are those exposed to counter-insurgency warfare. Within the households exposed to counter-insurgency warfare, those
households exposed to endogenous counterinsurgency warfare are less
likely to diversify than are those exposed to exogenous counterinsurgency
warfare. Importantly, non-poor households are less likely to diversify their
livelihood activities than are poor households, particularly in the context of
counter-insurgency warfare.

Adjusting Roles of Household Members

Besides adjusting the sources of livelihood and portfolio of livelihood activities as measures to reduce household susceptibility to counter-insurgency
warfare, the households in Bahr el Ghazal have equally adjusted the roles
and responsibilities of the members of households. The adjusted roles of
members of household in the 1990s resulted in a shift in the contribution
of each member of household to the overall household livelihood. While
the contribution of women to the overall household livelihood increased
during war in all the research communities, the contribution of other members declined, except that of men in Cuiebet and girls in Gogrial.

   The apparent increase in the contribution of women to the overall
household livelihood reflects the additional responsibilities that women have
assumed during war. One elderly woman during the community discussion
in Abyei commented that:

> *"Our society now is a society of women as we have now assumed not
> only all traditional roles of men towards family survival but even their
> role in traditional dancing"*

The apparent decline in the contribution of men and boys to household
livelihood is understandably attributed to the war that absorbed the male
population to engage in war efforts. For the community of Abyei area such
a decline in the contribution of boys is equally attributed to the permanent
migration of some members, particularly children, to northern Sudan, as
discussed in the next sub-section. The decline in the contribution of girls to
the household livelihood is largely attributed to the Dinka traditional perception of girls as a source of wealth through marriage that has been stifled

by war, either directly through the decline in the number of marriages, or indirectly through the apparent decline in bride-wealth. Besides these factors, the contribution of girls declined considerably during the war period in Abyei area, because of their permanent migration to northern Sudan. Unlike other research communities, the contribution of girls in Gogrial increased substantially, primarily because the source of livelihood shifted considerably to the gathering of wild foods, which is the traditional role of female members of household.

Investment in Human Assets: Off-Farm and Permanent Migration

There is a growing recognition that investment in human assets, besides promoting broad-based economic growth, can also reduce susceptibility to risk. The logic rural migration behaviour is imputed as part of their risk management strategies in development economics (Siegel and Alwang, 1999:28). It is generally argued that the households exposed to risk events widely use the *spatial* diversification of human assets, in the form of permanent or seasonal migration. While permanent migration (when household members migrate and send back remittances) tends to be an *ex ante* risk management measure, seasonal migration represents an *ex post* short-term response aimed at consumption smoothing or *ex ante* strategy depending on its nature.

Seasonal labour migration during the pre-war periods used to play an important economic role in the local economies and livelihood, particularly of the Dinka communities in northern Bahr el Ghazal. The monetisation of the Dinka economy in the 1960s and the 1970s encouraged a new pattern of labour migration, particularly to southern Kordofan and southern Darfur. According to Deng (1999:33), this labour migration fitted flexibly into the cultivation pattern of the Dinka: they finished with their fields first and could take advantage of the later rains to work on the fields in Darfur and Kordofan through sharecropping. Besides seasonal agricultural labour migration, there were also opportunities for Dinka youth to obtain employment as domestic servants or construction workers in most major towns in northern Sudan. Labour migration became a major means of earning money in the Dinka economy, thus reducing the sale of cattle to buy essential commodities as well to acquire more livestock and to marry (Ryle, 1989:13). Given variations in the climatic conditions between Bahr el Ghazal and western Sudan, this seasonal labour migration and off-farm employment activities in urban centres in northern Sudan became an important and effective livelihood risk management strategy to reduce the potential impact of drought and other shocks in the pre-war periods.

With the eruption of civil war and the intensification of counter-insurgency warfare in northern Bahr el Ghazal in the 1980s, seasonal agricultural labour migration was entirely disrupted and almost ceased to exist in the 1990s. While this disruption has had a profound impact on the livelihoods of Dinka communities in northern Bahr el Ghazal, it had also affected livelihoods in western Sudan by the acute shortage of seasonal labour from Dinka. It is widely believed and reported that the increased incidents of abduction, forced labour and slavery, which have been experienced by Dinka communities in northern Bahr el Ghazal, were directly linked to the acute labour shortage in Darfur and Kordofan in western Sudan.

As a result of the increased insecurity and intensification of counter-insurgency warfare in northern Bahr el Ghazal in the 1980s, some members of the households migrated permanently to the major towns and cities of northern Sudan. While this permanent migration is seen as an effective strategy to reduce the susceptibility of some household members to civil war, it is also a means of engaging some members in off-farm employment activities with the potential for sending remittances. Equally, reallocating some members of households to northern Sudan provides opportunities for their human development, particularly for children, since there are far better social services in northern Sudan.

Using the data on permanent migration from the household surveys as shown in Table 5.3, it is apparent that an average of 1.87 members of the sample households migrated permanently to northern Sudan in the 1990s. The households in Abyei area have the highest average members (4.07) of household who permanently migrated to northern Sudan compared to other research communities. This surprising high proportion of outmigration of household members in Abyei area is mainly attributed to their proximity to northern Sudan and more intensification of counter-insurgency warfare in Abyei area than other areas in Southern Sudan. Besides these two factors, there is a tendency among Dinka to use the extended family rather than the restricted definition of household and to include members of the extended family who helped (e.g. remittance) them during difficulties and those affected by war (abduction, slavery and death).

Table 5.3: Level of Permanent Migration in the 1990s[12]

Mean Household Members
Permanently Migrated in the 1990s

Research Communities	*--Initial Level of Household Wealth Status--*			
	Poor	Middle	Non–Poor	Total
Abyei	2.6	4.12	4.58	4.07
Gogrial	0.61	0.54	0.76	0.62
Cuiebet	0.15	0.33	0.15	0.22
Total	**1.03**	**2.02**	**2.21**	**1.87**

In general, the non-poor households tend to have more members permanently migrated (2.21) than do poor households (1.03). However, such
variation is significant in Abyei area, where non-poor households have
significantly higher numbers who have permanently migrated (4.58), almost
double that of poor households (2.6). Such variation between poor and
non-poor households in terms of the average number of members who
have permanently migrated is either insignificant (Gogrial) or does not exist
(Cuiebet) in the other research communities as, shown in Table 5.4.

This positive relationship between migration and wealth is largely related
to household size and structure, which affect the ability of a household
to supply labour to the non-farm sector. As rich households or families
with multiple conjugal units tend to be larger in size with more members
than poor households, they are able to supply their 'labour surplus' to work
off-farm. Another significant entry barrier to off-farm markets for poor
households in the context of Bahr el Ghazal region is the high transaction
costs (transport cost, search cost, information) that are more likely to be
afforded by rich households from their own sources, particularly livestock.

---

12   Ideally the data of members of household who have permanently migrated could have been related to the household size to obtain more informed trend.
However, due to the lack of data on the initial household size we used only the
average number of members of household who have migrated, which still provides
an illuminating trend.

Interestingly, most household members who have permanently migrated are women and children, as they are the most likely victims of civil war particularly counter-insurgency warfare. The perceived status of women as neutral, less harmful and suspicious allows them to move freely across and between the fighting parties. Besides taking care of children and engaging in casual labour work in northern Sudan, the Dinka women have become the only communication link and a crucial factor in sustaining family union between the divided members of families in the divided warring Sudan.

Another important aspect of permanent migration is the receipt of remittances by the household from its migrant members. Generally, remittances play an important role in risk management, as they usually tend to be inversely correlated with total household income. In the context of Bahr el Ghazal region remittance receipts constitute a major off-farm household activity in the lower-conflict areas of northern Sudan, with a minor but significant stabilising impact on household income in the higher-conflict area of Bahr el Ghazal region. Comparing remittances received by households during the famine in 1998, the Abyei community received significantly more remittances than the other communities, as shown in Table 5.4.

While about 56 per cent of sample households in Abyei area received remittances during the Bahr el Ghazal famine in 1998, only 8 and 5 per cent of the sample households respectively received remittances in Gogrial and Cuiebet areas. The pattern of remittances received in 1998 is consistent with the permanent members of household migrating to northern Sudan. While slightly more non-poor sample households (55 per cent) received remittances than did poor households (45 per cent) in Abyei area; there is not much difference between poor and non-poor households in the other research communities.

Table 5.4: The Remittances During Famine in 1998

Research Communities	Receipt of Remittances in 1998	*--Initial Level of Household Wealth Status--*			
		Poor	Middle	Non-Poor	Total
Abyei	No	16 (55%)	46 (41%)	31 (45%)	93 (44%)
	Yes	13 (45%)	67 (59%)	38 (55%)	118 (56%)
Gogrial	No	37 (97%)	89 (89%)	62 (92%)	188 (92%)
	Yes	1 (3%)	11 (11%)	5 (8%)	17 (8%)
Cuiebet	No	33 (100%)	36 (92%)	25 (93%)	94 (95%)
	Yes	0 (0%)	3 (8%)	2 (7%)	5 (5%)

Risk Mitigation Strategies: Reducing Potential Impact

Generally, risk mitigation strategies aim at reducing the potential impact if the risk event were to occur, and they include livelihood strategies, such as *asset portfolio management, insurance and hedging*, as discussed in Chapter 3. Importantly, asset and livelihood activities portfolio management includes the diversification of assets and livelihood activities, the holding of stock and investment in social capital, while insurance covers marriage, family and community arrangements and hedging covers extended family and future contracts.

In the context of the research communities of Dinka of Bahr el Ghazal region, the main livelihood activities, as discussed earlier include farming, animal husbandry, fishing and the gathering of wild foods. The most relevant livelihood activities for the analysis and discussion in this section will be farming and livestock management. Holding of stock (livestock and food) as precautionary savings will also be discussed under each of the traditional livelihood activities (farming and livestock). Investment in social capital and informal insurance arrangements are discussed under insurance and extended family and future contracts are analysed under hedging.

Asset Portfolio Management:

Generally **diversification** is often cited one of the common risk reduction as the primary pre-emptive household response to risk (Reardon, 1997; Ellis,

1998). However, there are misconceptions and confusion over the determinants of diversification and whether diversification is always a component of the *ex ante* household risk management strategies, as discussed in Chapter 2. While some researchers impute the determinants of diversification to either choice or necessity (Ellis, 2000), others emphasise risk (Bryceson, 1996) and differences in households' ability, location and access to credit (Dercon and Krishnan, 1996).

The concept of diversification is well-founded in finance theory, particularly assets portfolio theory. This theory was originally developed within the context of a risk-averse individual investor who is concerned with how to combine different shareholdings, in order to build an investment portfolio that would maximise the amount of expected return, given a specified level of risk. However, the importance of portfolio theory does not lie so much in its determinants (expected return and risk), but in the fact that the risk of the portfolio is *less than* the weighted average risk of the individual constituent investment. In other words, the determinants upon which portfolio theory is founded support the wisdom of the old adage of 'not keeping all your eggs (investment) in one basket', and the idea that risk can be reduced through diversification (Lumby, 1994:239). Portfolio theory is fundamentally based on the investors' behaviour axioms of general risk aversion (people dislike risk), rationality and consistency, which largely explain why people adopt diversification as the most rational investment decision and as an efficient risk management strategy. It is also recognised in asset portfolio theory that not all risk can be diversified away, because of the systematic risk (non-diversifiable risk) that affects all firms and hence cannot be eliminated by diversification (Lumby, 1994).

Portfolio theory, particularly diversification, has been gradually applied in development studies, particularly in household economic modelling, to examine the motives for and the determinants of livelihood diversification (Singh *et al.*, 1986; Ellis, 1993). In particular, the household economic model predicts diversification as a function of on-farm returns to labour time compared to off-farm earning opportunities (Ellis, 2000). In other words, risk factors provoke both on-farm and off-farm diversification as ways of spreading perceived risk and reducing the adverse impact of failure in any single branch of household activity. Assuming households behave like investors, the concept of portfolio theory has been applied in the context of poor rural households to show the link between vulnerability and the level of diversification of the portfolio of activities (Alderman and Paxon, 1992).

The attempts to draw parallels from the use of portfolio theory in finance in the context of development studies, have been challenged by many researchers on the ground of its irrelevance to social relations and non-financial assets (Folbre, 1986; Hart, 1992; Siegel and Alwang, 1999). The real challenge to the use of diversification in development studies is whether it is a part of risk management strategies or coping strategies, or whether it is considered as a result of voluntary decisions or involuntary actions (Dercon and Krishnan, 1996). Ellis (2000:55) classifies the motives for diversification into either necessity (involuntary and distress reasons) or choice (voluntary and proactive reasons), which correspond respectively to the coping and risk management determinants of diversification. Ironically, Ellis (2000) considers the diversification that is associated with natural disasters and civil disasters, including civil war, as a coping mechanism that is conceptually and in practice different from the risk management determinants of diverse livelihood patterns.

It is arguable whether such a distinction between the determinants of diversification that are triggered by necessity or choice does exist as the primary motive (necessity or choice), for diversification is triggered by risk events regardless of their sources. Our argument, as elaborated in Chapter 3, is that any livelihood strategy adopted by households as *ex ante* or *ex post* strategies to confront any type of risk events is an integral part of household risk management strategies. Specifically, diversification, as one of the livelihood strategies adopted by households prior to the occurrence of a risk event, is considered as an important component of household *ex ante* risk management strategies. In the light of this understanding, our focus will be on livelihood rather than on asset diversification.

Diversification within Livelihood Activities: Farming and Crop Production:

Crop production is an important livelihood activity in *Bahr el Ghazal* region that allows households to adopt a wide range of diversification forms to reduce the anticipated and actual adverse effect of risk events. These forms of diversification within crop production include *enterprise* diversification (planting different crops and inter-cropping), *spatial* diversification (planting in different fields), *temporal* diversification (staggered plantings) and *varietal* diversification (e.g. use of drought-resistant varieties) (Siegel and Alwang, 1999:26). Other forms of diversification that are responses to uncertain resource availability include *input* diversification (using low-risk inputs such as new technology), *market* diversification (alternative sources of purchasing inputs and selling outputs) and *vertical* integration (own production of inputs and own processing of outputs).

Before discussing and analysing the various forms of diversification, it is important to assess the level of crop production during the 1990s to gauge the effectiveness of the risk management strategies adopted by households. As discussed earlier and based on community survey data, there are apparent variations across research communities in terms of the contribution of farming to overall household livelihood. Data from the household survey are used to assess further the level of the contribution of farming to household livelihood in the 1990s, as shown in Table 5.5. It is clear that while 74 per cent of sample households in Abyei area agreed that their level of farming had increased in the 1990s, almost all sample households (97 percent) in Gogrial had experienced a decline in the level of farming and its contribution to household livelihood.

Table 5.5:

Level of Household Crop Production in the 1990s

		--Initial Level of Household Wealth Status--			
Research Communities	Crop production in the 1990s compared with pre-war periods	Poor	Middle	Non-Poor	Total
Abyei	Decreased	2 (7%)	34 (30%)	14 (20%)	50 (23%)
	The Same	1 (3%)	5 (4%)	0 (0%)	6 (3%)
	Increased	26 (90%)	74 (66%)	55 (80%)	155 (74%)
Gogrial	Decreased	37 (97%)	98 (98%)	64 (96%)	199 (97%)
	The Same	0 (0%)	1 (1%)	1 (1%)	2 (1%)
	Increased	1 (3%)	1 (1%)	2 (3%)	4 (2%)

Source: Household Survey/SPSS Output

Interestingly, despite the majority of sample households in Abyei area accepting that there had been an increase in the level of farming in the 1990s, there are variations between households, with poor households (90 per cent) realising an increased level of farming more than non-poor households did (66-80 per cent). These results about the level of farming and its contribution to household livelihood were further confirmed when we analysed the question in the household survey that asks about the level of farm size in the 1990s compared to pre-war periods. While most households in Abyei area consider their average farm size has increased in the 1990s, compared to pre-war periods, the households in other research communities asserted that their average farm size had instead shrunk.

These results about the level of farming and the size of farms in the 1990s are not enough without considering the actual trend of production in the 1990s. Relying on local and specific events in each of the research communities, a question was included in the sample household survey to retrieve data on the level of the household harvest of cereals for the past five years.

Although the data about the level of harvest might not be exact because of the problem of accurate recollection of the past, they do provide important trends about the level of farm production in the 1990s. The data indicate that while the average cereals harvest in Abyei has been steadily and progressively increasing even during the year of famine in 1998, the reverse trend is seen in other research communities, with harvests reaching their lowest levels in 1998, and recovering slightly afterwards. This enormous increase in agricultural production in Abyei is attributed as discussed below to increased market opportunities and adaptation to new opportunities created by exogenous counter-insurgency warfare.

For example, in Abyei area the average cereal harvest in 1999 reached as high as 1,690 kilograms and that exceeded the average harvest of sorghum (1,100 kg) that was estimated in 1980 in the pre-war periods (Huntington et al, 1981). This suggests that crop production in 1999 in Abyei area was not only higher than in pre-war periods, but even provided a surplus of about 30 per cent over consumption requirements (about 3 kgs daily per household) (Huntington et al, 1981:48). Compared to other research communities, the sample households in Gogrial area experienced the lowest level of crop harvest in the 1990s, one that was far lower than the minimum sorghum consumption requirements.

The real question is how can we explain the variations in the level of farming and production trends across the research communities who were exposed to different types of risk? Could we attribute such variations to their locality, ability, sources of risk, behaviour towards risk or lack of diversification, as is usually suggested? As other aspects, such as sources of risk and behaviour towards risk, have been discussed in previous chapters, we will focus on diversification as one of the livelihood strategies that has recently received increased attention in development economics.

Although there are various forms of diversification of crop production, the relevant forms in the context of the Dinka research communities include *enterprise, varietal, spatial, market* and *storage* is also included as an important risk strategy in the context of civil war. As most of the research communities have adopted most of these forms of diversification, the focus of the analysis and discussion is on the level of diversification in Abyei area, which shows a somewhat aberrant pattern.

Enterprise Diversification:

In order to assess the enterprise and varietal diversification, the data generated from community perception surveys are used, as shown in Table 5.6. It is clear that while the research communities used to plant a number of varieties and different crops on their fields, such a pattern persisted in the 1990s with an apparent change in proportions allotted to each crop, except in Abyei area where mono-cropping of sorghum predominantly prevailed in the 1990s. This suggests that while enterprise diversification was adopted by households in Gogrial and Cuiebet, households in Abyei area adopted only one type of crop (sorghum) and ceased to plant other crops on their fields in the 1990s. The data generated from household surveys also provide similar findings that suggest that almost all the sample households in Abyei area abandoned other crops and specialised only in the production of sorghum, while other communities maintained a similar portfolio of different crops to that which existed in pre-war periods.

Table 5.6: Level of Enterprise Diversification in the 1990s

Farm Land allotted (in %) to each crop planted in the 1990s

Research Communities	Periods	Sorghum	Maize	G/Nuts	Sesame	Others
Abyei	Before War	52%	8%	10%	20%	10%
	1990s	98%	2%	0%	0%	0%
Gogrial	Before War	22%	19%	44%	15%	0%
	1990s	37%	20%	23%	13%	7%
Cuiebet	Before War	36%	0%	28%	18%	8%
	1990s	29%	0%	52%	11%	8%

During the pre-war periods, the farmers of Abyei area used to plant a number of varieties of sorghum (*ruath, ngai* and *anguol*) and also planted amounts of sesame, groundnuts, maize and okra interspersed among the sorghum. The planting, sequencing and interspersing of these crops fit well into the annual agricultural cycle (April through January) that is conditioned by the rainfall pattern and topography of the area. The garden close to the house is sown first with fast maturing varieties of sorghum (*ngai*), maize, and other crops, that are harvested in late August for daily meals and snacks, then the large field is sown with varieties of slower maturing sorghum (*ruath*) that is harvested in October. The sorghum stalks are cut at the base, allowing new shoots to sprout and accompanied sometimes with some replanting, depending on the level of moisture, which produces a smaller second harvest (*anguol*) that constitutes about 30 per cent of the original harvest (Huntington *et al*, 1981).

The civil war was in many ways a blessing in disguise, particularly in the context of farming systems in Abyei area. The massive displacement in Abyei area in the 1980s resulted, as discussed in Chapter 4, in the rapid regrowth of shrubs that affected the pattern of rainfall, increased the level of moisture and provided new opportunities for the farming system in Abyei area. As the planting time of the short maturing sorghum (*ngai*) and other crops, such as groundnuts, sesame, maize and okra, coincided with the start of Arab militia activities in April/May, when they returned northward with the start of the rains, the farmers shifted their focus away from these crops.

Varietal Diversification:

The research communities adopted in one way or another a form of varietal diversification in the 1990s, as indicated by an increase in the area of a household's field allotted to the different crops. While households in Gogrial adopted new short-maturing and drought-resistant sorghum varieties, the households in Cuiebet area adopted a more short-maturing and drought-resistant variety of groundnuts (*terkeka*) than their traditional variety (*monyjang*). The adoption of new varieties of crops resulted in an apparent increase in the areas allotted to these new varieties, as shown in Table 5.6.

Unlike other research communities that adopted new varieties of crops to confront drought in the 1990s, households in Abyei area adjusted their portfolio of local sorghum varieties to respond to counter-insurgency warfare and the new environmental opportunities created by civil war. The long-maturing sorghum (*ruath*), which is planted after *ngai* in May, became less attractive because the timing of its planting coincided with counter-insurgency activities, and it was also reliant on early rains, which became increasingly erratic in the 1990s. As a result of these environmental constraints and the threats of raids by Arab militias, the farmers in Abyei area gradually shifted away from *ruath* in the 1990s and became increasingly interested in investing more in the second harvest (*anguol*) that is less dependent on rainfall but more dependent on soil moisture. The timing of *anguol* (October-December) is opportune, because of relative stability (the high water levels in River Kiir provide a natural deterrent to the raids from Arab militias) and adequate soil moisture during October-December.

In most cases the long-maturing sorghum (*ruath*) is planted not only for harvest, but importantly to provide ratoons that are supplemented by more replanting, as a result of higher moisture than during the pre-war periods. As a result of the drastic change in the farming systems in Abyei, it is not surprising that farmers adopted mono-cropping (sorghum), with a shift towards specific varieties of sorghum (*anguol*) to make use of opportunities and to minimise risks. On the basis of the community perception survey, while the *ruath* variety used to constitute about 44 per cent of the household sorghum harvest in pre-war periods, its contribution has declined to about 36 per cent. The contribution of *anguol* increased from 37 per cent during pre-war periods to about 54 per cent in the 1990s. This shift to investing more in one planting season, or in one variety of sorghum (*anguol*), is primarily aimed at reducing susceptibility to the occurrence of counter-insurgency warfare in Abyei rather than being a mere *varietal diversification* to reduce the effects of drought.

Spatial Diversification:

Using the data from the household surveys to assess the level of spatial diversification across the research communities, the study finds that the households exposed to counter-insurgency warfare tended to have a lower number of fields compared to pre-conflict periods, while drought-prone communities tended to have a higher number of different fields during the 1990s as shown in Table 5.7. For example, while the mean number of household fields in the 1990s was about 1.3 and 1.8 in Abyei and Gogrial areas respectively, the average number of fields in Cuiebet area was about 4.1, as shown in Table 5.7.

Interestingly, the difference between the number of fields during the 1990s and the pre-conflict periods is statistically significant across all the research communities. Comparing the mean number of household fields in the pre-war periods with that in the 1990s, the results of the Wilcoxon statistical test[13] show a significantly lower number of fields in Abyei and Gogrial, while a significantly higher number of fields is found in Cuiebet in the 1990s. In other words, while the households exposed to counter-insurgency warfare reduced their number of fields in the 1990s, the drought-prone households adopted spatial diversification in the 1990s. The difference between the average number of fields planted by poor and non-poor households is significant in the pre-war periods, while with non-poor households having more fields, such difference is insignificant and was eroded in the 1990s, particularly in Gogrial and Abyei areas.

---

13   The Wilcoxon statistical test is a non-parametric test that is used for testing the null hypothesis that two population means are equal. Like other non-parametric tests, it makes no assumption about the shape of distribution of the two variables and is more powerful, statistically, than other tests (Puri, 1996:68).

Table 5.7: Level of Spatial Diversification in the 1990s

Average Number of Fields Planted by Sample Households

| | | --Initial Wealth of Sample Households -- | | | |
Research Communities	Periods	Poor	Middle	Non-Poor	Average
Abyei	Pre War	1.69	1.77	2.12	1.87
	1990s	1.34	1.25	1.41	1.31
Gogrial	Pre War	4.00	4.58	4.82	4.55
	1990s	1.74	1.80	1.85	1.77
Cuiebet	Pre War	3.00	3.00	2.88	2.98
	1990s	4.06	4.09	4.37	4.13

Source: Household Surveys/SPSS Output

Interestingly, despite the fact that households in Abyei and Gogrial were equally exposed to drought, as well as counter-insurgency warfare, they opted not to take spatial diversification as an effective livelihood strategy to confront counter-insurgency warfare. This finding further confirms that diversification is not always the best risk management option for households exposed to the risk of civil war. This finding also clearly challenges, at least in the context of civil war, the dominant argument in the risk literature that the more households are exposed to risk events, the more they diversify to confront the risk events.

Access to Markets:

Proximity to markets and infrastructure is a critical asset to households, as it influences the availability and accessibility of goods and services, as well as the level of household diversification of its cropping activities. In the context of counter-insurgency warfare in Bahr el Ghazal region, access to markets that are in government-held areas plays a crucial role in providing not only goods and services but also information related to risk events, such as counter-insurgency warfare. This makes market diversification - alternative sources of purchasing inputs and selling outputs - a critical livelihood option for households that are exposed to the risk of counter-insurgency warfare.

Generally, the contribution of markets and exchange to household livelihood has not vanished during the current civil war, but has instead persisted and even increased in some cases, as discussed earlier. Using data from the household surveys to assess the level of their access to markets in the 1990s, the results show that while about 56 per cent of households in Abyei considered access to markets increased in the 1990s, about 77 per cent of households in Gogrial area agreed that this level of access had declined as shown in Table 5.8. Of great interest is the variation in responses within households, particularly in Abyei area, where more non-poor households (65 per cent) experienced the increase in their level of access to markets in the 1990s than did poor households (45 per cent).

This significant but important difference between poor and non-poor households regarding the level of access to markets is primarily attributed to the increased reliance of the non-poor on markets in the 1990s, particularly those households that reverted to pastoralism. In Gogrial area there is not much difference in the responses of households to the level of access to markets in the 1990s, but slightly more poor households (26 per cent) experienced an increase in the level of this contribution than did non-poor households (21 per cent). This again shows the drastic change in the wealth structure of the households exposed to endogenous counter-insurgency warfare in Gogrial area in the 1990s.

Table 5.8: Level of Household Access to Markets in the 1990s

Research Communities	Crop production in the 1990s compared with pre-war periods	--Initial Level of Household Wealth Status--			
		Poor	Middle	Non-Poor	Total
Abyei	Decreased	11 (38%)	40 (35%)	18 (26%)	69 (33%)
	The Same	5 (17%)	12 (11%)	6 (9%)	23 (11%)
	Increased	13 (45%)	61 (54%)	45 (65%)	119 (56%)
Gogrial	Decreased	25 (66%)	80 (80%)	52 (78%)	157 (77%)
	The Same	3 (8%)	2 (2%)	1 (2%)	6 (3%)
	Increased	10 (26%)	18 (18%)	14 (21%)	42 (20%)

Source: Household Survey/SPSS Output

The Abyei market is an important link between south and north and it used to be one of the largest livestock markets in the Sudan, which used to supply the markets in the major towns in the north, including Khartoum, with good quality Dinka oxen. Despite the fact that civil war has greatly reduced its role, the Abyei market continues to be pivotally the major source of basic commodities (salt, sugar, medicines, cloth, etc), that are supplied from the north to most parts of Bahr el Ghazal region.

Interestingly, the Abyei market because of its huge business potential, had encouraged the fighting parties (the government forces and the local rebel forces) to cooperate and to allow free movements of traders and the civilian population, because of their vested economic interests. Given their free movement, women together with children became increasingly the most reliable members of households to access these markets in the government-held towns. While the government armed forces in Abyei town virtually monopolised the trading and market activities, the local rebel forces (SPLA) benefit from the high taxes levied on traders and individuals who moved in and out of the market.

This practice around and in Abyei market confirms the observation made by Keen (1998:12) that: "the distinction between war and peace may be hazy, and the two may not necessarily be opposites". The female members of households, because of their perceived neutral role that allows them easy movement, are becoming more involved in trading activities, particularly accessing markets in the government-held areas than during pre-conflict period. Besides these markets in the government-held areas, the local communities in the SPLM-held areas created local markets that allows free interaction between Arab nomads and the Dinka communities. These markets, besides facilitating trading activities, have become increasingly important as they provided a forum for resolving grass-root conflicts between the Dinka and Arab nomads (Deng, 1999).

Besides access to market in Abyei town, the community of Abyei developed during the 1990s informal exchange system with their southern neigbouring communities of Twic Dinka. The mono-cropping (sorghum) system adopted by farmers in Abyei area, besides coping with the capricious rainfall pattern and threats of Arab raids, is largely conditioned by the market opportunities of sorghum that is in short supply in the region immediately to its south (Twic area). The farmers in Twic area had experienced an erratic rainfall pattern (drought and floods) during the 1990s, and this compounded with less arable land and insecurity contributed to a severe limitation to food production and an increased vulnerability to food insecurity. As a result, the households in Twic area became increasingly dependent on sorghum production in Abyei area, which is bartered for livestock or seasonal labour. The farmers in Abyei area started supplying sorghum also to the much drier areas to the north, particularly to the residents in the government-held town of Abyei, as their crop production had been constrained by drought and insecurity. These market opportunities for sorghum, which is in short supply in the much wetter areas to the south and the much drier areas to the north, make farmers in Abyei area to specialise more in sorghum production. One elderly key informant man in Abyei area commented during the community discussion that:

> *'What is keeping us on our land, which is the most insecure area in the whole of Sudan, is not only related to our patriotic feeling of protecting it but more importantly to the market opportunities of sorghum that has tied us further to our ancestral land.'*

Holding of Stocks: Livestock and Grain

The holding of stocks is the most common form of asset diversification for risk management (Binswanger and Rosenzweig, 1993; Devereux, 1993; Reardon and Vosti, 1995; Udry, 1995; Dercon; 1996; Carter and May, 1999). Physical assets are generally broad and they are usually classified into productive assets, household assets and stocks. In the context of the research communities in Bahr el Ghazal region, the most relevant category of physical assets in the analysis of the household risk management and livelihood strategies is the holding of stocks (livestock and food) as precautionary savings.

Holding of Grain Stocks: The Level of (A-)Symmetric Information:

Generally, the holding of food stocks as precautionary savings plays an important role in risk management, particularly in counter-insurgency warfare, as they have the advantage of being fairly liquid, and can be consumed or sold to smooth consumption. However, these attributes of food stocks that make farmers invest in them equally make them immediate targets and susceptible to militia raids. In particular, their attributes, such as lumpiness and immobility, make grain stocks increasingly susceptible to Arab raids and also make their management, particularly storage, an arduous task. The challenge of storage during war was summed up by statement of one key informants during focus group discussion that *"Planting sorghum is less harder than its storage"*.

The holding of grain stocks and the associated risk, particularly in the context of counter-insurgency caused communities to drastically change their traditional storage system. The data from the household surveys clear show that while all households exposed to both types of counter-insurgency warfare (Abyei and Gogrial) changed their traditional storage systems, the households exposed to drought did not change their storage systems in the 1990s.

The painful process of storage; from harvest, threshing, digging the underground storage and the storage of sorghum, is illustrated by photographs 5.1-5.6 that were taken during research fieldwork in Abyei area in 2000. These photographs show that the entire traditional surface storage systems have been transferred underground with a high labour input and with harvest losses that exceeded 25 per cent of the aggregate harvest, as reported by key informants during the community focus group discussion. In spite of these losses and the additional costs of underground stores, farmers in Abyei area managed to conceal and protect their grain stocks from Arab militia raids, and their continuous production of sorghum indicated that such a system is profitable and efficient with considerable rationality.

The timeliness of sorghum underground storage in Abyei area is crucially important in reducing the potential susceptibility of grain stocks to the raids of Arab militias, and subsequently changed the gender roles and community social networks in farming and crop production during the 1990s. Generally, the storage of sorghum that is harvested in November/December must finish in mid-December and early January, prior to the arrival of Arab militias in January/February, and such urgency necessitates collective action and shared labour and roles between and among members of the community; particularly men and women.

Photographs 5.1–6:
Storage Process and Stages in Abyei Area during the 1990s

The stored sorghum must remain untouched until the rains start in April/ May, when Arab nomads start returning northwards and also reduced the susceptibility of the stored sorghum to depreciation, as a result of high underground moisture or destruction caused by pests, such as monkeys. Interestingly, during my fieldwork households did not report the depreciation of stored sorghum as a result of high underground moisture and humidity, as this period (January-April) is extremely hot, but they complained instead about the destruction caused by monkeys. Of great interest is that when these underground stores were opened in May, it coincided well with the opportune time when the limited sorghum harvest in Twic area got exhausted and used up.

During the pre-war periods, the farming activities particularly harvesting and threshing like any other livelihood activity in Dinka society were strictly and traditionally apportioned by sex. Cleaning, sowing, and weeding were done by both men and women. But for the harvest, men used to chop sorghum stalks and women cut sorghum heads, and threshed and stored the harvest as a prelude to their (female) cooking duties (Huntington *et al*, 1981). During the 1990s these roles and others changed drastically, with men assuming more responsibilities in harvesting, threshing and storage, as shown in photographs 5.1-5.6.

Besides the erosion of apportioning agricultural activities by sex, mutual labour assistance clubs (*mat*) and beer parties became more institutionalised and practised in the 1990s to perform collectively the most critical agricultural activities, such as harvesting, threshing and underground storage. During the pre-war period, weeding and its timing used to be the most critical agricultural activity, because of the problem of a parasitic weed (striga) or 'witchweed', and the beer parties were optionally performed as part of weeding for those farmers who fell behind. Interestingly, Huntington *et al* (1981:47) observed that the labour provided for agricultural activities at the beer parties is as efficient as that of a sober person working alone.

Comparing the success of holding grain stocks in Abyei area in the face of exogenous counter-insurgency warfare with the experience of households exposed to endogenous counterinsurgency in Gogrial area, there was limited success in Gogrial in the 1990s, despite the drastic changes in the traditional storage system. The households in Gogrial area had tried various measures, including underground storage and on trees in the forest, of keeping their limited crop harvest, particularly that of grain and ground-nuts, but such measures did not reduce the susceptibility of these stocks to Dinka militia raids. The failure to hold stocks, as a risk mitigation strategy adopted by households to face Dinka militia activities in the 1990s, is largely related to the level of symmetric information between the potential victims (households) and the attackers (Dinka militias) as discussed in chapter 4. As most of the attackers came from within their communities, they had inside and detailed information, not only about the general household livelihood strategies, but even specific information about the particular strategies adopted by each individual household. During community group discussions in Gogrial area, I came across many horrific ordeals and accounts of how communities suffered at the hands of their sons, who had joined the Dinka militias in the 1990s and guided their activities and raids with detailed precision about underground storage and the location of their livestock.

One chief in Gogrial area said 'we tried first to hide our stocks in the forest (*bodiec*), then we buried our stocks in the form of a grave (*rang*), and then stored them underground in our own huts and cattle byres, but we did not succeed as we were failed by our own sons who revealed our survival secrets'. Another woman said 'we became victims of our own stored stocks, as we did not only lose our stocks but also we were brutally forced to carry such stocks when discovered by militias'. One elderly key informant narrated his personal experience when his own nephew joined the militias and directed them to his house to loot it. His nephew provided the Dinka militias with detailed information about his underground storage, which they then emptied, and he gained revenge by giving detailed information to the militias about the underground storage of his nephew's father inside the cattle byre (*Luak*). Unlike the situation in Gogrial area, information about household livelihood strategies, particularly the specific and detailed strategies adopted by each household in Abyei area, was not easily available to their attackers (Arab militias). The variation in the level of (a-)symmetric information about household livelihood strategies between victims and their attackers largely explains the variation in the level of effectiveness in the holding of stocks as a risk mitigation strategy in the 1990s.

Livestock Management:

Livestock as assets has the dual characteristic of being productive assets and stocks. Livestock, such as cattle, can be used as work animals and for transport, can be consumed (milk, meat or blood), represent a good store of value, and also serve as stocks that can be liquidated and have other social values. Unlike food stock that is stationary and lumpy, livestock are mobile and this makes them increasingly important for risk management strategies, particularly in the context of counter-insurgency warfare. All these attributes of livestock make them a popular means of precautionary savings and an effective means for household risk mitigation strategy. As cattle are hardly used for agricultural production and transport in the context of the Dinka research communities, we treat livestock as stocks rather than productive assets.

Animal husbandry, particularly cattle, is the primary feature of the Dinka economy and the significance of cattle goes beyond their economic value, as they are used to maintain social relations, religious values and political institutions[14]. The value of cattle in Dinka society, as described by Lienhardt (1961:27), is that of 'something to which men have assimilated themselves, dwelling upon them in reflection, imitating them in stylised action, and regarding them as interchangeable with human life in many social situations'. Cattle are not only part of Dinka life but they are the life (Keen, 1994). Despite the effect of the modernisation, the monetisation of their economy and even wars, cattle are still pivotal to Dinka livelihoods.

The management of livestock during pre-war period was very much conditioned by seasonality and organised around regular and seasonal migration between cattle camps in *toic*, "swampy areas", and *baai* "permanent settlements" or villages, that maximised the utilisation of livestock products and minimised the tension between animal husbandry and crop production. During the early rains (*Ker*) the fields are planted and cattle gradually return to camp near the villages to provide milk. In the early rainy season (*Ruel*) when mosquitoes are increasing, the cattle are brought home for protection

---

14   In Dinka the names of males are derived from the colours of oxen, while the names of females are derived from the colours of cows. The names of social structures, such as tribe, '*Wut*", which also means 'cattle camp', and clan, '*gol/dhien*' which also means 'cattle hearth', clearly show the dominant position cattle occupy, not only in the Dinka's economic life, but also in shaping spiritual and political institutions.

in the cattle byres at night. By the end of *Ruel* (*anyoic*) when crops are ripe, the cattle begin to graze farther away from villages and, as the pasture becomes exhausted in winter (*Rut*), the cattle are driven farther away along the upper reaches of the watercourses. During the dry season (*Mai*) the main cattle camp in *toic* begin to be used as water supplies and pastures become scanty near the permanent villages. The herding of cattle is generally collective except for the few cows kept permanently at home for milk. As a single family or household cannot protect its cattle alone, the co-operation of territorial groups - either a section of the tribe or a subsection - becomes necessary.

During the civil war in the 1990s, this traditional system of managing livestock changed drastically as a result of counterinsurgency warfare. This pattern of seasonal movement of livestock and their attributes make them susceptible to the counterinsurgency warfare in the 1990s. The attractive attributes of livestock made them a centre of household risk management strategies, and also made them the object of looting and raiding by the government militias. As a result, the management of livestock changed considerably, as well as their level of contribution to the overall household livelihood in the 1990s, as discussed earlier.

With increased counterinsurgency warfare in the 1990s, cattle owners were faced with two options either to directly manage their livestock, or to entrust or 'tethering' some animals to the custody of close relatives or friends. The custom of giving cattle in custody to others known as '*kuei*', is normally practised by the Dinka to minimise the risk of diseases or to disguise wealth, in order to escape the risk of cattle being claimed in discharge of kinship or other obligations, or of attracting the envy of less fortunate people. Other functions of *kuei* include: improving cross-breeding, creating space for one's herd, a form of assistance to relatives or friends and to accumulate independent and concealed wealth, particularly by young men (Deng, 1971).

According to the risk literature and on the basis of risk aversion and diversification arguments, it is rational that the strategy of entrusting or loaning cattle (*kuei*) would be practised more during counter-insurgency warfare in the 1990s than the direct management of cattle (Posner, 1980). On the basis of community survey, the practice of *kuei* declined considerably, while the direct management of livestock increased substantially during the 1990s among all the research communities, except those exposed to exogenous counter-insurgency warfare. The adult male household members became directly engaged in managing the household livestock, compared to youth management of livestock in the pre-conflict period. While about 15 per cent of the sample households in Abyei area adopted pastoralist livelihoods, as discussed earlier, the practice of *kuei* slightly increased with custodians now becoming more likely to be maternal relatives rather than paternal relatives or friends.

This practice of *kuei* increased among the households exposed to exogenous counter-insurgency warfare (Abyei) because the nature of risk has strengthened trust and specialisation. This necessitates that those households farming, but with limited number of livestock (poor households), opted to entrust their small number of livestock to those who have adopted a pastoralist livelihood in Twic area and away from Abyei area during the 1990s. This explains the apparent decline in the contribution of livestock to household livelihood in Abyei area, as livestock were kept far away from the area and this greatly reduced household access to livestock products in the 1990s.

In terms of the varietal diversification of cattle, the pastoralists have not changed the mix of the various types of cattle (cows, heifers, oxen and calves), except that the proportion of oxen declined considerably in the 1990s. The oxen were traditionally kept in the cattle camp for social value and their proportion declined in the 1990s, as they were the immediate targets of combatants, particularly the rebels, and of local authorities as a means of paying taxes (*moon*) for the war effort.

Social Capital and Hedging

Though it is generally accepted that social assets, household social ties and networks, can provide a form of informal insurance, there is no conclusive agreement over their effectiveness. Devereux (1999:15) emphasises that generic shocks such as drought are likely to make social safety nets least effective when they are most needed. In the context of civil war and particularly counter-insurgency warfare it is widely argued and perceived that social capital is one of its first casualties, and its absence perpetuates the occurrence of counter-insurgency warfare (Swift, 1993; de Waal, 1993a).

Besides the lack of consensus about the definition and effectiveness of social capital (Fine, 1999), agreement on its measurement is even further away and constitutes one of the greatest weaknesses of the social capital concept. There are, however, attempts to measure social capital through censuses of groups and group memberships and through survey data on levels of trust and civic engagement (Fukuyama, 2001). The measurement of social capital through a census of groups and memberships, as tried by Putnam (1993), has come under increasing criticism, particularly the observed inverse relationship between the size of a group, the numbers of such a group, and the problem of overlapping and multiple membership of individuals. A consensus is now building around the idea that internal cohesion within a given group, despite its subjective nature, is a critical qualitative measure of social capital. Besides the level of internal cohesiveness, Fukuyama (2001:13) added another dimension that captures the way in which such groups relate to outsiders that he termed as the 'radius of distrust' that positively affects the supply of social capital.

As the measurement of internal cohesiveness and the 'radius of distrust' is extremely difficult to capture through a census of groups and group membership, survey methods that generate data on trust and civic engagement as a proxy for social capital have been found more relevant. A general question that is used in surveys to qualitatively gauge the level of trust is 'Generally speaking, would you say that most people can be trusted or that you can't be too careful in dealing with people?' Despite the fact that there are manifold problems with such a general question, as it will not provide much precise information about the radius of trust or distrust, it has been used by the General Social Survey and World Values Survey to provide comparative data on social capital across countries (Fukuyama, 2001).

In order to measure the level of social capital in the 1990s, we asked a similar question but phrased slightly differently. We framed our question in such a way as to reflect attitudes toward co-operation in terms of kinship support, that captures not only internal cohesiveness but also on relation to outsiders. Specifically, we asked a household 'How would you compare the level of kinship support during the 1990s with that in the pre-war period?' The coded answer to this question is adequate to reflect not only the level of kinship support and co-operation from friends and family, but also the support from strangers and outsiders.

The Level of Social Capital in the 1990s: Trust and Co-operation:

The Dinka saying, "What is given circulates, and what is consumed is wasted" explains much about the importance and nature of the reciprocity system among the Dinka (Deng, 1971:268). Deng (1971) presented an account and baseline of Dinka social systems in the pre-war context that we used as a basis for assessing the status of social capital during the 1990s. The Dinka generally used to have social systems that worked towards maintaining equality and were more egalitarian than most other societies. Like other pastoralist societies, the social safety nets and traditional risk-pooling arrangements of the Dinka range from customary economic exchanges, such as generalised, balanced and negative reciprocity to customary redistribution systems, such as horizontal and vertical redistribution (Swift, 1993; Deng, 1999). The traditional Dinka social safety nets are well rooted in their social relations (*cieng*), their notions of human dignity (*dheeng*) and their communal ownership of wealth. The social relations of Dinka are largely determined and nurtured by marriage (*ruai*) and their notions of human dignity are reflected in values, such as pride, hospitality and generosity. These distinctive characteristics of Dinka society, such as gift-giving, reciprocal exchange, polygamy, bride wealth, the size of kinship, communal property rights, and the value placed on certain personality traits, such as generosity, can be explained as adaptations to risk, uncertainty or high information costs (Demsetz, 1967; Grossbard, 1976; Grossbard, 1978; Posner, 1980).

The Dinka communal right over property and wealth is primarily derived from their relationship to their Divinity (*yieth*), to which all wealth and property belong, and individuals are entrusted with control over wealth and property (Lienhardt, 1961:23). This mixture between individual and communal property rights among pastoralist societies is attributed by some economists to the scarcity of resources involved (Demsetz, 1967). In the context of rural Sudan, Evans-Pritchard (1940) explicitly pointed out that it is scarcity and not sufficiency that makes people generous in a community where everyone is likely to face difficulties. While there are social classes determined by wealth, there used to be no social barriers between these classes, as the strong spirit of equality among the Dinka did not permit the rich to look down on the poor or the poor to look up to the rich (Deng, 1971). The apparent emphasis on the human element in social relations is the main feature of Dinka society that used to bridge class barriers and differentiation. The virtues of wealth that are defined in the context of social prestige carry commensurate social responsibilities in Dinka society, as the rich are socially bound to assist the needy.

This inseparable link between wealth and social responsibilities is well reflected in the Dinka words *'adheng'* and *'ajak'*, which mean 'rich' and may also be translated as 'kind', 'generous', 'gentle' or in a word 'noble' (Deng, 1971:251). Thus calling a person 'rich' in Dinka is another way of describing what is expected of his/her relations with other people. The social relations in Dinka society; between individual and individual, and individual and community, as described by Deng (1971), are such that the individual is naturally conscious and responsive to the needs of others, and this deferential Dinka aspect of wealth paradoxically limits wealth accumulation.

In spite of these strong Dinka values that supply social capital and managed to survive modernisation, it is questionable whether such values persist during the civil war. This might have brought major changes to the way Dinka relate to each other. In order to assess the status of social capital (non-institutional) during civil war and counter-insurgency warfare in Bahr el Ghazal region in the 1990s, various measures as proxies for trust or distrust, co-operation and cohesiveness were used. These measures include *kinship support, traditional court settlements, and mutual labour assistance club (mat).*

The Level of Kinship Support in the 1990s:

The level of kinship support is used as a proxy for the level and status of social capital, particularly trust and co-operation, within the research communities and with their neighbouring communities during civil war and counter-insurgency warfare in the 1990s. Using the household survey data to assess the level of social capital stock in the 1990s as compared to pre-war period, the results as shown in Table 5.9 indicate that about 37 per cent of sample households in Abyei area experienced an increase in kinship support in the 1990s, while only 2 per cent of sample households in Gogrial area noticed an increase in the level of kinship support. An exceptionally high and significant percentage of sample households (94 per cent) in Gogrial area experienced a decline in the level of social capital stock in the 1990s.

Table 5.9: Level of Kinship Support in the 1990s

--Initial Level of Household Wealth Status--

Research Communities	Kinship support in the 1990s compared with pre-war periods	Poor	Middle	Non-Poor	Total
Abyei	Decreased	9 (31%)	43 (38%)	31 (45%)	83 (39%)
	The Same	10 (34%)	26 (23%)	14 (20%)	50 (24%)
	Increased	10 (35%)	44 (39%)	24 (35%)	78 (37%)
Gogrial	Decreased	34 (90%)	94 (94%)	65 (97%)	193 (94%)
	The Same	3 (8%)	3 (3%)	1 (2%)	7 (4%)
	Increased	3 (8%)	3 (3%)	1 (1%)	5 (2%)

Source: Household Survey/SPSS Output

Within the sample households in Abyei area, the poor and non-poor sample households provided similar pattern of responses about the level of social capital in the 1990s, with significantly more non-poor households (45 per cent) considering there had been a decline in the level of social capital than did poor households (31 per cent). In Gogrial area there is no significant variation in the level of responses, with more non-poor households (97 per cent) reporting a decline in the level of social capital than poor households (90 per cent). Conversely more poor households (8 per cent) in Gogrial area, though a small percentage, reported an increase in social capital than did non-poor households (1 per cent).

The findings on the status of social capital stock in the 1990s from sample surveys are also confirmed by findings from the community focus group discussions that show clearly that trust and co-operation within the households exposed to endogenous counter-insurgency warfare (Gogrial area) considerably eroded during the 1990s. The non-poor households, who were the immediate targets and victims of endogenous counter-insurgency warfare, significantly felt such a decline in the stock of social capital in Gogrial area. One elderly key informant in Gogrial area described the mistrust and bitter relations that existed in the 1990s when his own nephew, who had joined the government Dinka militias, described during their raids his relation with his elders as similar to the relationship between an eagle and its offspring[15].

Unlike the households exposed to endogenous counter-insurgency war-fare (Gogrial), the households in Abyei area did not experience a significant decline in the level of social capital stock in the 1990s, as the common threat from Arab militias (the radius of distrust) strengthened their internal cohesiveness, trust and co-operation. This finding suggests that the nature of counter-insurgency warfare explains much about the status of social capital in the context of civil war. The nature of endogenous counter-insurgency warfare as experienced by the communities of Gogrial in the 1990s created a climate of distrust and turned the community against itself, which resulted in weakened social capital, particularly social safety nets and kinship support.

Besides the climate of distrust created by endogenous counter-insurgency warfare, the profound depletion of assets, such as livestock, particularly among the non-poor households had greatly affected kinship support. Chief Ayii Madut of Gogrial rejected the argument that their *cieng* (way of life) had changed and attributed the weakened kinship support in the 1990s to the erosion of their asset-base, particularly livestock, that forced people to look inward and to struggle to save their own lives (Deng, 1999:61). Chief Ayii Madut supported his argument by comparing the famine of 1988 with that of 1998, arguing that people did not die in the same numbers in 1988, because people, particularly, the non-poor households, had livestock that made them able to help poor households during the famine of 1988.

The Level of Distrust: Traditional Court Settlements in 1998:

Another way of assessing the level of trust and co-operation is to use the level at which people resorted to courts to settle their claims during the critical period of famine in 1998. During the famine of 1998, the Dinka communities set up famine courts (*luok cok*) to enforce 'social contracts' (Deng, 1999). In fact the setting up of famine courts to enforce 'social contracts' is undoubtedly a good proxy for increasing social capital at com-munity level. However, as our focus is at household level, the act of resorting

---

15   The Dinka believe that eagles (*kuei*) delay having offspring till they become elderly as their offspring kill their parents immediately when they are grown up. Similar behaviour is also observed among some species of spiders as their offspring feed on the flesh of their mother immediately after they are hatched.

to famine courts to enforce social claims indirectly captures the level of mistrust and poor co-operation, as compared to the ideal situation where people voluntarily support each other, or fulfil claims without resorting to the courts or a third party[16]. The data generated from the household survey, as shown in Table 5.10 clearly show that a significant and high percentage of sample households (42 per cent) who resorted to traditional courts to settle their social claims in Gogrial area during the famine of 1998.

Table 5.10: Level of Social Claims[17]
Settlement in Traditional Courts in the 1990s

		--Initial Level of Household Wealth Status--			
Research Communities	Whether household was involved in court settlement in 1998?	Poor	Middle	Non-Poor	Average
Abyei	No	25 (86%)	91 (81%)	58 (84%)	174 (83%)
	Yes	4 (14%)	22 (19%)	11 (16%)	37 (17%)
Gogrial	No	24 (63%)	67 (67%)	27 (40%)	118 (58%)
	Yes	14 (37%)	33 (33%)	40 (60%)	87 (42%)
Cuiebet	No	31 (94%)	19 (49%)	20 (74%)	70 (71%)
	Yes	2 (6%)	20 (51%)	7 (26%)	29 (29%)

Source: Household Survey/SPSS Output

In Abyei area, the percentage of sample households who resorted to courts or to a third party to settle their claims in the 1990s was only 17 per cent, which is significantly lower than the level in Gogrial area. When looking closely at the variation within households, poor and non-poor households in Abyei area experienced a similar pattern of court settlements, with non-poor

---

16   This measure is in a way similar to the experiments conducted by the *Reader's Digest* to assess the level of trust through the number of lost wallets returned with their contents intact in each of 20 cities, selected from 14 different western countries. The percentage of wallets returned in each country closely tracks the World Value Survey measures (Knack and Keeefer, 1997).

17   These social claims include entrusted cattle (*kuei*), kinship assistance and unpaid bride wealth.

households having a slightly higher percentage (16 per cent) resorting to court settlement of their social claims. Interestingly the number of non-poor households subjected to court settlements in Gogrial area was significantly higher (60 per cent) than that of poor households (33 per cent). This could reflect the rapid depletion of assets (especially cattle) that was experienced more by non-poor households than by poor households and that pushed them to resort to pursuing their claims in courts during the famine in 1998. This finding again reaffirms that the level of trust and co-operation is more dented among households exposed to endogenous counter-insurgency warfare than among those exposed to exogenous counter-insurgency warfare.

Community Co-operation: Mutual Labour Assistance Clubs (Mat):

Besides assessing the level of co-operation and relations at household level, collective community actions to confront and adjust to changes in the external environment are equally important for assessing the level of co-operation and the status of social capital. Generally, the exogenous counter-insurgency warfare that was experienced by the communities in Abyei area in the 1990s strengthened solidarity among communities and subsequently enhanced their level of co-operation. This increased solidarity could be explained by their increased reliance on mutual labour farming assistance. Unlike farming during the pre-conflict period, the main livelihood activity of Abyei community, particularly crop production (sowing, weeding, harvesting and storage), became increasingly collectively performed through the traditional system known as *mat* during the 1990s. While such a system was optionally practised in a limited way during the weeding period, its practice has not only increased considerably in the 1990s in Abyei area, and covered almost all phases of sorghum production; particularly harvest and storage.

This traditional practice (*mat*) involves a regular system, whereby each household within the community invites members of the community to perform a certain activity on its farm and the inviting household will in return provide food and local beer. Though this practice was performed on a limited scale during the pre-conflict period, it is now widely practised and has become almost obligatory as the Arab militia raids necessitate urgency in performing farming activities in a timely fashion that are difficult for a household to perform alone. Failure of some households to participate in *mat* will result in social isolation and exclusion from social safety nets that are highly crucial during Arab militia raids and future invitations to perform *mat* on their farms will not be honoured.

Interestingly the use of *mat* in the underground storage of sorghum, the most sensitive and secret livelihood activity in Abyei area, shows the high level of mutual trust and confidence among households. There were very limited and insignificant reported cases of sorghum theft by individuals, who breached the code of confidentiality regarding the underground storage and who were severely punished and stripped of their *mat* membership. This high level of mutual assistance, confidence and trust has contributed to a significant reduction in the incidence of crimes in Abyei area. A local policeman during focus group discussion complained about the apparent decline in crimes in Abyei area by saying:

> *'Look at this prison (seigen) it has been empty since last season and I became without a job......everyone here seems to know all laws and abide by them....I really wonder about my future here as a policeman'.*

This practice of mutual labour assistance (*mat*), as necessitated by the Arab militia counter-insurgency warfare has apparently not only increased crop production, but has also renewed generalised reciprocity and egalitarian values. Besides strengthening kinship support and providing livelihoods, the spirit and practice of *mat* has also been used and extended by the community of Abyei to mobilise themselves to provide a communal security force to protect them against Arab militia counter-insurgency warfare. The phenomenon of *mat* has even been adapted to cover local relief efforts. Women in particular played an important role in local relief activities, that covered not only the victims of the Arab raids, but also the few households that returned from the north, as well as food-insecure individuals from southern Sudan, who seasonally migrate to Abyei area in search for food and causal labour.

In Gogrial area such mutual labour assistance practices used to exist, particularly in farming, in the pre-war period and totally vanished during the 1990s as a result of endogenous counter-insurgency warfare, which supplanted trust with mistrust and co-operation with lack of co-operation. This trend of increasing communal labour farming assistance in Abyei area apparently contradicts the narrative that non-commercial and communal exchange of labour is gradually being eroded and supplanted by the commercial labour exchange in the sub-Saharan Africa.

Marriages: Extending Social Ties

Marriage and social ties are other means of spatial diversification of the household's human assets, as well as expanding the risk pool for informal risk sharing and insurance arrangements. There is even a tendency to consider family arrangements such as marriage to be more akin to 'hedging' than 'insurance', as such arrangements are based on risk exchange (Holzmann and Jorgensen, 2000). Besides its apparent role as spatial diversification, insurance and hedging strategies, marriage provides social status and cohesion that are important determinants of household well-being.

Generally Dinka society is polygamous, even among those who have adopted Christianity[18]. The Dinka fabric of social relations and the basis of family are founded on marriage and bride wealth. When looking critically at the entire process of Dinka marriage, you will find in economic terms that the net flow of bride wealth will reach almost zero, with immense social relation multipliers and wealth redistribution effects in the future. Another important aspect of Dinka marriage is that it is not allowed within lineage (*alaraan*) or within friendship (*maath*). Interestingly the word 'marriage' (*ruai*) in Dinka is synonymous with the word 'relationship' (*ruai*), as Dinka see marriage in a wider context of social relationships (Deng, 1999:62). These characteristics of marriage in Dinka society, make marriage an important and effective means of social diversification and an insurance strategy for managing risks.

Marriage in Dinka society is an endless process that involves a series of claims, counter- claims, obligations and transfers of livestock between the groom's and bride's families and their extended families that usually engulfs the entire lineage and entire communities. The initial bride wealth (*hok ruai*) is a collective and legally enforced standardised contribution of cattle from the groom's family, his mother's family, his in-laws and friends (Deng, 1999). On the other hand, the bride's family upon receiving the bride wealth has

---

18   There has been an increase in the number of Dinka people who have adopted Christianity during the civil war. The data from the household survey indicated that about 18 per cent of households are Christians, while the rest still maintain their traditional beliefs.

a social obligation to pay (*arueth*), from their own cattle, to the groom's family to confirm mutual relationships and consolidate the social status and position of their daughter. Generally, *arueth* is largely dependent on the amount of actual bride wealth and it reaches sometimes up to one third of the bride wealth. The family of the groom does not usually urge immediate payment of *arueth*, which is loosely paid over a longer period, particularly during times of high need. The process of the payment of bride wealth (*hok ruai*) and *arueth* is also seen as an effective *ex ante* risk management strategy as well as a process of cross-breeding, as such cattle are carefully selected (Deng, 1999).

The process of marriage does not end with the payment of bride wealth and *arueth*, as a future series of payments and counter-payments becomes obligatory on both sides of the family. One important payment is *ariek*, which is usually paid by the family of the bride to the groom when one of the designated younger sisters of the bride gets married, and the number of cattle paid depends on the initial bride wealth. This marriage cycle goes on: when the daughter of the groom gets married the two families will be entitled to a standardised share from the bride wealth, and likewise the two families make standardised contributions to the marriage of the son. Throughout a woman's marital life, her agnatic kin maintain an interest in her affairs and come to her aid according to need, particularly when she does wrong to her husband; they usually appease him with the payment of a cow, known as *weng awec* (Deng, 1972). It is apparent from this complex process of marriage that divorce among the Dinka is strongly abhorred, rare and socially and economically undesirable, since the conditions for the return of bride wealth and other payments are extremely complex.

It is clear from the Dinka marriage system that the process of marriage involves strong social and economic relationships and binds people from different lineage with effective systems of claims and transfers of cattle, establishing an extremely interconnected society (Deng, 1999). This makes marriage an important strategic social diversification and a proxy indicator to assess the status of social capital during civil war. While there is little evidence from sub-Sahara Africa, Rosenzweig (1988) finds a statistically significant negative covariation between rainfall in a groom's home community and the bride's community in India. This evidence supports the hypothesis that marriage is a means of insuring against covariate risk (Siegel and Alwang, 1999, Posner, 1980).

In order to assess the level of marriage during the 1990s, the household survey specifically asked households to compare the number of wives in a family in the 1990s with the pre-war periods, and the responses are presented in Table 5.11. The families exposed to exogenous counter-insurgency war-fare (Abyei) had a significant increase in the level of marriage (44 per cent) in the 1990s, compared to the pre-war period. The level of marriage among the families in Gogrial area did not increase but overwhelmingly remained unchanged (90 per cent) in the 1990s. While in Abyei area, the non-poor families had a greater increase in the level of marriage (48 per cent) in the 1990s than did poor families, The slight and insignificant increase in the level of marriage in Gogrial area was higher among poor families (5 per cent) than among non-poor families (1 per cent). The families from Gogrial area did not have more marriages during the 1990s, partly because of the depletion of their livestock by counter-insurgency warfare and largely because of the nature of risk that created division and mistrust among the communities.

Although one must be careful not to reduce cultural practices to eco-nomic rationale, the finding of higher levels of marriage among families exposed to exogenous counter-insurgency (Abyei) than those exposed to endogenous counterinsurgency (Gogrial) shows that the nature of risk is crucially important in the choice of livelihood strategies. While the exter-nal and common threat from Arab militias made the community of Abyei strengthen their social ties through marriage within and beyond the Abyei area, The internal conflict engineered by Dinka militias among the commu-nity of Gogrial contributed to the disintegration and weakening of social ties in the 1990s. On the basis of this finding it is safe to conclude that marriage as a risk mitigation strategy was practised more by the community of Abyei area than by the community of Gogrial.

Table 5.11: Level of Marriage in the 1990s

--Initial Level of Household Wealth Status--

Research Communities	Number of wives in the 1990s compared with pre–war periods	Poor	Middle	Non–Poor	Total
Abyei	Decreased	3 (10%)	5 (4%)	3 (4%)	11 (5%)
	The Same	17 (59%)	57 (51%)	33 (48%)	107 (51%)
	Increased	9 (31%)	51 (45%)	33 (48%)	93 (44%)
Gogrial	Decreased	7 (18%)	5 (5%)	6 (9%)	18 (9%)
	The Same	29 (77%)	95 (95%)	60 (90%)	184 (90%)
	Increased	2 (5%)	0 (0%)	1 (1%)	3 (1%)

Source: Household Survey/SPSS Output

The effectiveness of marriage as a livelihood strategy is largely dependent on the level of covariation between the risk environment of the groom's and bride's communities. It is generally argued that informal social insurance arrangements, which provide members of the social network with a 'social contract' that entitles them to insurance in times of need, are not effective. Such a 'social contract' can easily be broken by covariate risk that simultaneously impacts on several members of the risk pool. The increased level of marriage among families in Abyei area occurred increasingly outside the community in the 1990s, particularly with families from Twic area to the south of their border. From the community perception survey in Abyei area, the level of marriage outside Abyei area during pre-conflict period was about 13 per cent, but this was mainly confined to chiefs and rich families as a symbol of special social status. During the civil war and in the 1990s, the level of marriage outside the Abyei community has significantly increased to more than 30 per cent. One key informant during the community focus group discussions said that:

> *'During this war we have realised the importance of marrying outside, particularly to the Dinka of Twic, as it has provided us with new social ties (ruai) that allow us easy access to new grazing land and refuge for our children and women'.*

Most of these marriages are now from the Twic area that lies on the southern boundary of Abyei area, with a different agro-climatic environment and less exposed to risk events, such as Arab militia counter-insurgency warfare. Besides the high marriage rate, Twic area is becoming a safe haven for the people of Abyei area to take refuge for themselves (especially children and elderly) and their livestock prior to Arab militia raids. One cattle camp leader (*majok wut*), who adopted pastoralism said during his interview that:

> *'We have decided to tie our lives to the cattle and to move with them to Twic area rather than risking them in Abyei area......we found it appropriate to invest more in marriage particularly in Twic area, not only to keep our stock to a manageable level but also to widen our social ties (ruai) to create a conducive environment for ourselves and our cattle'.*

These social relationships have also been strengthened with sorghum trading and agricultural labour opportunities in Abyei area. The finding of a higher number of marriages among households exposed to exogenous counter-insurgency warfare (Abyei) with other communities that have different environmental and risk conditions (Twic), suggests that marriage is an effective risk mitigation strategy, even in the context of civil war.

Hedging: Forward Bartering and Extended Family

The term 'hedging' is used in finance theory to mean 'avoiding' and, thus, if a risk is hedged, action is being taken to avoid it or at least to reduce exposure to it. While diversification is used to reduce unsystematic risk (idiosyncratic risk), hedging and options are used to manage the systematic risk (covariate risk) (Lumby, 1994). Hedging as discussed in chapter 3 is part of risk mitigation strategies and two strategies are analysed in the context of civil war; namely forward bartering and extended family.

Forward Bartering of Sorghum with Livestock:

Despite the considerable decline in the contribution of livestock to household livelihood in the 1990s, there has been a considerable but gradual acquisition of livestock through the bartering of sorghum with cattle in Abyei area. The high purchases of livestock, particularly cattle, in Abyei area were linked to sorghum production that is bartered with livestock from Twic area in its southern border. As discussed earlier, the sorghum is stored underground during the critical periods (January-May) of potential raids by the Arab militias, and these stored sorghum stocks are only used in May/June when the risk of attacks by Arab militias became minimal.

However, while households would be anxiously concerned about their stored sorghum because of potential Arab militia attacks, they would be equally concerned about disposing of their stored sorghum during the rainy season, so as to avoid storage losses caused by rains and potential underground moisture and humidity. On the other hand, households in Twic area, who normally face food shortage as a result of limited arable land and recurrent flooding and drought, have a high demand for sorghum during the hunger period (June/July), but are also concerned about the high prices of sorghum and the low prices of livestock at this time.

With these conditions faced by households and farmers in Abyei and Twic, they innovatively resort to forward bartering of sorghum with cattle, with prices fixed immediately after harvest in November/December, and actual payments taking place in May/June. These hedging measures and forward bartering had actually stabilised bartering prices and have greatly helped farmers to dispose and clear their stored sorghum stocks in a timely manner, while households in Twic area were able to sell their cattle at reasonable prices and terms of trade. With these innovative hedging measures adopted by households in Abyei area, they were able during the 1990s to acquire additional assets (cattle) that encouraged them to specialise in and increase sorghum production. This forward bartering also contributed in creating a vibrant local market in Abyei area that became the main market of sorghum during civil war for the food-deficit areas in Northern Bahr el Ghazal. Apparently such livelihood strategy was not available for the households exposed to exogenous counterinsurgency warfare in Gogrial area.

Extended Family: Household Structure

It has been gradually accepted that household composition, structure and the cohesion of family members are important assets that enhance the ability of households to adjust to changes in the external environment (Moser, 1998). In the context of the research communities in Bahr el Ghazal region, the structure of the household plays an important role, not only in mitigating risk, but it also reflects the level of kinship support, co-operation, and the social safety net. In particular, the evolution of the household structure from 'nuclear' to 'extended'[19] shows more about the level of support and provision of refuge or a safety net for vulnerable individuals, or about the conscious strategy to pool resources more effectively, such as food, space, income, and childcare (Moser, 1998:11).

Using the data from household surveys to trace the dynamic changes in the structure of households in the pre-war period in 1988 and during civil war in the 1990s, the results show a considerable and interesting change in the structure of households in both research communities (Abyei and Gogrial). While the number of extended households in Abyei area increased from 50 percent in 1988 to 57 percent in the 1990s, the number of nuclear households in Gogrial area increased from 39 percent in 1988 to 85 percent in the 1990s.

Interestingly, while there is no major variation among households in Gogrial area in the 1990s, non-poor households experienced a significant change in terms of an increasing number of nuclear households in the 1990s (79 per cent) compared with the level in 1988 (12 per cent). This enormous change in household structure, particularly the experience of non-poor households in Gogrial area, underlines the dynamics of asset depletion in the 1990s. This finding shows that with deteriorating livelihood conditions, as a result of intensification of endogenous counter-insurgency warfare, household co-operation dwindled and households started looking after their immediate household members in the 1990s.

Unlike the situation in Gogrial area, households in Abyei experienced an increase in the number of extended households with non-poor households experiencing the highest level (71 per cent), while poor households experienced a significant increase in the 1990s (45 per cent), compared to the level in 1988 (34 per cent). With the increasing common external threats from Arab militias in the 1990s, households in Abyei area became

---

19   The 'nuclear' household consists of husband and wife with their own children, while an 'extended' household consists of a 'nuclear' household and other dependent members.

more co-operative and pooled their resources effectively through forming extended households, thus improving their strategies to mitigate the effects of exogenous counterinsurgency warfare. Another explanation is that members of households with adults had died or gone to fight were absorbed into other households. As discussed earlier, the specialised farming activities in Abyei area in the 1990s made it almost impossible for a nuclear household to perform these activities that require speed and timeliness. It is natural for these households to adjust their structure and to incorporate more members to face these external challenges and to make use of opportunities in the 1990s.

Conclusions

This chapter is an attempt to apply the risk-livelihood-vulnerability framework to assess the *ex-ante* livelihood strategies adopted by households exposed to counter-insurgency warfare in the 1990s. In particular, the analysis of household livelihood strategies focuses on *ex ante risk management strategies* that are disaggregated into *risk reduction strategies* and *risk mitigation strategies.* Generally, households exposed to counter-insurgency warfare in the 1990s adopted a set of *ex ante* risk management strategies. Although the effectiveness of these livelihood strategies is discussed in chapter 6 in terms of vulnerability, it can be argued that effectiveness of these strategies has largely been conditioned by the nature and characteristics of risk, location, cumulative experience, and (a)symmetric information. The evidence provided in this chapter indicates that the livelihood strategies adopted by the households exposed to exogenous counter-insurgency (Abyei) performed better than those strategies adopted in the context of endogenous counter-insurgency (Gogrial), largely because of the characteristics of risk, location and importantly symmetric information.

Taking diversification as the most popular livelihood strategy used in development studies to assess the level of adjustment to changes in external environment, the results of a comparison of primary livelihood activities indicate that diversification is not always the best livelihood strategy option in the context of counter-insurgency warfare. Generally, the households exposed to drought tend to diversify their primary livelihood activities more than those households exposed to counter-insurgency warfare. Within the households exposed to counter-insurgency warfare, those exposed to endogenous counter-insurgency warfare tend to diversify their prima-ry livelihood activities less than those households exposed to exogenous counter-insurgency warfare. Interestingly, among the households exposed to exogenous counter-insurgency warfare, the non-poor households paradox-ically tend to diversify their primary livelihood activities less than the poor households. Similar findings are also observed from the results of the analysis and comparison of different forms of diversification in crop production, particularly *enterprise, varietal,* and *spatial* diversification, across the research communities and sample households.

Taking investment in social capital as one of the *risk mitigation strategies*, the results of various measures (*kinship support, structure of household, traditional court settlements and mutual labour assistance club*) of the level and stock of social capital indicate significant differences between households exposed to exogenous and endogenous counter-insurgency. The households exposed to exogenous counter-insurgency tend to have higher levels of social capital stock than those households exposed to endogenous counter-insurgency warfare. With increasing common threats from Arab militias, the households in Abyei have become more cohesive and co-operative with strong commu-nity-based risk sharing arrangements and invest more in social capital than do those households exposed to endogenous counter-insurgency warfare. The level of distrust and poor co-operation was more evident among the households exposed to endogenous counter-insurgency with non-poor households feeling it and being affected more than poor households.

Assessing the level of marriage, it has been shown that the external and common threat from Arab militias made households in Abyei strengthened and diversified their social ties through marriage, while the internal con-flict engineered by Dinka militias in Gogrial dented and weakened social ties. The households exposed to exogenous counter-insurgency not only increased the level of marriage within the Abyei community but they also extended their social ties through an increased level of marriage outside their community in Twic area, which has different climatic conditions.

CHAPTER SIX

Livelihood Outcomes:
Household Vulnerability and Resilience

·····-·-·-·-·-■■·····⟨⚛⟩·····■■·-·-·-·-·-·····

Introduction

The outcome of a risk event, such as counter-insurgency warfare is undoubtedly conditioned by the risk management and livelihood strategies adopted by households to reduce their susceptibility to such a risk event or to mitigate its potential impacts. The measurement of risk outcomes is a complex endeavour, as it is linked to vulnerability that is both *ex ante* and *ex post* and it is also associated with dynamic and complex processes. This implies that risk outcomes should be seen not as the last phase of vulnerability, but rather as a broad concept that includes the entire process of increasing vulnerability. In most poverty studies, the outcome of a risk event is measured in terms of vulnerability. Vulnerability in return is measured in terms of indicators related to the level of well-being and welfare loss in relation to a set of minimum level of survival (as measured by a poverty line or consumption requirement).

After discussing the sources and characteristics of the risk events faced by the research communities and the livelihood strategies they adopted in the 1990s to confront these risk events, the real question is 'what were the livelihood outcomes of their risk management strategies?' The aim of this chapter is to assess and analyse vulnerability during civil war, to understand better the communities and types of households that were most vulnerable, and to provide possible explanations for their vulnerability.

As vulnerability is a complex concept, its measurement in the context of civil war requires multi-dimensional indicators in order to capture the mutually constitutive experiences of vulnerability in the face of counter-insurgency warfare. The definition of vulnerability in chapter 2 provides the most relevant vulnerability indicators that are used in this chapter to assess household livelihood outcomes. These indicators are organised in this chapter around the level of *susceptibility, sensitivity* and *resilience*. The level of household susceptibility to counter-insurgency warfare, measured in terms of the displacement, is analysed in Section 2. The level of sensitivity, measured in terms of depletion of assets, is discussed and compared across and within research communities in Section 3. The level of household resilience, measured in terms of poverty dynamics and consumption level indicators, such as level of malnutrition and excess mortality, is analysed and discussed in Section 4. The main findings and conclusions of the chapter are presented in Section 5.

The Level of Susceptibility:[20]
The Curse of Assets

In spite of the fact that susceptibility to risk events could be perceived as livelihood outcomes, it is also an important ingredient in the household's perception of risk events that largely shapes and determines the choice of livelihood strategies. Importantly, understanding the level of household susceptibility to risk events, particularly counter-insurgency warfare, will help in assessing the research question regarding the exogeneity assumption and the relationship between the occurrence of counter-insurgency warfare and household assets. This in turn is hoped to shed light on whether greed and economic drive do sustain and trigger the occurrence of counter-insurgency warfare.

The main assumption in the literature of risk is that risk events are exogenous, and this assumption allows imputing vulnerability and susceptibility

---

20   The term 'susceptibility' is generally defined in the risk literature as 'the probability that a household will experience welfare loss from a given risky event' (Siegel and Alwang, 1999:5).

to risk events to the level of household asset ownership and management, rather than to the nature, sources and characteristics of risk events. It is generally argued that risk events are transmitted through assets and are not triggered by them, with the inherent assumption of an independent relationship between the occurrence of risk events and household asset ownership.

The discussion about the sustenance of civil war, particularly counter-insurgency warfare, in Chapter 5 clearly challenges this assumption, and suggests instead that greed and the criminal acquisition of assets, and to a lesser extent grievances, are largely the primary causes of counter-insurgency warfare. In other words, the occurrence of counter-insurgency warfare is hypothesised to be positively linked with the initial level of household assets holdings, as discussed in Chapter 3. This suggests that the occurrence of counter-insurgency warfare is not exogenous, but is primarily caused by the level of household and community asset ownership. Some researchers (Keen, 1994; Deng, 1999) have even argued, in the case of the Dinka of Bahr el Ghazal, that it is the wealth of the Dinka, rather than their poverty, that makes them susceptible to the risk of counter-insurgency warfare.

In order to assess the level of household susceptibility to counter-insurgency warfare, some direct effects of counter-insurgency warfare, such as the level of displacement, are used as proxy indicators for the level of household susceptibility in the 1990s. The data related to the level of displacement are generated from the household surveys and are analysed and compared both across and within research communities.

Level of Displacement: Proxying Susceptibility to Counter-insurgency:

In order to assess the relationship between the occurrence of counter-insurgency warfare and the initial level of household asset ownership, the frequency of household displacement during the 1990s was used to proxy the level of household susceptibility and exposure to counter-insurgency warfare. The level of displacement is the most appropriate proxy to capture this susceptibility as it reflects disruption of livelihoods, loss of assets and also lives. Using contingency tables[21] to cross-tabulate the initial level of

---

21   A contingency table is a table with a cell for every combination of values of two or more variables and shows the number of cases with each specific combination of values (Puri, 1996:70).

asset ownership by household category (poor, middle and non-poor) and the frequency of displacement in the 1990s, so as to assess the level of household susceptibility during the 1990s, the results are shown in Table 6.1.

Table 6.1: Level of Household Susceptibility to Counter-Insurgency Warfare

Risk Event	Status	--Initial Wealth --Frequency of household displacement in the 1990s--					
		None	Once	Twice	Thrice	More than Three	Total
Exogenous Counter Insurgency (Abyei)	Poor	0 (0%)	0 (0%)	2 (7%)	5 (17%)	22 (76%)	29
	Middle	0 (0%)	3 (3%)	1 (1%)	19 (17%)	90 (79%)	113
	Non-poor	0 (0%)	1 (1%)	2 (3%)	7 (10%)	59 (86%)	69
	Total	0 (0%)	4 (2%)	5 (%)	31 (15%)	171 (81%)	211
Endogenous Counter Insurgency (Gogrial)	Poor	0 (0%)	8 (21%)	14 (37%)	14 (37%)	2 (5%)	38
	Middle	0 (0%)	2 (2%)	25 (25%)	51 (51%)	22 (22%)	100
	Non-poor	0 (0%)	0 (0%)	18 (27%)	28 (42%)	21 (31%)	67
	Total	0 (0%)	10 (5%)	57 (28%)	93 (45%)	45 (22%)	205

Source: Household Surveys and SPSS Output

It is generally clear that every household experienced displacement during the 1990s in Abyei and Gogrial areas, with the overwhelming majority of households experiencing more than one displacement. The households exposed to exogenous counter-insurgency (Abyei) experienced a higher number of displacements (81 per cent were displaced more than three times) in the 1990s than those exposed to endogenous counter-insurgency warfare (Gogrial) (22 per cent were displaced more than three times). The non-poor households experienced a higher frequency of displacements than poor households, particularly among those exposed to endogenous counter-insurgency warfare (Gogrial). For example, while only 5 per cent of poor households in Gogrial area experienced displacement 'more than three times', about 31 per cent of the non-poor households experienced the same number of displacements. In other words the non-poor households experienced progressively higher numbers of displacement and were five times more likely to be displaced than were poor households during the 1990s in Gogrial area.

However, among the households exposed to exogenous counter-insurgency warfare in Abyei area, the poor and non-poor experienced similar patterns of displacement, with non-poor households experiencing slightly higher numbers of displacement. For example, while 76 per cent of poor households in Abyei area experienced displacement 'more than three times', 86 per cent of non-poor households experienced a similar level of displacement. These results strongly suggest that non-poor households were more susceptible to counter-insurgency warfare than were poor households, particularly the households that were primarily exposed to *endogenous counter-insurgency* warfare (Gogrial).

Assets Ownership and Susceptibility:

Besides the frequency of household displacement in the 1990s, we used other aspects of household susceptibility to counter-insurgency warfare to assess the level of correlation between the household's initial asset ownership and aspects of household susceptibility. The most relevant aspect of household susceptibility to counter-insurgency is the cattle looted by the government-supported militias (Dinka and Arab raiders). The initial level of household wealth is cross-tabulated with the most relevant aspects (displacement and looted cattle) of household susceptibility and the values of correlation and level of significance are presented in Table 6.2.

Generally, the statistical test (Pearson's R) that is used to measure statistical association, clearly shows a positive association between initial household asset ownership and the level of household displacement (susceptibility to counter-insurgency warfare) in Abyei and Gogrial area, as shown in Table 6.2. The strength of correlation between the initial level of asset ownership and displacement is about 5 times higher among households in Gogrial area (+0.302) than among those exposed to exogenous counter-insurgency (+0.062). Interestingly, it can be seen from Table 6.2 that the value of correlation in Gogrial area is not only positive but also significant, while it is positive but not significant in the context of exogenous counter-insurgency in Abyei area except in relation to the looted cattle.

Table 6.2: Statistical Association[22]:
Asset Ownership and Susceptibility in the 1990s

Correlation between Aspects of Susceptibility and Initial Wealth Status

Aspects of Hosuehold Succeptibility	Abyei Community	Gogrial Community
Displacement	+	+★
Looted Cattle	+★	+★

Source: Household Surveys and SPSS Output;
★Indicates significant at the 5% level

The results of the statistical association tests clearly suggest the significant and positive association between initial asset ownership and the level of susceptibility to endogenous counter-insurgency warfare, with non-poor households becoming more exposed to counter-insurgency warfare than the poor households. This finding is extremely important, as it challenges the exogeneity assumption and the posited asset-vulnerability argument in the context of endogenous counter-insurgency warfare. In other words, the argument that the more assets owned by a household the less vulnerable that household is, is not supported by this finding, at least in the context of endogenous counter-insurgency. Importantly, this finding also confirms that economic drive is one of the main factors that trigger and sustain the occurrence of counter-insurgency warfare.

The observed strong and significant link between household assets holdings and the occurrence of counter-insurgency warfare is largely related to the nature and characteristics of endogenous counter-insurgency warfare, as discussed in chapter 5. Most of these raids and counter-insurgency warfare campaigns targeted mainly household assets, particularly livestock as the mainstay of the Dinka livelihood, and subsequently made non-poor households more susceptible to these raids than poor households.

---

22   Spearman's rank correlation and Kendall's tau-b are nonparametric statistical tests that use differences between pairs of ranks to give a statistical association and a nonparametric version of the Pearson product moment correlation coefficient (Pearson's R) that measures the strength of the linear relationship for bivariate data for two variables (Puri, 1996:108). As Pearson's R, the correlation coefficient statistic, is the most commonly used statistic in correlation analysis, as it specifies the magnitude and direction of relation (Nachmias and Nachmias, 1996:420), we presented its results rather than other tests.

In the context of exogenous counter-insurgency warfare (Abyei), there is a significant positive link between initial level of wealth and the looted livestock but insignificant positive association between the level of initial wealth and displacement and that suggests a random pattern in the occurrence of Arab raids. In other words, unlike the raids of Dinka militias, which were more specific in targeting individual households, the raids of Arab militias were more general and did not target specific households. This difference in the association between the initial level of wealth and displacement in Abyei and Gogrial may be attributed to difference in the nature of a(-)symmetric information of counterinsurgency warfare as discussed in Chapter 4. While the Arab raiders did not have knowledge about livelihood strategies adopted by households in Abyei area, the Dinka raiders did have full knowledge of their victims in Gogrial.

It is clear also from Table 6.2 that the level of correlation between the looted cattle and the initial wealth status is considerable and positively significant among all households exposed to counter-insurgency warfare. In other words, the initially non-poor households in Abyei and Gogrial area experienced relatively higher cattle losses in the 1990s than did poor households. This finding suggests that, while the initially non-poor households were more susceptible to counter-insurgency warfare than were the poor households in Abyei and Gogrial areas, the level of susceptibility of the non-poor households was relatively higher in Gogrial area.

Household Characteristics and Level of Susceptibility:

Besides the initial household wealth status as a determinant of the level of susceptibility (displacement) to counter-insurgency warfare, we used other household characteristics, such as sex, education, age and marital status of the household head, to assess their correlation with the level of household susceptibility in the 1990s, as shown in Table 6.3. It is clear that the values of correlation between the level of displacement (susceptibility) and the other characteristics of the household approach almost zero, and are all statistically insignificant in both Abyei and Gogrial areas. As discussed earlier, the value of correlation between the level of displacement and initial household wealth status in Gogrial area is distinctively not only sizeable (+0.302), but also significant, while the correlation Abyei area is almost zero and insignificant and confirms the random pattern of exogenous counterinsurgency warfare. These findings clearly suggest that the main determinant of the level of household susceptibility to counter-insurgency warfare in the 1990s was the initial level of asset ownership. Other aspects, such as sex, age, marital status and level of education of the household heads, do not explain much the level of household susceptibility to counter-insurgency warfare in the 1990s.

Table 6.3: Household Characteristics and Level of Susceptibility in the 1990s

Correlation between Characteristics of Household Heads and Displacement

Hosuehold head Characteristics	Abyei Community	Gogrial Community
Initial Wealth	+	+★
Sex	–	–
Age	–	+
Marital Status	–	–
Education	–	+

Source: Household Surveys and SPSS Output;
★Indicates significant at the 5% level.

These results also confirm the "curse of assets" argument, as they made households susceptible to counter-insurgency warfare, particularly those households exposed to endogenous counter-insurgency in Gogrial area. The insignificant correlation between these household characteristics and the level of susceptibility shows that people were susceptible to counter-insurgency warfare simply because of their assets, not because they were old/young, educated/illiterate, or male/female.

The Level of Sensitivity[23]:
Asset Depletion and Poverty in the 1990s

One aspect of vulnerability is the extent to which the household's asset base is prone to depletion, following adjustments to risk events through livelihood strategies. In the context of the research communities in Bahr el Ghazal region, livestock, particularly cattle, constitute the most important livelihood assets and, therefore, become the relevant proxy for household's assets. The level of livestock depletion in the 1990s is measured either by livestock loss, livestock acquisition, and/or the trend in the level of household livestock ownership in the 1990s. Besides livestock, the status of human capital, measured in terms of abduction, conscription and migration during the 1990s, is also used to assess the level of household sensitivity to counter-insurgency warfare. The shift in the level of poverty in the 1990s will then attest to these dynamic changes in the level of household livestock ownership.

Trends in the Level of Household Livestock Ownership:

In order to assess the trend of livestock ownership in the 1990s, the data from household surveys about the average number of heads of cattle owned by different wealth groups in 1988, 1993 and 1998 are presented in Table 6.4. It is clear that while the level of household cattle ownership in 1998 declined by almost 60 per cent of the level in 1988 in Abyei area, households in Gogrial experienced about a 90 per cent decline in the level of their cattle ownership. The decline was significantly higher during 1993 - 1998 than during 1988 – 1993 particularly in Gogrial area when endogenous counter-insurgency warfare intensified.

By 1998 when famine occurred, the households in Gogrial had the lowest average cattle ownership (6 heads of cattle), which was only one-tenth of the average in 1988 (59 heads). Interestingly, the average household in Gogrial area, which used to own more cattle (59 heads) in 1988 than the average household in Abyei area (52 heads), had its average cattle ownership in 1998 reduced to one-third (6 heads) of the average household cattle ownership (20 heads) in Abyei area.

---

23   In the context of vulnerability and literature of risk as discussed earlier, the term 'sensitivity' refers to the extent to which the household's asset base is prone to depletion following adjustments to risk (Ellis, 1998).

Table 6.4:

Level of Household Cattle Ownership in the 1990s[24]

Average Number of Cattle Owned by Households

		--Initial Level of Household Wealth Status--			
Research Communities	Years	Poor	Middle	Non-Poor	Total
Abyei	1988	15.1	25.9	112.0	52.6
	1993	11.2	26.1	97.3	47.3
	1998	5.3	13.4	37.5	20.2
Gogrial	1988	5.9	54.4	97.0	59.3
	1993	16.8	47.0	40.7	39.3
	1998	1.6	7.8	6.7	6.3

Source: Household Survey/SPSS Output

It is of great interest to observe the variations in trend of the level of cattle ownership within and across households, as shown in Table 6.4. While the level of cattle ownership declined by 65 per cent during 1988 – 1998 among poor households in Abyei area, the non-poor households experienced almost the same level of decline (67 per cent). In Gogrial area, non-poor households experienced a higher and significant decline (93 per cent) in their level of cattle ownership during 1988 – 1998 than the decline experienced by poor households (72 per cent). In aggregate the households in Gogrial area experienced a significantly higher decline in their level of cattle ownership (89 per cent) during 1988 – 1998 than the level of decline experienced by sample households in Abyei area (62 per cent).

The rapid decline and depletion of livestock in the 1990s experienced by households exposed to counter-insurgency warfare, particularly non-poor

---

24   In spite of the fact that the data provided are generated from household surveys, they may not reflect the real average numbers of cattle owned by households, but instead reflect the trend, because of a general tendency among pastoralists not to reveal their actual number of stock. In other words, this assumes systematic over-reporting of past level of livestock ownership and under-reporting of the current level of ownership across the research communities.

households in general and Gogrial area in particular, shows that the asset base of non-poor households was more sensitive to counter-insurgency warfare. While the asset base of households in Abyei area was relatively sensitive to exogenous counter-insurgency, the rapid decline and depletion of the asset base of households in Gogrial area suggests that their level of sensitivity to endogenous counter-insurgency warfare was higher, particularly among non-poor households. In other words, the asset base of non-poor households was more sensitive to counter-insurgency warfare than that of poor households. Even within the non-poor households exposed to counter-insurgency warfare, the asset base of the non-poor households exposed to endogenous counter-insurgency was more sensitive than that of those exposed to exogenous counter-insurgency warfare.

In order to understand the main reasons for such a rapid decline and depletion of the asset base of sample households in the 1990s, the data relating to the level of cattle lost by households, as a result of looting by government-supported militias, are presented in Table 6.5. The actual number of cattle looted by the Dinka and Arab militias from these households in the 1990s constitutes a good indicator for the level of asset depletion and household sensitivity to counter-insurgency warfare. While households in Gogrial area had significantly higher average cattle losses (47.7 head) than those in Abyei area (38.5 head), non-poor households experienced cattle losses twice that of poor households in Gogrial, and four times that of poor households in Abyei area. This result again shows clearly that the asset base of non-poor households was more sensitive to counter-insurgency warfare in the 1990s than was that of poor households.

Table 6.5:
Cattle Looted and Household Initial Wealth Status[25]

Average Number of Cattle Looted From
Households in the 1990s

--Initial Level of Household Wealth Status--

Research Communities	Poor	Middle	Non-Poor	Total
Abyei	15.7	26.4	68.0	38.5
Gogrial	30	47.8	57.5	47.7

Source: Household Survey/SPSS Output

Besides cattle losses as a result of looting in the 1990s, it is equally important to assess the level of livestock purchases or sales as determinants of the level of household assets ownership. This is crucially important, as the apparent decline in the level of livestock ownership, as shown in Table 6.4, may conceal some important dynamics in the acquisition of livestock that took place during the 1990s. In order to avoid specificity and actual numbers, the sample households were asked whether they bought or sold more livestock (cattle and goats) during the 1990s, and their responses are provided in Table 6.6.

It is clear that during the 1990s, most sample households in Gogrial area sold more livestock (92 per cent), particularly non-poor households (97 per cent). Interestingly, about 46 per cent of sample households in Abyei area bought more livestock in the 1990s, while only 24 per cent of sample households sold more livestock. The percentage of poor households (38 per cent) who bought more livestock in the 1990s in Abyei was similar to the percentage of non-poor households (39 per cent), while middle-wealth households purchased significantly more livestock (51 per cent) than did the other groups.

This clearly suggests, that while there was a decline in the level of livestock ownership in the 1990s, there was a hidden and interesting process of asset

---

25   These figures may not reflect the actual numbers of cattle looted as there might be over-reporting but they provide the trend rather than the actual numbers.

accumulation, paradoxically in the midst of exogenous counter-insurgency warfare in Abyei area. This asset accumulation in Abyei area came as a result of increased specialisation in the production of sorghum and making use of sorghum market opportunities through a hedging strategy, as discussed in Chapter 5. Unlike households in Abyei area, the sample households, particularly the non-poor households in Gogrial area, in attempting to adjust to the impact of endogenous counter-insurgency warfare resorted to excessive sales of their livestock, which made their asset base highly sensitive in the 1990s.

Table 6.6:

Level of Livestock Acquisition by Households in the 1990s

		--Initial Level of Household Wealth Status--			
Research Communities	Livestock Purchases in 1990s compared with pre-war periods	Poor	Middle	Non-Poor	Total
Abyei	Sold More	8 (28%)	24 (21%)	20 (29%)	52 (24%)
	The Same	10 (35%)	31 (27%)	22 (32%)	63 (30%)
	Bought More	11 (38%)	58 (51%)	27 (39%)	96 (46%)
Gogrial	Sold More	27 (71%)	97 (97%)	65 (97%)	189 (92%)
	The Same	9 (24%)	3 (3%)	2 (3%)	14 (7%)
	Bought More	2 (5%)	0 (0%)	0 (0%)	2 (1%)

Source: Household Survey/SPSS Output

Human Assets: Slavery, Conscription and Migration:

It is estimated that 35,000 children and 16,000 women were abducted, particularly in Bahr el Ghazal region, by militias in the 1990s, either for forced labour or for slavery, and 38,000 children were conscripted into the army during the same period (UNICEF, 2000:141). Besides abduction and conscription, there has been a considerable permanent migration to northern Sudan, which resulted in considerable demographic changes, as shown in Table 6.7.

It is clear from Table 6.7 that, while there is no major significant difference between males and females within the age group 0-14 years in southern Sudan, there is a significant decrease in the population of males (40 per cent) and females (37 per cent) in the age group "15-39 years" and "40 years and above" respectively. These demographic changes are considerable in Bahr el Ghazal region compared to the overall situation in southern Sudan. For example, the proportion of the male population in the age group 15-39 in Bahr el Ghazal region reached 35 per cent in 2001, while that of the female population in the age group 40 and above was 31 per cent. The sharp decrease in the population of males in the most active age group (15-39 years) may be attributed to excessive demands through recruitment and conscription for this age group to be engaged in the fighting. The apparent decrease in the population of females in the older age group (40 years and above) may be attributed to displacement and migration, which affected more female household members than males.

Table 6.7:
Population Distribution in Bahr el Ghazal
and Southern Sudan, 2001

Study Population Distribution by Sex and Age Group

Regions	0-14 Years		15-39 Years		40 and Above	
	Male	Female	Male	Female	Male	Female
Bahr el Ghazal	1501 (56%)	1203 (44%)	429 (35%)	803 (65%)	478 (69%)	217 (31%)
Southern Sudan	6215 (54%)	5332 (46%)	2881 (40%)	4385 (60%)	2098 (63%)	1257 (37%)

Source: UNICEF (2002:9)

The data generated from the household surveys show that almost half of the sample households in Abyei area (50 per cent) lost at least one member of their household as a result of counter-insurgency raids, compared with 48 per cent of sample households in Gogrial area who lost at least one member.

However, the non-poor households in Abyei (71 per cent) and Gogrial (58 per cent) experienced a relatively higher death toll than did poor households. Similar trends were observed in the data relating to whether households had experienced any abduction of their members by Dinka militias for forced labour and by Arab militias for slavery in the 1990s. While about 64 per cent of sample households in Gogrial had at least one of their members abducted in the 1990s, 39 per cent of households in Abyei area had experienced the same, with non-poor households having a higher incidence (52 per cent) than poor households (31 per cent). This could be attributed to the fact that non-poor households tend to have more members than poor households, as well as having larger herds that were the immediate targets of these raids.

The Dynamics of Poverty in the 1990s: Poverty Transition Matrix

Given the variation in the level of susceptibility to counter-insurgency warfare and the sensitivity of the asset base in the 1990s across and within the research communities, it is important to assess the dynamics of poverty in the 1990s. In assessing these dynamics, the focus is less on making a distinction between transitory and chronic poverty, but more on the dynamics of transition and movement within and across various wealth groups (Baulch and McCulloch, 1998). Given the lack of panel data, the perception of household of its wealth status (poor, middle, non-poor) and community perceptions about a household's wealth status are used and then triangulated with the level of cattle ownership to determine the wealth status (poor, middle and non-poor) of a household.

In order to assess the number of households that moved in or out of the poor group in the 1990s, the data relating to the initial level of household wealth in the pre-war periods are cross-tabulated with their wealth status in the 1990s, as shown in Table 6.8. It is clear that there has been a significant transition and movement in the 1990s into the category of the poor group in Gogrial and Abyei areas. For example, while in Abyei area only 6.6 per cent of the sample households were non-poor in both pre-war periods and in the 1990s, approximately 38 per cent and 12 per cent of sample households were respectively middle and poor in both periods. Apparently, there was no sample household that either moved out of middle group or escaped the poverty group in Abyei area in the 1990s. On the contrary, over 26 per

cent (20.9 + 5.2) of the initially non-poor sample households fell into either
the middle (20.9 per cent) or poor (5.2 per cent) groups during the 1990s.
Finally, while less than 2 per cent of the initially poor sample households had
improved their status to middle wealth group in the 1990s, just over 15 per
cent of the initially middle wealth households moved into the poor group
in the 1990s.

Table 6.8: Poverty Dynamics:
Transition and Movement in the 1990s

Research Communities	Inital Household Wealth Status	--Level of Household Wealth Status in the 1990s--		
		Non-Poor	Middle	Poor
Abyei	Non Poor	14 (6.6%)	44 (20.9%)	11 (5.2%)
	Middle	0 (0%)	81 (38.4%)	32 (15.2%)
	Poor	0 (0%)	3 (1.4%)	26 (12.3%)
	Chi-square = 78.64	Kendall's tau-b = 0.457	N = 211	I = 0.573
Gogrial	Non Poor	0 (0%)	0 (0%)	59 (28.8%)
	Middle	0 (0%)	0 (0%)	96 (46.8%)
	Poor	0 (0%)	0 (0%)	36 (17.5%)
	Chi-square = 4.15	Kendall's tau-b = 0.111	N = 205	I = 0.195

Source: Household Survey/SPSS Output

The reported chi-square value (78.64) and kendall's tau-b[26] (0.457) statistic
tests both reject the hypothesis that the wealth status in Abyei area in the
pre-war periods is independent of the wealth status during the 1990s. This
apparent interdependence of the wealth status in both periods is further
supported by immobility measure (I)[27], as over 57 per cent of sample households did not change their wealth status in the 1990s, as indicated by the

---

26   Kendal's tau-b is a nonparametric version of a coefficient of the association between ordinal variables incorporating ties and is similar to Spearman's rank correlation (Puri,
1996; Nachmias and Nachmias, 1996).
27   The Immobility measure (I) has been suggested by Scott and Litchfield (1994) to
compare the persistence of different dimensions of poverty and is calculated as the sum of
the cell frequencies (trace (M)) along the leading diagonal of the square transition matrix (M)

sum (6.6 + 38.4 + 12.3) of the cells of the leading diagonal of the transition matrix in Table 6.8.

Interestingly, the non-poor sample households experienced the lowest immobility (6.6) in comparison to other wealth categories, and this clearly shows the apparent high mobility experienced by the non-poor households in the 1990s. In addition, the number of sample households below the leading diagonal of the transition matrix (1.4 per cent) is much lower than those above the diagonal (41.3 per cent) (20.9 + 5.2 + 15.2) and this clearly suggests the considerable increase in the incidence of poverty in Abyei area during the 1990s.

In Gogrial area, there was no single sample household that remained non-poor in both the pre-war period and the 1990s, and only 2 per cent and 17.5 per cent of sample households were respectively middle and poor groups in both periods, as shown in Table 6.8. During the 1990s, there was no sample household that escaped either from the middle group or the poor group. In contrast, just over 32 per cent of initially non-poor households fell into either the middle group (3.9 per cent) or poor group (28.8 per cent). In addition, while over 46 per cent of sample households, which were initially in the moderate poor group, moved to the poor group in the 1990s, only 1 per cent of initially poor households had improved their status to the moderately poor group.

It is not surprising that the reported Pearson chi-square (4.15) and Kendall's tau-b (0.111) statistic tests verified the null hypothesis that wealth status in Gogrial area in the 1990s is independent of pre-war wealth status. This is further supported by the low level of the immobility index (0.195) measured as sum of the cells (0 + 0.02 + 0.175) on the leading diagonal of Table 6.8, with non-poor and moderately poor households experiencing complete mobility (I = 0 and 0.012 respectively) to the poor group during the 1990s. Clearly, the number of poor households in the 1990s (79.5 per cent), measured as the sum of the cells (3.9 + 28.8 + 46.8) above the leading diagonal of Table 6.8, is considerably higher than those poor households (1 per cent) in the pre-war periods, measured as the sum of the cells below the diagonal.

---

divided by the number of individuals in the panel (N). The immobility measure (I) varies between zero, when there is a complete mobility, and one, when there is complete immobility (Baulch and Masset, 2003).

In order to compare the dynamics of entry to and exit from poverty in Abyei and Gogrial, the proportional hazards model is used as suggested by Cox (1972) and Baulch and McCulloch (1998) to calculate and compare the probability of entering/exiting poverty in the 1990s, as presented in Table 6.9. Given the fact that personal wealth ranking makes middle wealth status nearer to the non-poor than the poor group, the middle wealth status households are regrouped with the non-poor households in Table 6.8, so as to allow the calculation of reported probabilities of entering/existing poverty in Table 6.9, as suggested by Baulch and McCulloch (1998:14).

It is clear from Table 6.9 that the households exposed to endogenous counter-insurgency (Gogrial) were four times more likely to enter poverty (0.928) than were those households (0.236) exposed to exogenous counter-insurgency warfare (Abyei). In addition, the households exposed to exogenous counterinsurgency warfare (Abyei) were twice (0.103) as likely to escape poverty than were those households (0.053) exposed to endogenous counter-insurgency warfare (Gogrial). The incidence of poverty (77 per cent) among households exposed to endogenous counter-insurgency (Gogrial) was almost three times higher than that of households exposed to exogenous counter-insurgency warfare (Abyei).

Table 6.9:
Simple Poverty Entry and Exit Probabilities in the 1990s[28]

Research Communities	Probability of Entering Poverty in the 1990s	Probability of Escaping Poverty in the 1990s	Poverty Head Count, 1990s (%)
Abyei	0.236	0.103	32.7
Gogrial	0.928	0.053	76.6

Source: Calculated from Table 6.8

Household Characteristics and Incidence of Poverty in the 1990s:

In order to understand better the dynamics of poverty in the 1990s, we cross-tabulated household characteristics with wealth status in the 1990s. The values of *Pearson Correlation* and *the level of significance* are presented in Table 6.10 to trace any significant correlation between these characteristics and the incidence of poverty in the 1990s.

In Abyei area, the initial household wealth status has a sizeable (+0.500) and significant positive correlation with the wealth status in the 1990s. This clearly suggests that the initial wealth status of households largely explains household wealth status in the 1990s. The correlation between the sex of household heads and wealth status in the 1990s is negative (- 0.179) but significant, which suggests that female-headed households were mostly poorer than male-headed households in the 1990s.

---

28   If the middle households group is treated as poor households, then the results in Table 6.9 will be different. The probability of entering poverty will respectively be 0.8 and 1.00 in Abyei and Gogrial area, while the probability of escaping will be zero in both areas. The poverty head count in the 1990s will be 93.4 per cent in Abyei area and 100 per cent in Gogrial area.

Table 6.10:

Household Characteristics and Level of Poverty in the 1990s

**Correlation between Characteristics of Household
and Wealth Status in the 1990s**

Characteristics of head of hosuehold	Abyei Community	Gogrial Community	Cuiebet Community
Initial Wealth	+★	+	+★
Sex	-★	-★	-
Age	-	+	-
Marital Status	-★	-	-
Education	+★	+	+

Source: Household Surveys and SPSS Output,
★ Indicates significant at the 5% level

A similar negative but significant correlation pattern is also observed in the marital status of the household heads, suggesting that households headed by widows were poorer than those headed by married couples. Interestingly, the relationships between household characteristics and the incidence of poverty among households exposed to drought in Cuiebet have similar patterns to those households exposed to exogenous counter-insurgency warfare in Abyei area, as shown in Table 6.10. This could be attributed to the similar characteristics, particularly the random pattern, between drought and exogenous counter-insurgency warfare, as discussed in Chapter 4.

In Gogrial area, the initial wealth status of households is positively (+0.111) but insignificantly correlated with their wealth status in the 1990s. This suggests, unlike the situation in Abyei, that the initial wealth status of households in Gogrial area does not greatly explain their wealth status in the 1990s, as initially non-poor households became poor in the 1990s, as a result of endogenous counter-insurgency warfare. The correlation between the sex of the household heads and their wealth status in the 1990s is not only negative but also significant, and shows that households headed by females tend to be poorer than those headed by males.

It is clear from Table 6.10 that, while household characteristics, such as

initial wealth status, sex and marital status influence the probability of entry
to and escape from poverty in Abyei area, only the sex of the household
heads affects the wealth status of households in Gogrial area. Other household characteristics, such as age and education, did not affect the wealth
status of the research communities in either Abyei or Gogrial areas in the
1990s.

Level of Resilience[29]: Downward Movement in Well-Being

The third dimension of vulnerability is the level of resilience, which assesses the ability of the household to resist a downward spiral movement
in well-being. The main obvious measure of this downward movement in
well-being at the household level is the level of consumption. Given the
level of exposure to counter-insurgency warfare, and the livelihood strategies adopted by households, there is a need to assess to what level these
households had been successful in smoothing their consumption in the
1990s. In assessing the level of household resilience in the 1990s, the level
of malnutrition is used as well as famine excess mortality experienced by
sample households during the famine of 1998.

The Level of Malnutrition in 1998:

The household survey data on the number of household members admitted
to any feeding programme during the famine of 1998 were cross-tabulated with the initial level of household wealth, as presented in Table 6.11.
Apparently no household in Abyei area had any of its members admitted
to the feeding programmes in 1998, while an average of 1.95 and 2.55
household members respectively were admitted to the feeding programmes
in Gogrial and Cuiebet areas. Interestingly, while the initially non-poor
households had more average numbers admitted to feeding programmes
(2.69) than poor households (1.08) in Gogrial, the non-poor households in
Cuiebet had fewer average members (0.85) admitted than did poor households (3.91).

---

29   In the context of vulnerability and the literature of risk, as discussed earlier,
the term 'resilience' refers to the household's ability to resist the downward movement in
well-being (Moser and Holland, 1997).

It is not surprising that the initially non-poor households in Gogrial area had become less resilient in the 1990s as a result of the rapid depletion of their asset base caused by endogenous counter-insurgency warfare. The non-poor households who were exposed to drought in Cuiebet area were more resilient than were poor households in the 1990s, as their initial asset base helped them to resist the downward movement in their well-being.

Table 6.11: Household Wealth Status and Level of Malnutrition in 1998

Average Number of Household Members Admitted into Feeding Programmes

--Initial Level of Household Wealth Status--

Research Communities	Poor	Middle	Non-Poor	Total
Abyei	0	0	0	0
Gogrial	1.08	1.78	2.69	1.95
Cuiebet	3.91	2.56	0.85	2.55

Source: Household Survey/SPSS Output

Household Members and Level of Malnutrition:

In order to assess which household members suffered most from the down-ward movement in household well-being, household survey data on the number of members of households admitted to feeding programmes are disaggregated, according to the main household members, as presented in Table 6.12. Generally, children had higher average numbers admitted to feeding programme than did adults. Among children admitted to feeding programmes in Gogrial, female children had a lower average (0.65) than that of male children (0.76). Comparing these results with the aggregate secondary data from the nutrition survey conducted in Bahr el Ghazal in 1998 (UNICEF, 1998), the nutrition survey results clearly show that the malnutrition rate was higher in male children than in female children.

Table 6.12: Members of Household Admitted into Feeding Programme in 1998

Average Number of Household Members Admitted into Feeding Programme

Research Communities	--Children--		--Adults--	
	Female	Male	Female	Male
Abyei	0	0	0	0
Gogrial	0.65	0.76	0.28	0.26
Cuiebet	0.85	0.73	0.53	0.44

Source: Household Survey/SPSS Output

The sex differentials in the malnutrition rate become apparent and significant, as the level of malnutrition worsens as is evident in the level of severe malnutrition. These findings show that more male children suffered (57 per cent) from severe malnutrition than did female children (43 per cent) (UNICEF, 1998). Contrary to evidence in South Asia (Das Gupta, 1987; Harris, 1995), these results seem not to suggest any preferential treatment among Dinka male children during famine and food crisis. Although the Dinka concepts of immortality, procreation and lineage continuation favour male infants, they do not lead to preferential treatment of male children during a food crisis, because female children, according to Dinka culture, are seen as a source of wealth through bride wealth.

Household Characteristics and Level of Malnutrition:

Besides the members of households who were less resilient in the 1990s as a result of counter-insurgency warfare, it is important to know the types of households that suffered most. The numbers of household members admitted into the feeding programmes in 1998 (proxy of level of malnutrition) are correlated with the characteristics of household heads in Gogrial and Cuiebet as there was no single member of sample households in Abyei area admitted to a feeding program in 1998. The results as shown in Table 6.13 show that the initial wealth status is significantly important in determining the level of malnutrition. While the correlation between the initial wealth status and level of malnutrition in Gogrial area is positive and sizeably significant, the level of the correlation in Cuiebet area is negative and significant. This finding suggests that while the initial level of wealth in Gogrial area made households paradoxically less resilient in the 1990s, it had been an important factor in making the non-poor households exposed to drought more resilient than poor households in Cuiebet area.

Table 6.13: Household Characteristics and Level of Malnutrition in 1998

Correlation between Household Characteristics and Malnutrition of Head of Household

Characteristics of head of hosuehold	Gogrial Community	Cuiebet Community
Initial Wealth	+★	-★
Sex	-	+
Age	+	-
Education	+	-

Source: Household Surveys and SPSS Output;
★ Indicates significant at the 5% level

Another interesting finding is the association between the sex of the head of household and the level of malnutrition in Gogrial area, as the negative and insignificant correlation suggests that female-headed households were more resilient than male-headed households. While such association is positive and insignificant in the case of households exposed to drought in Cuiebet area. This finding in Gogrial area could be attributed to the fact that households were becoming increasingly reliant on gathering wild foods, as discussed in Chapter 5. Also other characteristics of household such as age and education are insignificant but provide contrasting correlation with malnutrition suggesting households headed by older people and more educated admitted more members to the feeding centres in Gogrial area, which is a reverse in Cuibet area.

Level of Famine Excess Mortality[30] in 1998:

Famine mortality is undoubtedly the lowest level of the downward spiral of vulnerability and clearly captures the end results of household efforts to survive and to resist downward movement in its well-being. In addition to the level of malnutrition, the famine mortality data in 1998 were used to assess the level of household resilience in the 1990s. Having from the household survey the famine mortality data and initial wealth status of research communities, it is possible to partially test the link between famine mortality and the initial household wealth. This link will also shed light on the importance of the nature of counter-insurgency warfare and the efficacy of livelihood strategies adopted by various sample households during the 1990s.

As the famine mortality data from household survey show similar findings to those observed in the level of malnutrition and, given that the number of sample households was too small to represent the entire population, the qualitative data from the community surveys are used. The qualitative data from both women and men focus group discussions suggest generally higher famine mortality among non-poor than poor households in Gogrial area, while higher famine mortality was observed among poor households than non-poor households in Cuiebet area.

Though the data from the community survey might not be precise, their qualitative trend strongly suggests a considerable and higher mortality among non-poor households than among poor households in the context of households exposed to endogenous counter-insurgency warfare (Gogrial). This astonishing finding of a positive, significant correlation between initial wealth and mortality in the context of counter-insurgency warfare (Gogrial) is related to the nature of risk, as discussed in Chapter 5. The households in the Gogrial community had tried to adopt various risk management strategies that failed to be effective, as these strategies were known by the government militia raiders, who happened to be from within the communities and had detailed inside information about these strategies. The households in Gogrial area were forced to rely heavily on harvesting natural resources

---

30   The famine excess mortality data generated from household surveys may not provide exact numbers, as households might have included the members of their larger extended family. However, such data do indicate trend in excess famine mortality rather than actual numbers.

particularly, wild foods. The non-poor households as a result suffered most in terms of rapid and sudden depletion of their livestock, with considerable social and psychological trauma.

Household Members and Level of Famine Mortality

The trend in famine mortality differentials among the members of households is crucially important in understanding the level of household resilience in the 1990s. The disaggregated famine mortality data show that while female children had a slightly lower than average mortality rate than male children, the famine mortality differential was significant among adult members, with women's average mortality being nearly half of that of men (0.26) in Gogrial area. In Cuiebet a similar pattern was observed among children, but among adults there was a slightly higher mortality rate among adult women than among men.

The community surveys in Gogrial and even Cuiebet area indicate significant sex mortality differentials, with male members (boys and men) having a higher mortality rate than female members of household. Deng (1999:18) observes the same pattern of sex mortality differentials with women accounted for 17 per cent and men accounted for about 23 per cent of the total excess famine mortality in Gogrial area in 1998, while children accounted for about 60 per cent with no significant sex differentials in famine excess mortality (Deng, 1999:18).

This apparent sex mortality differential has been generally observed in most famines and is usually attributed to the higher level of female body fat, a greater propensity for males to migrate and the reduction in conceptions (Dyson, 1993). In addition to these factors, the situation in Bahr el Ghazal in the 1990s suggests that the stigma attached to wild foods – the most available means of accessing food during famine – tend to benefit females and even poor households more than males and rich households respectively. Deng (1999) argues that in Dinka society, there are certain wild foods which, although they have a high calorific value, are eaten exclusively by children and women and not by adult males, merely for the sake of pride and dignity. During the community surveys, both men and women key informants attributed the low famine mortality rate among female members to the early upbringing of children, as female children are brought up with a culture of tolerance and endurance (*lier piou* (cold heart)) in Dinka society.

Household Characteristics and Famine Mortality:

In order to understand better the level of vulnerability in the 1990s, the main characteristics of sample households are cross-tabulated with famine mortality, so as to assess the level of resilience across different wealth groups in various research communities. Generally, similar results to those found in the malnutrition data are affirmed by the results of correlation between the main characteristics of household heads and famine mortality. The initial wealth status of households in Gogrial area is not only positively correlated with famine mortality, but that such correlation is considerable (+0.723) and statistically significant. Unlike the situation in Gogrial area, the correlation between initial wealth status and famine mortality among sample households in Cuiebet was negative (–0.386) and significant. This suggests that while more members from non-poor households died during famine than those from poor households in Gogrial area in 1998, poor households had higher average famine mortality than non-poor households in Cuiebet.

This finding of low resilience among the non-poor households in Gogrial area affirms further the earlier findings relating to the increasing susceptibility and sensitivity of non-poor households in the 1990s as a result of endogenous counter-insurgency warfare. This finding is also inconsistent with the commonly held view in the famine literature that imputes famine to poverty, with relatively rich groups in society usually surviving famine. Though it is true that there is a positive relationship between poverty and famine in relatively stable societies, or in societies exposed to exogenous shocks, such as drought, as is the case in Cuiebet, the 1998 famine in Gogrial area suggests that this relation does not hold true among households exposed to endogenous shocks.

Female-headed households have emerged into the policy arena of development studies and entered popular rhetoric, because of their growing prevalence and concerns regarding the well-being of children (Waite, 2000). It is generally argued that the emergence of female-headed households is attributed either to women's emancipation from patriarchal constraints (Tinker, 1990), or women's greater assertiveness and autonomy (Jackson, 1996), or an awareness of 'class consciousness among women' (Chant, 1997). Importantly, in rural communities particularly in Africa, however, the growing population of female-headed households is imputed less to women's choice, but attributed more to economic hardship and the commercial-isation of the rural economy that has resulted in more frequent divorce and abandonment by men of their households. Also AIDS is increasingly creating female-headed households in many parts of Africa. The emergence and growing population of female-headed households have undoubtedly provided the springboard for concern that female-headed households are disproportionately represented in the poorer sections of society and are consequently the most vulnerable.

Rather than entering the debate about the 'feminisation of poverty and vulnerability', the focus here is on the gendered experience of vul-nerability in the context of the Sudan's civil war. Generally, the number of female-headed households has considerably increased during the civil war. The results of household surveys show that women in Abyei and Gogrial headed about 34 per cent and 43 per cent of the sample households re-spectively. The emergence of female-headed households came as a result of the bitter realities of war, as husbands are either soldiers sent far away from their families for many years, or husbands who have died as a result of war. Generally, as discussed earlier, female-headed households were more likely to be in the poor group than were male-headed households in the 1990s, as shown in Table 6.10. However, the level of poverty among female-headed households does not necessary imply that they were more vulnerable or less resilient than the male-headed households in the 1990s.

In Gogrial area, the correlation between the famine mortality and sex of head of households is negative but insignificant. This suggests, though insig-nificant, that female-headed households may have had less famine mortality than male-headed households during the famine of 1998. One possible explanation is the fact that the increasing reliance on the collection of wild foods might have benefited female-headed households. Deng (1999:12) observes, that in responding to famine in 1998, female-headed households performed similarly to or even better than male-headed households because of wild food collection or the targeting of relief food aid, which favours female-headed households, as they are believed to be more vulnerable than male-headed households.

Conclusion

The chapter focuses on vulnerability as the apparent livelihood outcome of the risk management strategies adopted by households exposed to counter-insurgency warfare and drought in Bahr el Ghazal region in the 1990s. Vulnerability is an important element of household well-being and is a fluid and dynamic concept, which is more suitable for a life course perspective that captures the process of change (Moser, 1998). Although household well-being is often juxtaposed with poverty, it is argued that poverty is only one dimension, as other aspects of 'ill-being', such as vulnerability, are important elements of household well-being. The most important elements of vulnerability, such as *susceptibility, sensitivity* and *resilience,* have been used to compare and analyse the livelihood outcomes of households exposed to various risk events such as endogenous counter-insurgency, exogenous counter-insurgency and drought.

The key findings of the link between risk events and the outcome of livelihood strategies in terms of vulnerability are summarised in Table 6.14 In terms of susceptibility and sensitivity, households exposed to counterinsurgency warfare (exogenous and endogenous) exhibit similar livelihood outcomes with non-poor households more affected than poor households and the reverse is true in the case of drought. Interestingly, households exposed to exogenous counterinsurgency warfare were more resilient than those exposed to drought with non-poor were more resilient than the poor and households facing endogenous counterinsurgency warfare with all households less resilient; particularly the non-poor.

The findings summarise the hypothesised links between risk events, livelihood strategies and vulnerability as presented in the *'Risk-Livelihood-Vulnerability'* framework that was discussed in Chapter 3. While the nature of risk is important, the characteristics of risk are more crucial in understanding household vulnerability, particularly in the context of civil war. The findings from the households exposed to drought (Cuiebet) confirm the 'standard' pattern of vulnerability in the literature. In the case of civil war, the level of vulnerability differs considerably between those exposed to exogenous and endogenous counterinsurgency warfare and this points to the context specificity

The major finding that is different from the literature is the pattern of vulnerability to endogenous shocks such as endogenous counter-insurgency warfare (Gogrial), which clearly and surprisingly indicates the positive link between vulnerability and initial level of household wealth. This finding came as result of proxy indicators related to the elements of vulnerability, particularly *susceptibility*, *sensitivity* and *resilience* that consistently show high vulnerability among non-poor households who were exposed to endogenous counterinsurgency warfare. This finding is mainly related to the distinctive characteristics of endogenous counter-insurgency warfare, particularly symmetric information, year-round duration, specificity, high correlation with other risk events, limited past experience and post-period threat. Besides these characteristics of endogenous counter-insurgency warfare, the characteristics of non-poor households, particularly their limited capacity to absorb shocks, susceptibility to trauma and inflexibility to adopt to new ways of livelihood such as reliance on wild food collection, all contributed to their increased vulnerability. This pattern of vulnerability could be hypothesised to be a 'standard' pattern for endogenous shocks and this will certainly require more validation and verification from researches in other case studies in different contexts.

Table 6.14: Summary of Links between Risk Events, Livelihood Strategies and Vulnerability

Status of Household Vulnerability in the 1990s

Risk Events	Susceptibility	Sensitivity	Resilience
Endogenous Counter-insurgency (Gogrial)	More among non-poor households than poor households	Higher among non-poor households than poor households	Low among all households, particularly among non-poor households
Exogenous Counter-insurgency (Abyei)	Random pattern among all households, but slightly more among non-poor households	Higher among non-poor households than poor households	High among all households (poor and non-poor)
Drought (Cuiebet)	More among poor households than non-poor households	Higher among poor households than non-poor households	Higher among non-poor households than poor households

CHAPTER SEVEN

Conclusions:
Risk-Livelihood-Vulnerability Nexus

┄┄┄▪┄▪┄▪■━◍━■▪┄▪┄▪┄┄

Introduction

This book set out a framework in an attempt to gain a nuanced understanding of household vulnerability and resilience in the context of civil war and located this framework in the larger context of the dimensions of the characteristics of risk events, livelihood strategies and vulnerability as livelihood outcome. The dearth of under-standing of risk-related behaviours in the civil war has made existing studies in risk and livelihood literature unwittingly equating these behaviours with risk-related behaviours in the context of other risk events, or even ruled out any rational risk management behaviour in the context of civil war. By juxtaposing risk-related behaviours in the context of civil war and those in other risk events, or even questioning any rational behaviour in the context of civil war, these studies have failed to heed the subtle and complex risk behaviours, which occur in the environment of civil war. In fact, there are few attempts in rural development literature that have been made to link risk events in a systematic way to livelihood strategies and their outcomes. The framework set out in this study has come to be called the Risk-Livelihood-Vulnerability Framework and it attempts to provide the link between risks, livelihood strategies and their outcomes in terms of vulnerability and resilience, and subsequently identifies constraints on rural livelihoods and actions to remove them.

In this regard, the study attempted to unravel and understand better household livelihood strategies in the context of the civil war by delving into comparative empirical inquiries at household level in Bahr el Ghazal region in southern Sudan. As discussed in the introductory chapter, the study addressed the core hypothesis that people surviving in the prolonged and protracted violent environment do take livelihood strategies to confront civil war by analyzing the three elements of the risk-livelihood-vulnerability framework. First, this research inquired into the risk events faced by the research communities in the 1990s with a focus on the aetiology and conduct of civil war. The types and characteristics of counter-insurgency warfare were examined and compared with other sources of risk, such as drought, to assess the level of exposure of the research communities to these risk events in the 1990s. Second, this study examined the ex-ante risk management strategies, particularly the risk reduction and risk mitigation livelihood strategies including assessing and examining the status of and investment in social capital, as one of the risk mitigation livelihood strategies, in the context of civil war. Finally, the study investigated, analysed and compared the level of household vulnerability, which is measured in terms of susceptibility, sensitivity and resilience, as a livelihood outcome of the livelihood strategies adopted by households in the 1990s.

The Key Empirical Findings

As civil wars are caused by multiple factors and sustained by greed and economic interests, the livelihoods of communities living in prolonged violent conflict environment are less affected by the direct war between governments and rebels but more by the ways the civil wars are conducted and sustained; particularly counterinsurgency warfare. The evolution and conduct of the civil war in Sudan indicate the dominance of greed, need grievances and psychological pay-offs in sustaining civil war in the 1990s in southern Sudan and affecting as well the rural livelihoods.

The key finding of this research is that households exposed to counter-insurgency warfare do take a rational course of actions, particularly ex-ante risk management strategies, to confront the effects of civil war. The diversification of primary livelihood activities was found to be less evident among households exposed to counter-insurgency warfare than among those exposed to drought. Also, it has been shown that social capital is not necessary the causality of civil war as its status during counter-insurgency warfare was found to be context-specific and largely determined by the type and characteristics of the counter-insurgency warfare. It was found also that the level of vulnerability as the outcome of livelihood strategies adopted during the civil war is context-specific. Paradoxically, the level of vulnerability among households exposed to endogenous counter-insurgency warfare was significantly found to be positively associated with their initial wealth status, with non-poor households becoming more vulnerable than poor households.

Understanding the Characteristics of Risk:

The narrative analysis of counter-insurgency warfare shows that factors such as need and greed at all levels, economic crisis and deliberate political and economic agendas at a national level, and fear and psychological pay-offs at a micro level, largely explained the rapid growth and intensity of counter-insurgency warfare in southern Sudan in the 1990s. While the government of Sudan used counter-insurgency warfare to deflect the grievances resulting from its unpopular policies and to wage and sustain its war cheaply against rebels in the south, the greed, need, fear and economic drive of its militias mainly sustained counter-insurgency warfare in the 1990s.

The most interesting finding is the perception of households about the risk events faced in the 1990s, as they attached more importance to counter-insurgency warfare, which had more direct and profound effects on their livelihoods than the conventional warfare between the government and the rebels. Interestingly, the non-poor households attach relatively more importance to counter-insurgency warfare than do poor households, who in turn attach more importance to drought than do non-poor households. This finding implicitly suggests that non-poor households were more concerned about counter-insurgency warfare in the 1990s than were poor households.

A distinction is made between exogenous counter-insurgency, which originates from outside the community, and endogenous counter-insurgency, which emanates from within the community. Endogenous counter-insurgency warfare was perceived by households to have more profound negative effects on rural livelihoods than any other forms of conflict. Unlike other sources of risk (drought and exogenous counter-insurgency warfare), it has been shown that endogenous counter-insurgency warfare has distinctive characteristics, including specificity, year-round occurrence, symmetric information and a high correlation with other sources of risk. These have had profound effects on the choice of livelihood strategies and livelihood outcomes in southern Sudan in the 1990s.

Livelihood Strategies: Level of Diversification

There are few or no attempts in the risk and rural development literature to link the choice of livelihood strategies with the risk events, particularly in empirical studies. The risk events are assumed to be exogenous and would not as such explain variation in the choice of the livelihood strategies adopted by households. In most cases, household livelihood strategies, particularly livelihood diversification, are linked to poverty reduction policies or to assets, rather than to sources of risk. One salient feature of the Risk-Livelihood-Vulnerability framework is that it provides just such an opportunity of linking risk events and the choice of livelihood strategies. The comparative analysis of ex-ante risk management strategies across research communities shows that households exposed to counter-insurgency warfare adopted a set of livelihood strategies in the 1990s. Those strategies adopted by households exposed to exogenous counter-insurgency warfare not only outperformed those strategies adopted by households exposed to endogenous counter-insurgency warfare, but also they were innovative.

One striking example of such an innovative livelihood strategy is the hedging strategy, the forward bartering of sorghum with livestock, adopted by households exposed to exogenous counter-insurgency warfare to minimise susceptibility to risk and to make the best use of market opportunities. This strategy is essentially a futures market that is used by households as a tool to avert sorghum potential losses as a result of storage and counter-insurgency warfare raids by accepting lower terms of trade (bartering of sorghum with livestock) as a premium to avoid the risk of losing their sorghum stock. It is interesting and surprising that futures markets do exist even in the midst of civil war and this clearly indicates that households in the 'war zone' are not only proactive but they are also innovative in their livelihood strategies.

With respect to diversification as the most popular livelihood strategy in development studies, the key finding about diversification can be summarised fairly succinctly, as the commonly held view of the apparent evidence of diversification in rural areas is less tenable in the context of civil war. The results of a comparative analysis of primary livelihood activities indicate that diversification is not always the best livelihood strategy option in the context of counter-insurgency warfare. Generally, the households exposed to drought tend to diversify their primary livelihood activities more than do those households exposed to counter-insurgency warfare. The comparison of primary livelihood activities during the pre-war period and during the war in the 1990s also shows that households exposed to counter-insurgency warfare in the 1990s adopted less diversified livelihood activities.

For example, while increasing numbers of the households exposed to exogenous counter-insurgency adopted pure pastoralism, nearly half of the sample households exposed to endogenous counter-insurgency reverted from previously diversified agro-pastoralism to pure farming in the 1990s. This finding clearly suggests that households exposed to endogenous counter-insurgency warfare diversified their primary livelihood activities less in the 1990s than did those exposed to exogenous counter-insurgency warfare. Interestingly, among the households exposed to exogenous counterinsurgency warfare, the non-poor households paradoxically tended to diversify their primary livelihood activities less than did the poor households. Similar findings are also observed from the results of the comparative analysis of different forms of diversification in crop production, particularly enterprise, varietal, and spatial diversification, across the research communities and sample households.

The Status of Social Capital during Civil War:

Discussion of social capital has largely been confined to debates on development and civil society and it has been assumed it has very little to say about the civil war because it is always more associated with co-operation and trust than with conflict and violence. It is generally assumed that violent conflict has a negative effect on social capital, and war zones are considered to be 'zones of social capital deficiency' (Goodhand et al, 2000:390). The

Risk-Livelihood-Vulnerability Framework provides an opportunity for not only treating investment in social capital as one of the livelihood strategies but also importantly for relating the status of social capital to risk events, such as counterinsurgency warfare.

Taking investment in social capital as one of the risk mitigation strategies, the results of various measures (kinship support, the structure of the household, traditional court settlements and mutual labour assistance clubs) of the level and stock of social capital indicate significant differences between households exposed to exogenous and endogenous counter-insurgency warfare. The households exposed to exogenous counter-insurgency tend to have higher levels of social capital stock than do those households exposed to endogenous counter-insurgency warfare. With increasing external common threats from Arab militias, the households in Abyei area have become more cohesive and co-operative, with strong community-based risk-sharing arrangements and have invested more in social capital than have those households exposed to endogenous counter-insurgency warfare in Gogrial. The level of mistrust and poor co-operation was more evident among the households exposed to endogenous counter-insurgency than among those exposed to exogenous counter-insurgency, with non-poor households feeling and being affected more than poor households.

Specifically, while the overwhelming majority of households exposed to endogenous counter-insurgency warfare experienced a decline in kinship support in the 1990s, nearly 40 per cent of the sample households exposed to exogenous counter-insurgency warfare experienced an increase in kinship support. Equally, a significant and higher proportion of the households exposed to endogenous counter-insurgency warfare resorted to traditional courts in the 1990s to settle their social claims, compared to the insignificant level among households exposed to exogenous counter-insurgency warfare. Also, the household structure among those exposed to endogenous counter-insurgency has become increasingly nuclear, while an extended household structure was more evident among those exposed to exogenous counter-insurgency warfare.

The practice of the mutual labour assistance club has apparently increased not only crop production but has also renewed generalised reciprocity and egalitarian values among households exposed to exogenous counter-insurgency warfare, while such practices have vanished in Gogrial area. These findings suggest that the nature of counter-insurgency warfare explains much of the differential variation in the level and status of social capital in the context of civil war. Specifically, the nature of endogenous counter-insurgency warfare, as experienced by households in Gogrial area in the 1990s, created a climate of mistrust and turned the community against itself, which dented co-operation and weakened social capital.

Taking marriage as an important and effective social diversification and insurance strategy in Dinka society, higher incidences of marriage were found among communities exposed to exogenous counter-insurgency warfare than among those exposed to endogenous counter-insurgency warfare. The external and common threat from Arab militias made households in Abyei area to strengthen and diversify their social ties through marriage, while the internal conflict engineered by the Dinka militias in Gogrial area dented and weakened social ties. The communities exposed to exogenous counter-insurgency had not only increased the level of marriage among their own community, but they extended further their social ties to mini-mise the radius of mistrust through an increased level of marriage with the neighbouring community, which has different climatic conditions and less exposed to the raids of Arab militias.

Livelihood Outcome: The Level of Vulnerability and Resilience

In most literature on risk and development studies, the level of a household vulnerability is associated with assets and poverty and is rarely linked with risk events, particularly in empirical studies. The analysis of the level of household vulnerability in this book was guided by the Risk-Livelihood-Vulnerability Framework that links sources of risk not only to the choice of livelihood strategies but also to the level of vulnerability. The most relevant three proxies of the three elements (susceptibility, sensitivity and resilience) of vulnerability have been used to compare the livelihood outcomes across research communities.

Using the frequency of household displacement as a proxy indicator for the level of household susceptibility to counter-insurgency, the results of the comparative analysis show that households exposed to exogenous count-er-insurgency warfare were more susceptible to counter-insurgency warfare than were those exposed to endogenous counter-insurgency warfare. While the initially non-poor households experienced a significantly higher number of displacements than did poor households in Gogrial area, the non-poor and poor households experienced a similar pattern of displacement in the Abyei area. The comparison of the correlation between the characteristics of household head (initial wealth status, sex, age, marital status and education) and the level of susceptibility (displacement) distinctively shows a significant and positive correlation between the initial wealth status and the level of susceptibility, particularly in the context of endogenous counter-insurgency warfare. These findings undoubtedly suggest that non-poor households were significantly more susceptible to counter-insurgency warfare than were poor households. The random pattern (insignificant difference) in the level of susceptibility among poor and non-poor households in Abyei area and the significant difference in the level of susceptibility between poor and non-poor households in Gogrial area could largely be attributed to the difference in the characteristics of counter-insurgency warfare.

In the context of the Dinka research communities, the level of livestock ownership, rather than the level of resources generally, was used as a proxy for the household asset base to measure the level of household sensitivity to counter-insurgency warfare in the 1990s. The comparative analysis shows that households exposed to endogenous counter-insurgency experienced a considerable and higher decline in their asset base in the 1990s than did those exposed to exogenous counterinsurgency warfare. Generally, initially, non-poor households experienced micro-socialmore rapid depletion of their livestock than did poor households. Even within initially non-poor households, the asset base of those households exposed to endogenous counter-insurgency warfare depleted at a higher rate in the 1990s than that of those households exposed to exogenous counter-insurgency warfare.

In terms of cattle losses resulting from looting by government-supported militias (Dinka and Arab) in the 1990s, households exposed to endogenous counter-insurgency warfare had significantly higher average cattle losses than those exposed to exogenous counter-insurgency warfare, with non-poor households experiencing higher average cattle losses than non-poor households. Despite this rapid depletion of livestock during the 1990s, the overwhelming majority of households (poor and non-poor) exposed to exogenous counter-insurgency warfare bought more livestock, while those exposed to endogenous counter-insurgency warfare, particularly non-poor households sold much more livestock. These findings of the rapid depletion of livestock, as a result of looting or excessive sales, all suggest that the asset base of households exposed to endogenous counter-insurgency warfare was more sensitive than those exposed to exogenous counter-insurgency warfare. The asset base of the initially non-poor households was more sensitive to counter-insurgency warfare than was that of poor households, particularly in the context of endogenous counter-insurgency warfare. In other words, these findings show again that initially non-poor households were more vulnerable than poor households, particularly in the context of endogenous counterinsurgency warfare.

With the rapid depletion of the household asset base in the 1990s, the proportion of poor households in Abyei area almost doubled in the 1990s, while that of households exposed to endogenous counter-insurgency warfare more than quadrupled. The poverty dynamics and transition were more drastic among households exposed to endogenous counter-insurgency as an overwhelming majority of initially non-poor households became poor in the 1990s, while a small and insignificant percentage of the initially non-poor households exposed to exogenous counter-insurgency warfare became poor. While the incidence of poverty in the 1990s was positively and significantly correlated to initial wealth status among households exposed to drought and exogenous counter-insurgency warfare, such correlation was positive but insignificant among households exposed to endogenous counter-insurgency warfare. This insignificant correlation between initial wealth status and the wealth status in the 1990s clearly indicates the rapid depletion and sensitivity of the asset base of households exposed to endogenous counter-insurgency warfare.

The comparative analysis of the levels of malnutrition and famine excess mortality in 1998 shows that the households exposed to endogenous counter-insurgency warfare experienced higher rates of malnutrition and excess famine mortality, while those exposed to exogenous counter-insurgency warfare did not experience any. Among households exposed to endogenous counter-insurgency warfare, the initially non-poor households had higher levels of malnutrition and excess famine mortality than did poor households. However, among the households exposed to drought, the level of malnutrition was higher among poor households than among initially non-poor households. The values of correlation between the level of malnutrition and excess famine mortality and the characteristics of the household head distinctively indicate that initial wealth status has a significantly positive value among households exposed to endogenous counter-insurgency warfare. However, the correlation between the level of malnutrition and excess famine mortality, and initial wealth status among households exposed to drought, was negative and significant. This finding undoubtedly suggests that, while the initial level of wealth made households exposed to endogenous counter-insurgency warfare less resilient in 1998, it had been an important factor in making initially non-poor households exposed to drought more resilient than poor households. One important finding is that the marital status of household heads rather than the sex of household head was found to be more important in explaining the level of household vulnerability, particularly in the context of endogenous counter-insurgency warfare.

Implications for Understanding and Research:

These major empirical findings, although drawn from the case studies from three communities, shed light on some subtle gaps in our understanding of civil wars and the behaviours of households caught up in war zones. The strong and excessive focus on the political economy of civil wars has resulted not only in sweeping generalisations, but has also stifled any 'fine-grained' micro social analysis at the community and household level. These sweeping generalisations about aspects of civil war have not come under empirical scrutiny to either prove or refute them, as the methodological problems of researching complex social process and household behaviour in war zones have restricted empirical studies.

These major empirical findings from a general case study of civil war in Sudan and the two specific case studies of research communities exposed to different types of counter-insurgency warfare in southern Sudan all point to complexity and context-specificity. They have as well theoretical implications for our understanding of conduct civil war, livelihood diversification, social capital and vulnerability as well as enriching academic literature and identifying new avenues of future research.

How Civil War Is Perceived by Communities?

The way communities perceived civil war is important not only to understand how they confront violent conflict but also how to support them during the civil war. Understanding the rural livelihoods of communities surviving with civil wars is less about the causation of civil war but more about its conduct. What is more relevant for rural communities is the manner and ways in which civil wars are pursued and conducted, rather than their primary causes and conventional warfare between rebels and governments. The analysis of the evolution and progressive growth of counter-insurgency warfare in Sudan has shown the variation across the research communities in their level of exposure to counter-insurgency warfare and civil war. This clearly suggests that even within a given 'war zone' it is difficult to make sweeping generalisations, as variation exists across communities. As the literature on civil war focuses on meso-factors at a national level, the case of Sudan's civil war suggests the need to consider not only global factors but also micro factors at a community level that provide a better understanding of and context-specificity for civil wars.

Is Diversification Always the Best Livelihood Strategy Option?

It is a commonly held view, with considerable empirical evidence from many case studies, that rural households do indeed engage in multiple activities and rely on diversified income portfolios. It has been generally observed that the poor households, especially those facing food security, market and credit constraints, tend to be more diversified in terms of cropping activities (Fafchamps, 1992; Alwang, et. al., 1996; Barrett, 1997; Alwang and Siegel, 1999; Little et al., 2001). In sub-Saharan Africa, the more diverse the income portfolio, the better-off is the rural household, while elsewhere a common pattern is for the very poor and the comparatively well-off to have the more diverse livelihoods than middle-income households, who display less diversity (Ellis, 2000). However, when non-farm income diversification is considered, the evidence from various case studies in Africa indicates the empirical regularity of a positive association between income diversification and wealth, because of the existence of substantial entry or mobility barriers (Barrett et al, 2001:327).

What is apparent in the literature and in empirical studies on diversification is that, although the risk has been identified as one of the natural determinants of diversification, it hardly features in the analysis of diversification. In most case studies, the choice of diversification is associated with transaction costs, location, assets and entry or mobility barriers with the source of risk, predominantly climatic risk, playing an insignificantly explanatory role. There is an apparent absence in rural development literature of any comparative analysis of diversification strategies across households exposed to different sources of risk. The findings related to livelihood diversification clearly point to the important role played by the sources of risk in determining the level and type of diversification strategies. Specifically, sweeping generalisations about the common pattern of livelihood diversification in the context of climatic risk or macro-economic shocks in rural sub-Saharan Africa may not be tenable in the context of civil war. Even within the context of civil war, as shown by the case of Sudan's civil war, it is difficult to draw common patterns in livelihood strategies, including diversification, as communities in conflict areas are differently exposed to various types of counter-insurgency warfare and levels of civil war. The variation in the level of diversification of the primary livelihood activities adopted by households in the research communities exposed to different types of counter-insurgency warfare in southern Sudan point again to the complexity and context-specificity of livelihood strategies adopted in the context of civil war.

As this study has primarily focused on the effect of counter-insurgency warfare on the choice of risk management strategies and the level of livelihood diversification, there is a need for future research to assess and disentangle the effects of insurgency warfare on the choice of household livelihood strategies. Equally, as this study focuses on the effect of counter-insurgency warfare on the level of diversification of primary livelihood activities, future research needs to use more rigorous methods, such as a livelihood diversity index method, and to incorporate other combinations of various livelihood activities that have not been considered in this study.

Is Social Capital Always a Casualty of Civil War?

Since the concept of 'social capital' entered the international development lexicon, it has seen progressive growth and recognition in promoting economic growth and fostering good governance, but it has also invited heated debates. These debates around 'social capital' are described at times as 'generating much more heat than light!' (Edwards, 1999:4). As the conceptualisation of 'social capital' pays scant attention to issues of power, inequality and social differentiation, while emphasising co-operation and co-ordination, it conceptually rules out any positive role to be played by conflict in the processes of social change (Goodland et al., 2000). In other words, the conceptualisation of 'social capital' has generally assumed that violent conflict has a negative effect on social capital.

However, some researchers (Duffield, 2000; Keen, 2000) challenge this premise and argues instead that violence is less about social breakdown than about the creation of new forms of social relations. The case of Sri Lanka is one of the rare studies that provide empirical evidence which questions the belief that violent conflict inevitably erodes social capital (Goodland et al., 2000). However, Goodland et al. (2000:401) observed also that in a war zone, social capital is strengthened and deepened in the more stable areas, while it is depleted in front-line areas suffering from chronic insecurity. In a way, this empirical finding, paradoxically, supports the assumption that violent conflict undermines social capital.

The empirical findings of this study clearly questioned any simplistic assumption that conflict erodes social capital. While it is true that certain types of social capital have been a casualty of civil war, particularly among communities exposed to endogenous counter-insurgency warfare, there has been deepening and strengthening of bonding social capital among communities exposed to exogenous counter-insurgency warfare. This finding has made it clear that 'fine-grained' social analysis in 'war zone' is best understood in its wider context, within which social, economic and political processes interact. A better understanding of the determinants of the livelihood strategies adopted by households to confront any risk requires a thorough understanding of the characteristics of risk events to which households are exposed. The comparative analysis of the level and status of social capital among communities exposed to different types of counter-insurgency warfare in southern Sudan has again challenged any generalisation, and clearly pointed to complexity and context-specificity.

As this study has focused only on non-institutional (norm rather than form), normative ('good' rather than 'good or bad' in terms of the outcomes they generate) and bonding (intra-group solidarity) aspects of social capital in the 'war zone', the other aspects of social capital merit further exploration and research. In particular, understanding structural social capital that involves trust in rebel institutions (as the de facto state) and other wider social institutions, such as traditional structure, civil society organisations and non-governmental organisations (local and international) will shed more light on these debates on the status of social capital during the civil war. Another important aspect of social capital that merits further research in the context of civil war is the bridging aspect of social capital, particularly inter-community solidarity and broader societal networks, such as the relations between rebel combatants and communities. As the normative analysis of social capital may downplay its perverse outcomes, future research on social capital requires the examining not only of the amount of social capital but also of its quality, such as the level of social inclusion and cohesion.

Are Poor Households Always the Most Vulnerable?

There are common consensus and cumulative empirical evidence in the risk, poverty and rural development literature that unambiguously suggest the empirical regularity of a negative association between vulnerability and wealth, including assets and income. It is commonly argued that poor households are more susceptible to risk, less resilient with a higher sensitive asset-base than are non-poor households because they have fewer tools (assets) at their disposal to defend against risk events and thus suffer proportionally greater welfare losses for given levels of risk. Specifically, Swift (1989), Chambers (1989), Moser (1998) and Siegel and Alwang (1999) presented arguments or frameworks that closely linked vulnerability to asset ownership and generally suggested that the more assets people have, the less vulnerable they are.

This commonly held view and the sweeping generalisation of a negative association between vulnerability and the level of asset ownership have not been questioned, as the findings from a huge body of empirical studies were convincingly overwhelming. There is, however, a growing thinking and empirical studies that have started questioning this sweeping generalisation about vulnerability and asset ownership. In particular, Glewwe and Hall (1998) question this general assertion about vulnerability, using the case study of Peru that shows how subsistence and poor farmers in rural areas were less vulnerable to economic shocks than were high-income earners in the urban areas. In the context of civil war, there is also different thinking (Duffield, 1993; Keen, 1994), which has questioned this general assertion of vulnerability in the context of the 'asset transfer economy' and has suggested instead a positive association between wealth and vulnerability in the case of Dinka community in the Sudan.

As echoed in the earlier findings, the underlying problem in the risk and rural development literature is that, while the risk is conceptually and theoretically emphasised as an important determinant in household risk management strategies and vulnerability, in particular, it is seldom incorporated in the empirical analysis. Risk events and their characteristics are generally assumed as exogenous factors and subsequently have no bearing in explaining the differential vulnerability among households. While it is a common fact that assets play an important role in determining the level of household vulnerability, assets such as livestock become directly susceptible to risk events such as counterinsurgency warfare.

One unique and salient feature of this study is its distinctive attempt to compare the level of vulnerability across households exposed to drought and different types of counter-insurgency warfare. This comparative analysis of the level of vulnerability clearly shows that it is not always true that poor households are necessarily more vulnerable than non-poor households, particularly among households exposed to endogenous counter-insurgency warfare. Another important finding is that it is not always true that all the households (the entire community) subjected to an 'asset transfer economy' in the context of counter-insurgency warfare are vulnerable, as households in the Abyei area have shown a remarkable example of a high level of resilience. In particular, the study has shown that the 'standard' pattern of vulnerability during drought and identified different patterns of vulnerability during endogenous and endogenous counter-insurgency warfare.

As cited before, the problem of the general assertion on the negative or positive association between vulnerability and wealth is that it tends to reduce a complex situation that can only be better understood in a specific context, to a simple and generic phenomenon. A future research agenda in the area of vulnerability might need to focus on developing a greater understanding of the nature and characteristics of risk events, and how such risk events are perceived by different wealth-income groups of households, rather than focusing only on assets, wealth or income. Despite the fact that this study has attempted to provide a different and hypothesised 'standard' pattern of vulnerability to endogenous shocks, there is a need for more rigorous vulnerability modelling for endogenous shocks, such as endogenous counter-insurgency warfare. In addition, there is a need for more case studies from different contexts to validate this new pattern of vulnerability to endogenous shocks, such as endogenous counter-insurgency warfare.

Implications for Policy and Intervention

As highlighted in the introductory chapter, there is a need to improve on understanding of risk-related behaviours and livelihood strategies adopted by households in the 'war zone' areas. This call for a better understanding of rural livelihood strategies is heightened by the increasing incidence of civil wars that are sweeping rapidly into rural areas and have overtaken drought as the main risk event faced by rural communities. This study with its case studies has come up with some findings that might be of some value for policy decisions and practical approaches to rural livelihoods. In concluding this study, I attempt to draw the implications of some relevant findings for policy and practice.

Peace-Building: Local vs. National Level

The perceptions of the research communities about the sources of risk clearly demonstrate that what is more important for their livelihoods is the conduct of the civil war, particularly counter-insurgency warfare, rather than conventional warfare between the rebels and the government. Also, the case studies of the communities exposed to counter-insurgency warfare have also indicated that conventional warfare between the rebels and government has produced bitter inter- and intra- communities conflicts that have had a more profound impact on rural livelihoods. One policy implication is that while peace efforts tend to focus on the main warring parties (rebels and government) at the national level, it is equally important that peace efforts should also be directed at the grass-root level to address these inter- and intra-community conflicts.

Specifically, the donors and NGOs should support during civil war traditional mechanisms of conflict resolution and grass-root peace initiatives that will eventually contribute to the settlement of the major civil war between rebels and the government. Also during the post-conflict period, strengthening the local traditional mechanisms for achieving inter- and intra- community justice, healing and reconciliation to be prioritized. If these local conflicts are not adequately addressed, the peace agreements signed by elites at the national level may not be sustainable and with the likelihood of a new wave of conflicts may erupt.

Development Alongside Relief during Civil War:

There is an on-going debate among policymakers and analysts about the relationship between 'relief' and 'development', particularly in the context of civil war. The debate about applying the principle of linking relief and development in the context of civil war has come under increasing criticism, to the extent that many consider it a dead issue, or at least one they would prefer not to discuss (White and Cliffe, 2000). Yet, despite this apparent despair, the discussion around the need to broaden aid objectives from pure survival support to rehabilitation or development is still very much alive in the context of civil war. One apparent criticism of the relief-development divide debate is that it is constructed from the point of view of aid programmes, with little relevance to the concerns of intended beneficiaries, as well as paying insufficient attention to context. In other words, the relief-development divide debate seems often to be stuck at the level of generalities and has subsequently suffered from inadequate contextualisation, as there is a wide range of variation in the level of humanitarian crises across communities in the war zones (White and Cliffe, 2000:315).

The case studies covered in this study clearly demonstrate the variation in the level of communities' exposure to counter-insurgency warfare, ranging from communities that are in relatively secured and stable areas to those communities who are in front-line areas with chronic insecurity. Even within the communities exposed to counter-insurgency warfare, there are those households who were exposed to exogenous counterinsurgency warfare and were able to adopt more effective livelihood strategies than other households. This variation among communities in a 'war zone', in terms of their exposure to civil war and their livelihood strategies and vulnerability, makes it extremely difficult to make any generalisation.

The experience of households exposed to exogenous counter-insurgency warfare in the Abyei area has shown that, even in the midst of civil war, some households have adopted innovative livelihood strategies that need to be supported with 'development intervention'. However, the disparate situations of households exposed to endogenous counterinsurgency warfare in the Gogrial area make pure relief intervention a necessity. The apparent policy implication is that the choice of 'relief intervention' or 'rehabilitation/ development intervention' in the context of civil war largely depends on a better understanding of the context.

Also, the comparative analysis of livelihood strategies adopted by households exposed to different types of risk events echoes the need for contextualisation, because of the apparent variations in the choice and effectiveness of these livelihood strategies. The practical policy implication of this finding is the need to understand the context within which livelihood strategies are relevant and effective. For example, as shown in the case studies, while some livelihood strategies, such as diversification, work well in some risk contexts such as drought, they may not necessarily be effective in other risk contexts, such as counter-insurgency warfare.

Investment in Social Capital during Civil War:

As the case studies in this study have demonstrated that social capital has been a casualty of civil war in certain contexts and strengthened and deepened in other contexts, it is likely that in the midst of civil war there could be opportunities to enhance social capital. In most cases of civil war, the external actors with a limited understanding and knowledge of community-level dynamics and social relations tend, with an inherent assumption of social capital as a casualty of conflict, to focus on engineering social capital through indigenous NGOs and civic organisations. In the case of southern Sudan, the external actors, guided by the simplistic assumption that conflict undermines social capital, embarked on engineering civil society through support and the proliferation of handpicked indigenous NGOs, without adequate knowledge of the context. As remarked by Edwards (1999), focusing on a number of NGOs and civic organisations may be the easiest areas in which to influence social capital in the short run, but in the long run they may not be especially important in the grand scheme.

While a focus on the form of social capital is important, other aspects of social capital, such as its norms with attributes of trust, tolerance and co-operation, are equally important in promoting social capital during civil war. The variation in the status and investment in social capital among households exposed to counter-insurgency warfare indicates the need to map out the status of social capital, which will help in identifying the areas of intervention that may create an enabling environment for social capital formation. For example, in the case study of Abyei area, where intra-community solidarity has been strengthened during civil war, the appropriate intervention would be to focus on inter-community solidarity, particularly with their Arab neighbours, while consolidating intra-community solidarity. In the Gogrial area, where there has been a rapid depletion of social capital, as a result of endogenous counter-insurgency, it may require a different mix of interventions that will focus increasingly on intra-community solidarity.

One policy implication is that any external intervention should be based on a comprehensive analysis and understanding of the context and should aim at creating an enabling environment, rather than engineering its own social capital formation intervention. During the post-conflict period, there is an urgent need for the government to rehabilitate the traditional social support networks as well as developing formal social security systems for the war-affected population. It is equally important also that the government conduct social capital survey immediately after the peace agreement in order to map the status of social capital and to guide its social security safety nets programmes.

Be Mindful also of the Non-Poor during Civil War:

The initially non-poor households are the real casualties of civil war and the main losers, particularly in the context of counter-insurgency warfare, as clearly demonstrated by the comparative analysis of the level of vulnerability across research communities. Specifically, the case study of the Gogrial area has provided convincing evidence that shows the positive association between vulnerability and wealth. This finding, besides challenging the commonly held view of the negative association between vulnerability and wealth, it also has an important policy implication during the war and post-conflict periods. One obvious policy implication during the civil war is that the targeting of relief assistance should be guided by a better and thorough understanding of the dynamics of poverty and vulnerability, rather than by using pre-war criteria that might have changed drastically during a civil war.

During the 1990s, and specifically during the famine in Bahr el Ghazal in 1998, the external actors established women-led relief committees to distribute food aid. This externally imposed relief targeting committee, besides reflecting the outsiders' perception gender balance and vulnerability, made women be more socially vulnerable and undermined the traditional social safety nets as well as the existing traditional institutions that have a better understanding of the local context (Deng, 1999:85). Another important finding of this study is the fact that women-headed households and female members of the household are not always the most vulnerable, but that households headed by widows and male household members are found to be increasingly vulnerable. This finding has also important implications in targeting food aid, as these important dynamic changes in vulnerability during civil war need to be well understood and contextualised.

The analysis of poverty dynamics during the civil war in Southern Sudan in the 1990s has clearly shown the drastic increase in the incidence of poverty reaching as high as 100 per cent in some areas, particularly areas affected by counter-insurgency warfare. This clearly shows the rapid erosion and depletion of assets base of all households including the initially non-poor households that moved to a poor group during the current civil war. The apparent and clear policy implication is the need for clear poverty reduction strategy to address the special needs of the war-affected communities of Southern Sudan. On top of these pressing needs is to build-up assets, particularly the restocking of livestock among the agro-pastoralist communities through livestock loans.

INDEX

BIBLIOGRAPHY

Adams, R., 1998, 'Remittances, Investment, and Rural Asset Accumulation in Pakistan', *Economic Development and Cultural Change* 47 (1): 155-73

Africa Watch, 1990, *Denying the 'Honour of Living': Sudan a Human Rights Disaster*, New York, Washington, London: Africa Watch.

Ahmed, A., 1988, 'Why the Violence?', in *War Wounds: Sudanese People Report on their War*, London: The Panos Institute.

Ahmed, I., 2000, 'Remittances and Their Impact in Post-war Somaliland', *Disasters* 24 (4): 382-89.

Alderman, H., 1996, 'Saving and Economic Shocks in Rural Pakistan', *Journal of Development Economics* 51 (2): 343-366.

Alderman, H. and Paxson, C., 1992, *Do the Poor Insure? A Synthesis of the Literature on Risk and Consumption in Developing Countries,* Policy Research Working papers, Agricultural Policies, WPS 1008, World Bank.

Ali, A., and Elbadawi, I., 2002, *Prospects for Sustainable Peace and Post-Conflict Economic Growth in the Sudan*, Nairobi: African Economic Research Consortium (AERC), paper presented at AERC workshop on Post-Conflict Economies in Kampala in July 2002.

Alwang, J., Siegel, P., and Jorgensen, S., 1996, 'Seeking Guidelines for Poverty Reduction in Rural Zambia', *World Development,* 24 (11): 1711-1724.

Anderson, J., 1973, 'Sparse data, climatic variability and yield uncertainty in response analysis', *American Journal of Agricultural Economics*, 55 (1).

Antle, J., 1987, "Econometric Estimation of Producer's Risk Attitudes", *American Journal of Agricultural Economics,* 69(3): 509-22.

Arrow, K., 1971, *Essays in the Theory of Risk-Bearing,* Amsterdam: North-Holland Publishing Company.

Baber, R., 1998, *The Structure of Livelihoods in South Africa's Bantustans: Evidence from Two Settlements in Northern Province,* unpublished doctoral thesis, Magdalen College, Oxford.

Bandura, A., 1980, 'The Social Learning Theory of Aggression', Ch. 6 in Falk, R. and Kim, S. (ed), *The War System: An Interdisciplinary Approach,* Boulder, Colorado: Westview Press.

Barrett, C., 1997, 'Food Marketing Liberalisation and Trade Entry: Evidence from Madagascar', *World Development* 25 (5): 763-778.

Barrett, C., Reardon, T., and Webb, P., 2001, 'Nonfarm income diversification and household livelihood strategies in rural Africa: concepts, dynamics, and policy implications', *Food Policy* 26: 315-331.

Baulch, B. and Masset, E., 2003, "Do Monetary and Nonmonetary Indicators Tell the Same Story About Chronic Poverty? A Study of Vietnam in the 1990s", *World Development,* 31 (3): 441-453.

Baulch, B., and McCulloch, N., 1998, 'Being Poor and Becoming Poor: Poverty Status and Poverty Transitions in Rural Pakistan', *IDS Working Paper* No. 79, Brighton: Institute of Development Studies.

Bebbington, A., 1999, 'Capitals and Capabilities: A Framework for Analyzing Peasant Viability, Rural Livelihoods and Poverty', *World Development,* 27 (3): 2021-2044.

Bem, D., 1980, 'The Concept of Risk in the Study of Human Behaviour', Ch. 1 in Dowie, J., and Lefrere, P. (ed), *Risk and Chance: Selected Readings,* Milton Keynes: The Open University.

Bender, D., 1967, 'A refinement of the concept of household: Families, coresidence and domestic functions', *American Anthropologist* 69 (5): 493-504.

Bernstein, P., 1996, *Against the Gods: The Remarkable Story of Risk,* New York: John Wiley & Sons.

Besley, T., 1995, 'Nonmarket Institutions for Credit and Risk Sharing in Low-income Countries', *Journal of Economic Perspectives,* 9 (3): 115-128.

Bevan, P., and Joireman, S., 1997, 'The Perils of Measuring Poverty: Identifying the 'Poor' in Rural Ethiopia', *Oxford Development Studies,* 25 (3): 315-343.

Binswanger, H., 1980, "Attitudes Towards Risk: Experimental Measurement in Rural India", *American Journal of Agricultural Economics* 62

(3): 395-407.

Binswanger, H., 1981, "Attitudes towards risk: Theoretical implications of an experiment in rural India", *Economic Journal* Vol. 91: 867-89.

Binswanger, H., and Rosenzweig, M., 1993, "Wealth, Weather Risk and the Composition and Probability of Agricultural Investments", *Economic Journal,* Vol. 103: 5-21.

Binswanger, H., and Sillers, D., 1983, "Risk Aversion and Credit Constraints in Farmers' Decision-Making: A Reinterpretation", *The Journal of Development Studies.* 20(1): 5-21.

Bruce, J. and Lloyd, C., 1997, 'Finding the Ties that Bind: Beyond Headship and Household', in Haddad, L., Hoddinott, J. and Alderman, H., 1997, *Intrahousehold Resource Allocation in Developing Countries: Models, Methods, and Policy*, Baltimore: John Hopkins.

Bryceson, D., 1996, 'Deagarianisation and Rural Employment in Sub-Saharan Africa: A Sectoral Perspective', *World Development*, 24 (1): 97-111.

Buchanan-Smith, M. and Davies, S., 1995, *Famine Early Warning and Response: The Missing Link,* London: IT Publications.

Carney, D., 1998, 'Implementing the Sustainable Rural Livelihoods Approach', in D. Carney (ed), *Sustainable Rural Livelihoods: What contribution Can We Make?*, London: Department of International Development.

Carney, D., 1998, 'Implementing the Sustainable Rural Livelihoods Approach', Ch. 1 in Carney, D. (ed), *Sustainable Rural Livelihoods: What Contribution Can We Make?*, London: Department for International Development.

Carter, B., Hancock, T., Morin, J., and Robins, N., 1996, *Introducing RISKMAN Methodology: The European Project Risk Management Methodology*, Norwich: The Stationery Office.

Carter, M., 1991, *Risk, Reciprocity and Conditional Self-Insurance in the Sahel: Measurement and Implications for the Trajectory of Agricultural Development in West Africa,* Department of Agricultural Economics Staff Paper No.333, University of Wisconsin.

Carter, M., 1997, 'Environment, Technology, and the Social Articulation of Risk in West Africa Agriculture', *Economic Development and Change*, 45 (3): 557-591.

Carter, M., and May, J., 1999, 'Poverty, Livelihood and Class in Rural South Africa', *World Development*, 27 (1): 1-20.

Cater, N., 1986, 'Sudan: The Roots of Famine', Oxford: Oxfam.

Chambers, R. (ed.), 1989, "Vulnerability: How the Poor Cope", *IDS Bulletin,* 20(2): 1-7.

Chambers, R., 1994, 'The Origins and Practice of Participatory Rural Appraisal', *World Development,* 22 (7): 953-969.

Chambers, R., and Blackburn, J., 1996, 'The Power of Participation: PRA and Policy', *IDS Policy Brief,* Brighton: Institute of Development Studies.

Chambers, R. and Conway, R., 1992, 'Sustainable Rural Livelihoods: Practical Concepts for the 21st Century', *IDS Discussion Paper* No. 296, Brighton: Institute of Development Studies

Chang, H., 1997, 'Coking Coal Procurement Policies of the Japanese Steel Mills: Changes and Implications', *Resources Policy,* 23 (3): 125-135.

Chant, S., 1997, *Women-headed Households: Diversity and Dynamics in the Developing World,* London: St. Martin's Press.

Checchi, F., Testa, A., Warsame, A., Quach, L., and Burns, R. 2018. "South Sudan: Estimates of Crisis-attributable mortality". London: London School of Hygiene and Tropical Medicine.

Choucri, N, 1986, "Demographics and Conflict", *Bulletin of the Atomic Scientists.* 42: 24-5.

Christensen, G., 1992, 'Sensitive Information: collecting data on live-stock and informal credit', Ch. 8 in Devereux, S., and Hoddinott (ed), 1992, *Fieldwork in Developing Countries,* Hertfordshire: Harvester Wheatsheaf.

Christian Aid, 2001, *The Scorched Earth: Oil and War in Sudan,* London: Christian Aid.

Churchill, W., 1940, *The River War: An Account of the Conquest of the Sudan,* London: Eyre and Spottiswoode.

Cliffe, L., and Luckham, R., 1999, 'Complex Political Emergencies', *Third World Quarterly* 20 (1): 27-50.

Cliffe, L., and Luckham, R., 1998, 'Complex Political Emergencies and the State: Towards an understanding of recent experiences and an approach for future research', *COPE Working Paper 2,* Centre for Development Studies, University of Leeds.

Cliffe, L., and Luckham, R., 2000, 'What happens to the State in Conflict?: Political Analysis as a Tool for Planning Humanitarian Assistance', *Disasters* 24 (4):291-313.

Coate, S., and Ravallion, M., 1993, "Reciprocity without commitment:

Characterization and performance of informal insurance arrangements", *Journal of Development Economics* 40: 1-24.

Cohen, J., 1964, *Behaviour in Uncertainty*, New York: Basic Books

Collier, P., 1998, 'The Political Economy of Ethnicity', *CSAE Working Paper 98-8,* Oxford: Centre for the Study of African Economies.

Collier, P., 2000, "Economic Causes of Civil Conflict and Their Implications for policy", *mimeo,* Washington DC: World Bank.

Collier, P., and Hoeffler, A, 1998, "On Economic Causes of Civil War", *Oxford Economic Papers,* 50: 563-73.

Collins, R., 1962, *The Southern Sudan, 1883-1898: a struggle for control,* New Haven and London:

Collins, R., 1971, *Land Beyond the Rivers: The Southern Sudan: 1889-1918,* New Haven and London: Yale University Press.

Collins, R., 2001, *Oil, Water, and War in the Sudan*, manuscript.

Cook, S., 1966, 'The Obsolete "Anti-Market" Mentality: A Critique of the Substantive Approach to Economic Anthropology', *American Anthropologist,* 68 (2): 323-345.

Corbett, J., 1988, 'Famine and household coping strategies', *World Development*, 16 (9): 1099-1112.

Cox, D., 1972, "Regression Models and Life-tables", *Journal of the Royal Statistical Society*, B (34): 187-220.

Crehan, K., 1992, 'Rural Households: Making a Living', in Bernstein, H., Crow, B. and Johnson, H. (ed), *Rural Livelihoods: Crises and Responses*, Oxford: Oxford University Press.

Czukas, K., Fafchamps, M., and Udry, C., 1998, 'Drought and Saving in West Africa: Are Livestock a Buffer Stock', *Journal of Development Economics* 55 (2): 273-305.

Da Corta, L., and Venkateshwarlu, D., 1992, 'Field methods for economic mobility', Ch.7 in Devereux, S., and Hoddinott, J. (ed), 1992, *Fieldwork in Developing Countries*, Hertfordshire: Harvester Wheatsheaf.

Dalton, G., 1961, 'Economic Theory and Primitive Society', *American Anthropologist,* 63 (1): 1-25.

Daly, M., 1986, *Empire on the Nile: The Anglo-Egyptian Sudan 1898-1934,* Cambridge.

Daly, M., 1993, 'Broken bridge and empty basket: the political and economic background of the Sudanese civil war' in Daly, M. and A. Sikainga,

'*Civil War in the Sudan*', London: British Academic Press.

Das Gupta, M., 1987, "Selective discrimination against female children in rural Punjab, India", *Population and Development Review,* 13: 77-100.

Davies, S., 1993, "Are Coping Strategies a Cop Out?", *IDS Bulletin* 24(4): 60-72.

Davies, S., 1996, *Adaptable Livelihoods: Coping with Food Insecurity in the Malian Sahel,* London: Macmillan.

de Soysa, I., 2000, 'The Resource Curse: Are Civil Wars Driven by Rapacity or Paucity?' in Berdal, M. and D. Malone (Eds.), 2000, *Greed and Grievances: Economic Agendas in Civil Wars,* London: Lyne Rienner Publishers Inc..

de Waal, A., 1989, *Famine That Kills: Darfur, Sudan, 19884-85*, Oxford: Oxford University Press.

de Waal, A., 1990, 'A re-assessment of entitlement theory in the light of the recent famines in Africa', *Development and Change*, 21 (3): 469-490.

de Waal, A., 1993a, "War and famine in Africa", *IDS Bulletin* 24(4): 33-40.

de Waal, A., 1993b, 'Some Comments on Militias in the Contemporary Sudan', in Daly, M. and A. Sikainga, '*Civil War in the Sudan*', London: British Academic Press.

de Waal, A., 1996, "Contemporary warfare in Africa: Changing context, changing strategies", *IDS Bulletin* 27(3): 6-16.

de Waal, A., 1997, *Famine Crimes: Politics and Disaster Relief Industry in Africa,* Oxford: James Currey.

De Waal, 2018. *Mass Starvation: The History and Future of Famine.* Polity Press.

Deaton, A., 1992, "Saving and Income Smoothing in Cote D' Ivoire", *Journal of African Economies* 1(1): 1-24.

Deaton, A., 1997, *The Analysis of Household Surveys: A Microeconomic Approach*, Baltimore: Johns Hopkins University Press.

Demsetz, H., 1967, 'Toward a Theory of Property Rights', *American Economic Review* 57: 347-53.

Deng, F., 1971, '*Tradition and Modernization: A Challenge for Law among the Dinka of the Sudan*', New Haven: Yale University Press.

Deng, F., 1972, '*The Dinka of the Sudan*', Illinois: Waveland Press.

Deng, F., 1986, *The Man Called Deng Majok: A Biography of Power, Polygyny and Change,* Yale University Press, New Haven.

Deng, F., 1995, 'War of Visions: Conflict of Identities in the Sudan', Washington, D.C.: Brookings Institution.

Deng, L., 1999, "Famine in the Sudan: Causes, Preparedness and Response: A Political, Social and Economic Analysis of the 1998 Bahr el Ghazal Famine", *IDS Discussion Paper 369*, Brighton: Institute of Development Studies.

Deng, L., 2002a, "Confronting Civil War: a comparative study of household assets management in Southern Sudan", *IDS Discussion Paper 381*, Brighton: Institute of Development Studies.

Deng, L., 2002b, 'The Sudan Famine of 1998: Unfolding of the Global Dimension', *IDS Bulletin* 33 (4): 28-38.

Deng, L., 2003, 'Education in Southern Sudan: War, Status and Challenges of Education for All Goals', Paper Prepared for EFA Monitoring Report, Paris: UNESCO.

Deng, L., 2013, "Changing Livelihoods in South Sudan", *ODI Humanitarian Practice Network Issue No. 57*.

Deng, L., 2010a, "Livelihood Diversification and Civil War: The Case of Dinka Communities in the Sudan's Civil War", *Journal of Eastern African Studies Vol 4 (3), pp. 381-399*.

Deng, L., 2010b, "Social Capital and Civil War: The Case of Dinka Communities in the Sudan's Civil War", *Journal of African Affairs 109 (435) pp. 231-250*.

Deng, L., 2008, "Are Non-poor always less vulnerable? The Case of Households exposed to protracted civil war in Southern Sudan", *Journal of Disasters 32 (3)*.

Deng, L., 2007, "Increased Rural Vulnerability in the Era of Globalization: Conflict and Famine in Sudan in the 1990s", in Devereux, S., 2007 (eds.), "*The New Famines: Why famines persist in an era of globalization*", London: Routledge Inc.

Deng, L., 2002, "The Sudan Famine of 1998: Unfolding of the Global Dimension", *IDS Bulletin* 33 (4).

Dercon, S., 1993, *Risk, Crop Choice and Savings: Evidence from Tanzania*, Centre for the Study of African Economies, Working Paper Series No. 93 (2), Oxford.

Dercon, S., 1996, 'Risk, Crop Choice and Savings: Evidence from Tanzania', *Economic Development and Cultural Change* 44 (3): 485-514.

Dercon, S., 2000, 'Income risk, coping strategies and safety nets', *Working Paper* No. 26, Oxford: Centre for the study of African Economies.

Dercon, S. and Krishnan, P., 1996, 'Income Portfolios in rural Ethiopia and Tanzania: choices and constraints', *Journal of Development Studies*, 32 (6): 850-875.

Devereux, S., 1993, "Goats before ploughs: dilemmas of household response sequencing during food shortages", *IDS Bulletin* 24(4): 52-59.

Devereux, S., 1999, '*Making Less Last Longer: Informal Safety Nets in Malawi*, IDS Discussion Paper 373, Brighton: Institute of Development Studies.

Devereux, S., 2000, 'Famine in the twentieth century', *IDS Working Paper* 105, Brighton: Institute of Development Studies.

Devereux, S., 2001a, 'Sen's Entitlement Approach: Critiques and Counter-critiques', *Oxford Development Studies*, 29 (3): 245-263.

Devereux, S., 2001b, 'Famine in Africa', Chapter 5 in S. Devereux and S. Maxwell (eds), *Food Security in Sub-Sahara Africa*, London: ITDG Publishing.

Devereux, S., and Hoddinott, J., 1992, 'Issues in data collection', Ch.2 in Devereux, S., and Hoddinott (ed), 1992, *Fieldwork in Developing Countries*, Hertfordshire: Harvester Wheatsheaf.

Devereux, S. and Naeraa, T., 1996, 'Drought and survival in rural Namibia', *Journal of Southern African Studies*, 22 (3): 421-440.

Dillon, J., 1971, 'An expository review of Bernmoullian decision theory in agriculture: Is utility futility?', *Review of Marketing and Agricultural Economics*, 39 (1).

Downing, T., 1991, 'Vulnerability to Hunger in Africa', *Global Environmental Change* Vol. 1 (5).

Dr`eze, J. and Sen, A., 1989, *Hunger and Public Action*, Oxford: Clarendon Press.

Duffield, M., 1993, "NGOs, Disaster Relief and Asset Transfer in the Horn: Political Survival in a Permanent Emergency", *Development and Change* 24: 131-157.

Duffield, M., 2000, 'Globalization, Transborder Trade, and War Economies', in Berdal, M. and D. Malone (Eds.), 2000, *Greed and Grievances: Economic Agendas in Civil Wars,* London: Lyne Rienner Publishers Inc..

Dyson, T., 1993, 'Demographic Responses to Famine in South Asia', *IDS Bulletin,* 24 (4): 17-26.

Edkins, J., 1996, 'Legality with a vengeance: famines and humanitarian relief in "complex emergencies', *Journal of International Studies*, 25 (3): 547-575.

Edwards, M., 1999, 'Enthusiasts, Tacticians and Sceptics: The World Bank, Civil Society and Social Capital', Ford Foundation: Social Capital, Governance and Civil Society Unit.

Eibner, J., 2001, 'Two Goats Can Free a Slave in Sudan', *International Herald Tribune 29th June*.

Elbadawi, I, and Sambanis, N., 2000, "Why are there many civil wars in Africa? Understanding and Preventing Violent Conflict", *Journal of African Economies* 9(3): 244-269.

Ellis, F., 1993, *Peasant Economics: Farm Households and Agrarian Development*, Cambridge: Cambridge University Press.

Ellis, F., 1998, "Household Strategies and Rural Livelihood Diversification", *Journal of Development Studies*, 35(1): 1-38.

Ellis, F., 2000, *Rural Livelihoods and Diversity in Developing Countries*, Oxford: Oxford University Press

Eswaran, M. and Kotwal, A., 1990, 'Implications of Credit Constraints for Risk Behaviour in Less Developed Economies', *Oxford Economic Papers*, 42 (2): 473-482.

Evans-Pritchard, E., 1940, *The Nuer: A Description of the Modes of Livelihood and Political Institutions of a Nilotic People*, Oxford: Clarendon Press.

Fafchamps, M., 1992, 'Solidarity Networks in Preindustrial Societies: Rational Peasants with a Moral Economy', *Economic Development and Cultural Changes* 41 (1): 147-174.

Falk, R. and Kim, S., 1980, *The War System: An Interdisciplinary Approach*, Boulder, Colorado: Westview Press.

Farrington, J., Carney, D., Ashley, C. and Turton, C., 1999, 'Sustainable Livelihoods in Practice: Early Applications of Concepts in Rural Areas', *ODI Natural Resource Perspectives* No. 42, London: Overseas Development Institute

FEWS/USAID, 1999, *Southern Sudan Monitoring Report*, Nairobi: Famine Early Warning Systems.

Fine, B., 1999, 'The Developmental State Is Dead – Long Live Social Capital?', *Development and Change*, 30: 1-19.

Folbre, N., 1986, 'Hearts and Spades: Paradigms of Household Economics', *World Development*, 14 (2): 245-256.

Fukuyama, F., 2001, 'Social capital, civil society and development', *Third World Quarterly*, 22 (1): 7-20.

Gagnon, G., and Ryle, J., 2001, *Report of an Investigation into Oil Development, Conflict and Displacement in Western Upper Nile, Sudan*, Sudan Interagency Reference Group of Canada.

Galtung, J., 1980, 'A Structural Theory of Imperialism', in Falk, R. and Kim, S. (ed), *The War System: An Interdisciplinary Approach*, Colorado: Westview Press.

Gittelsohn, J. and Mookherji, S., 1997, 'The Application of Anthropological Methods to the Study of Intrahousehold Resource Allocation', in Ch. 10 in Haddad, L., Hoddinott, J. and Alderman, H. (ed), 1998, *Intrahousehold Resource Allocation in Developing Countries: Models, Methods, and Policy*, Baltimore: John Hopkins.

Glewwe, P., and G. Hall, 1998, 'Are Some Groups More Vulnerable to Macroeconomic Shocks than Others? Hypothesis Tests Based on Panel Data from Peru', *Journal of Development Economics*, 56: 181-206.

Goodhand, J., Hume, D., and Lewer, N., 2000, 'Social Capital and the Political Economy of Violence: A Case Study of Sri Lanka', *Disasters* 24(4): 390-406.

Gottman, J., 1945, 'Bugeand, Gallieni, Lyautey: the development of the French colonial warfare', in Earle, E. (ed), *Makers of Modern Strategy: Military Thought from Machiavelli to Hitler*, Princeton: Princeton University Press.

Gray, J., 1961, *A History of the Southern Sudan, 1839-1889*, London: Oxford University Press.

Green, R., 1997, 'Bureaucracy and Law and Order' in J. Faundez (ed.), *Good Government and the Law*, Basingstoke: St. Martin's Press.

Grisley, W., 1980, *Effect of Risk and Risk Aversion on Farm Decision-Making: Farmers in Northern Thailand*, PhD thesis University of Illinois.

Grossbard, A., 1976, 'An Economic Analysis of Polygyny: The Case of Maiduguri', *Current Anthropology* 17.

Grossbard, A., 1978, 'Toward a Marriage between Economics and Anthropology and a General Theory of Marriage', *American Economic Review* 68 (2): 33-37.

Gurr, T. (ed.), 1970, *Why Men Rebel*, Princeton: Princeton University Press.

Haddad, L., Hoddinott, J. and Alderman, H., 1997, *Intrahousehold Resource*

Allocation in Developing Countries: Models, Methods, and Policy, Baltimore: John Hopkins.

Harriss, B., 1995, "The intrafamily distribution of hunger in South Asia" in J. Dreze, A. K. Sen, and A. Hessian (eds), *The Political Economy of Hunger: selected essays*, Oxford: Clarendon Press.

Hart, G., 1992, 'Imagined Unities: Constructions of "The Household" in Economic Theory', Ch.6 in Ortiz, S., and Lees, S. (ed), *Understanding Economic Process,* Lanham, NY: University Press of America.

Hart, G., 1995, 'Gender and Household Dynamics: Recent Theories and Their Implications', in Quibria, M. (ed), *Critical Issues in Asian Development: Theories, Experiences and Policies*, Oxford: Oxford University Press.

Hazell, P., 1982, "Application of Risk Preference Estimates in Firm-Household and Agricultural Sector Models", *American Journal of Agricultural Economics* 64(2): 385-90.

Henderson, K., 1939, 'A Note on the Migration of the Messeria Tribe into South West Kordofan', *Sudan Notes and Records*, 32.

Hendrickson, D, Mearns, R, and Armon, j, 1996, "Livestock Raiding Among the Pastoral Turkana of Kenya: Redistribution, Predation and the Links to Famine", *IDS Bulletin* 27(3):17-30.

Hey, J., 1979 (ed), *Uncertainty in Microeconomics*, Oxford: Martin Robertson and Co. Ltd.

Holt, P., and Daly, M., 1988, *A History of the Sudan: From the Coming of Islam to the Present Day*, London and New York: Longman.

Holzmann, R. and Jorgensen, S., 2000, 'Social Risk Management: A new conceptual framework for Social Capital Protection, and beyond', *Social Protection Discussion Paper No. 6*, World Bank: Social Protection, Human Development Network.

Homer-Dixon, T., 1995, 'The Ingenuity Gap: Can Poor Countries Adapt to Resource Scarcity', *Population and Development Review* 21 (3): 587-612.

Homer-Dixon, T. (Eds.), 1999, *Environment, Scarcity and Violence*, Princeton: Princeton University Press.

Hoogeveen, J., 2000, 'Risk and insurance by the poor in developing countries', Washington: World Bank, Disaster Management Facility, mimeo report.

Human Rights Watch, 1999, *Background Paper on Slavery and Slavery Redemption in the Sudan.*

Huntington, R., Achroyd, J. and Deng, L., 1981, 'The Challenge for Rainfed Agriculture in Western and Southern Sudan: Lessons from Abyei', *Africa Today, 2nd Quarter.* 43-53.

ICG, 2002, 'God, Oil and Country: Changing the Logic of War in Sudan', *ICG Africa Report* No. 39, Brussels: International Crisis Group Press.

Jackson, C., 1996, 'Rescuing Gender from the Poverty Trap', *World Development*, 22 (3): 489-504.

Jodha, N., 1975, 'Famine and Famine Policies: Some Empirical Evidence', *Economic and Political Weekly* 10 (2).

Johnson, D., 1988, 'The Southern Sudan', *Report No. 78*, London: Minority Rights Group.

Kaplan, R., 1994, 'The Coming Anarchy', *Atlantic Monthly*, January: 44-77.

Karam, K., 1980, 'Dispute Settlement among Pastoral Nomads in the Sudan', Masters thesis, University of Birmingham.

Keen, D., 1990, 'A Disaster for Whom?: Local Interests and International Donors during Famine among the Dinka of Sudan', *Disasters* 15 (2): 150-165.

Keen, D., 1994, *The Benefits of Famine: A Political economy of famine in South-west Sudan, 1983-1989,* Princeton: Princeton University Press.

Keen, D., 1997, 'A rational kind of madness', *Oxford Development Studies* 25 (1): 67-75.

Keen, D., 1998, "The Economic Functions of Violence in Civil Wars", *Adelphi paper 320,* Oxford: The International Institute for Strategic Studies.

Keen, D., 2000, 'Incentives and Disincentives for Violence' in Berdal, M. and D. Malone (Eds.), 2000, *Greed and Grievances: Economic Agendas in Civil Wars,* London: Lyne Rienner Publishers Inc..

Kinsey, B., Burger, K. and Gunning, J., 1998, 'Coping with Drought in Zimbabwe: Survey Evidence on Responses of Rural Households to Risk', *World Development,* 26 (1): 89-110.

Knack, S., and Keefer, P., 1997, 'Does Social Capital Have and Economic Payoff?: A Cross-Country Investigation', *Quarterly Journal of Economics* 62 (4): 1251-1288.

Kogan, N., and Wallach, M., 1967, 'Risk taking as a function of the situation, the person, and the group', in *New Directions in Psychology III*, New York.

Kuol, L., 2014, "Confronting Civil War: The Level of Resilience in Abyei Area During Sudan's Civil War in the 1990s", *Journal of Civil Wars.* Volume 16(4). pp 468-487.

Lesch, A., 1998, '*Sudan Contested National Identities*', Oxford: James Currey.

Lienhardt, G., 1958, 'The Western Dinka: Tribes without Rulers', in Middleton, J. and Tait, D. (eds), *An examination of the association between the political structure and the kinship system of the Dinka and of the religious undertones permeating them*, Oxford: Oxford University Press.

Lienhardt, G., 1961, '*Divinity and Experience: The Religion of the Dinka*', Oxford: Clarendon Press.

Lim, Y. and Townsend, R., 1994, 'Currency, Transaction Patterns, and Consumption Smoothing: Theory and Measurement in ICRISAT Villages', mimeo report.

Lipton, M., 1977, *Why Poor People Stay Poor: Urban Bias in World Development*, London: Temple Smith.

Little, P., Smith, K., Cellarius, B., Coppock, D., and Barrett, C., 2001, 'Avoiding Disaster: Diversification and Risk Management among East African Herders', *Development and Change*, 32 (3): 401-434.

Luckham, R.; Ahmed, I.; Muggah, R.; White, S., 2001, 'Conflict and Poverty in Sub-Saharan Africa: An Assessment of the Issues and Evidence', *IDS Working Paper* 128, Brighton: Institute of Development Studies.

Lumby, S., 1994, *Investment Appraisal and Financial Decisions*, London: Chapman and Hall.

Mahmud, U., and Baldo, S., 1987, *Al Daien Massacre: Slavery in the Sudan*, Khartoum: Human Rights Violations in the Sudan.

Marchione, T., 1996, 'The Right to Food in the Post-Cold War era, *Food Policy* 12 (1): 83-102.

Mawson, A., 1990, 'Murahaleen Raids on the Dinka, 1985-89', *Disasters* 15(2): 137-149.

Messer, E., 1983, 'The household focus in nutritional anthropology: An overview', *Ecology of Food and Nutrition* 5 (4).

Morduch, J., 1991, "Consumption Smoothing Across Space: Tests for Village-Level Response to Risk", *Harvard University. Mimeo.*

Morduch, J., 1995, "Income Smoothing and Consumption Smoothing", *Journal of Economic Perspectives,* 9: 103-114.

Morduch, J., 1998, 'Between the Market and State: Can Informal

Insurance Patch the Safety Nets?', *Development Discussion Paper* No. 621, Harvard: Harvard Institute for International Development.

Moscardi, E. and de Janvry, A., 1977, "Attitudes Toward Risk Among Peasants: An Econometric Approach", *American Journal of Agricultural Economics,* 59(4): 710-6.

Moser, C., 1998, "The Asset Vulnerability Framework: Reassessing Urban Poverty Reduction Strategies", *World Development,* 26(1): 1-19.

Moser, C., and J. Holland, 1997, 'Household Responses to Poverty and Vulnerability, Volume 4: Confronting Crisis in Cawama, Lusaka, Zambia', Urban Management Programme, Report No. 24, *The World Bank*: Washington.

Myers, N., 1987, "Population, Environment, and Conflict", *Environmental Conservation,* 14(1): 15-22.

Nachmias, C. and Nachmias, D., 1996, *Research Methods in the Social Sciences,* London: St. Martin's Press, Inc.

Naeraa, T., Devereux, S., Frayne, B. and Harnett, P., 1993, 'Coping with drought in Namibia: informal social security systems in Caprivi and Erongo, 1992', *NISER Research Report 12,* Windhoek: University of Namibia.

Norusis, M., 1997, *SPSS 7.5 Guide to Data Analysis,* New Jersey: Prentice-Hall Inc..

Nyaba, P., 1997, *The Politics of Liberation in South Sudan: An Insider's View,* Kampala: Fountain.

Pingali, L. and Binswanger, P., 1986, *Population Density, Market Access, and Farmer-Generated Technical Change in Sub-Saharan Africa,* Agriculture and Rural Development Department Research Unit, The World Bank.

Platteau, J., 1997, 'Mutual Insurance as an Elusive Concept in Traditional Rural Communities', *The Journal of Development Studies,* 33 (6): 764-796.

Popkin, S., 1979, *The Rational Peasant: The political economy of rural society in Vietnam,* Berkeley: University of California.

Posner, R., 1980, 'A Theory of Primitive Society, with Special Reference to Law', *Journal of Law and Economics* 23(1): 1-53.

Preston, D., 1994, 'Rapid Household Appraisal: A Method for Facilitating the Analysis of Household Livelihood Strategies', *Applied Geography,* 14: 203-213.

PRIO, 2019. "Conflict Trends in Africa, 1989-2918". Oslo: Peace Research Institute Oslo (PRIO).

Puri, B., 1996, *Statistics in Practice: An illustrated Guide to SPSS,* Oxford: Oxford University Press Inc..

Putnam, R., 1993, *Making Democracy Work: Civic Traditions in Modern Italy*, Princeton: Princeton University Press.

Reardon, T., 1997, 'Using Evidence of Household Income Diversification to Inform Study of the Rural Nonfarm Labour Market in Africa', *World Development,* 25 (5): 735-747.

Reardon, T., and Vosti, S., 1995, 'Links Between Rural Poverty and the Environment in Developing Countries: Asset Categories and Investment Poverty', *World Development,* 23 (9): 1495-1506.

Reardon, T., Delgado, C., and Malton, P., 1988, 'Coping with Household-Level Food Insecurity in Drought-Affected Areas in Burkina Faso', *World Development* 16 (9): 1065-74.

Riezler, K., 1943, 'On the Psychology of the Modern Revolution', *Social Research* X: 320-336.

Rodeghier, M., 1996 *Survey with confidence: A practical guide to survey research using SPSS,* Chicago: SPSS Inc..

Rosenzweig, M., 1988, "Risk, Implicit Contracts and the Family in Rural Areas of Low-Income Countries", *The Economic Journal,* 98: 1148-1170.

Rosenzweig, M., and Binswanger, H., 1993, "Wealth, Weather Risk and the Composition and Profitability of Agricultural Investments", *The Economic Journal,* 103: 56-78.

Rosenzweig, M., and Stark, O., 1989, "Consumption Smoothing, Migration, and Marriage: Evidence from Rural India", *Journal of Political Economy,* 97(4): 905-26.

Ryle, J., 1989, 'Displaced Southern Sudanese in Northern Sudan with Special Reference to Southern Darfur and Kordofan', Save the Children (SCF-UK), mimeo report.

Sachs, J., and Warner, A., 1999, 'Natural Resource Abundance and Economic Growth', *NBER Working Paper* 5398, Boston: National Bureau of Economic Research.

Saeed, A., 1982, 'The State and Socioeconomic Transformation in the Sudan: The Case of Social Conflict in Southwest Kordofan', Ph.D. dissertation, University of Connecticut.

Sanderson, L., and Sanderson, N., 1981, *Education, Religion and Politics in Southern Sudan, 1899-1964,* London: Ithaca Press; Khartoum: Khartoum

University Press.

Scoones, I., 1995, 'Investigating difference: applications of wealth ranking and household survey approaches among farming households in Southern Zimbabwe', *Development and Change*, 26: 67–88.

Scoones, I., 1998, "Sustainable Rural Livelihoods: A Framework for Analysis," *IDS Working Paper* No. 72, Institute for Development Studies: Brighton.

Scott, C., and Litchfield, J., 1994, "Inequality, mobility and the determinants of income among the rural poor in Chile, 1968–1986", *Discussion Paper* 53, London: Development Economics Research Programme, London School of Economics.

Scott, J., 1976, *The Moral Economy of the Peasant: Rebellion and Subsistence in Southeast Asia,* New Haven: Yale University Press.

Seaman, J., 2000, 'Making Exchange Entitlements Operational: The Food Economy Approach to Famine Prediction and the RiskMap Computer Programme', *Disasters* 24 (2): 133–153.

Sen, A., 1981, *Poverty and Famines: An essay on entitlement and deprivation,* Oxford: Oxford University Press.

Siegel, P. and Alwang, J., 1999, "An Asset-Based Approach to Social Risk Management: A Conceptual Framework", *Social Protection Discussion Paper No.*9926, Social Protection, Washington: The World Bank.

Sillers, D., 1980, *Measuring Risk Preferences of Rice Farmers in Nueva Rcija, Philippines: An Experimental Approach,* Yale University.

Singh, I., Squire, L., and Strauss, J., 1986, *Agricultural Household Models,* Baltimore: Johns Hopkins University Press.

Sinha, S., and Lipton, M., 1999, *Undesirable Fluctuations, Risk and Poverty: A Review,* World Bank, mimeo report.

Slivard, R., 1996, *World Military and Social Expenditures,* Washington: World Priorities.

Spaulding, J., 1982, 'Slavery, Land Tenure and Social Class in the Northern Turkish Sudan', *International Journal of African Historical Studies* 15 (1).

SPSS Inc., 1998, *SPSS Basic 8.0 for Windows User's Guide,* Chicago: SPSS Inc..

SRRA, 1998, 'The Looming Famine in Bahr el Ghazal Region', *Monitoring Report,* Sudan Relief and Rehabilitation Association.

Stark, O., 1991, *The Migration of Labour,* Cambridge, Mass.: Basil Blackwell.

Stewart, F., Humphreys, F. and Lea, N., 1997, 'Civil conflict in developing countries over the last quarter of a century: an empirical overview of economic and social consequences', *Oxford Development Studies* 25 (1): 11-42.

Stiglitz, J., 1974, 'Incentives and risk sharing in sharecropping', *Review of Economic Studies*, 41 (2): 219-255.

Swift, J., 1989, "Why Are Rural People Vulnerable to Famine?", *IDS Bulletin* 20(2): 8-15.

Swift, J., 1993, "Understanding and Preventing Famine and Famine Mortality", *IDS Bulletin,* 24(4): 1-16.

Swift, J. (ed.), 1996, 'War and Rural Development in Africa', *IDS Bulletin* 27(3): 1-5..

Swift, J., 1998, *Factors influencing the Dynamics of Livelihood Diversification and Rural Non-Farm Employment in Space and Time,* Rural Nonfarm Project, Chatham, UK: Natural Resources Institute, mimeo report.

Thompson, R., 1966, *Defeating Communist Insurgency: Experiences from Malaya and Vietnam*, London: Chatto.

Tinker, I., 1990, *Persistent Inequalities: Women and World Development,* Oxford: Oxford University Press.

Townsend, R., 1994, 'Risk and insurance in village India', *Econometrica* 62 (3): 539-591.

Trinquier, R., 1964, *Modern Warfare: A French View of Counterinsurgency*, New York.

Udry, C., 1995, 'Risk and Saving in Northern Nigeria', *American Economic Review,* 85 (5): 1287-1300.

UNHCR, 2018. "Global Trends: Forced Displacement in 2018". Geneva: UNHCR.

UNICEF/OLS, 1998, *Nutrition Assessment in Southern Sudan, June 1998*, Nairobi: UNICEF/Operation Lifeline Sudan (OLS).

UNICEF/OLS, 2000, *Progress of Regions: Multiple Indicator Cluster Survey Results in Southern Sudan, 2000,* Nairobi: UNICEF/Operation Lifeline Sudan (OLS).

UNICEF/SRRA, 2002, *The Status of Basic Education, Water and Sanitation Coverage, Diarrhoea Prevalence and Cost in Southern Sudan*, Nairobi: UNICEF

USAID, 1998, AIMS Project, various country studies, Washington: USAID.

von Braun, J., T. Teklu and P. Webb, 1998, *Famine in Africa: Causes, Responses, and Prevention,* Baltimore: John Hopkins University Press.

Waite, L., 2000, 'How is Household Vulnerability Gendered?: Female-headed Households in the Collectives of Suleimaniyah, Iragi Kurdistan', *Disasters* 24 (2): 153-172.

Walker, T., 1980, *Decision Making by Farmers and by the National Agricultural Research program on the Adoption and Development of Maize Varieties in El Salvador,* PhD dissertation Stanford Food Research Institute, Stanford, California.

Walker, T. and Ryan, J., 1990, *Village and Household Economies in India's Semiarid Tropics,* Baltimore: Johns Hopkins University Press.

Watson, F., 2002, 'Why are there No Longer 'War Famines' in Contemporary Europe?': The Case of the Besieged Areas of Bosnia 1992-5', *IDS Bulletin* Vol. 33 (4): 39-47.

Watts, M., 1983, *Silent Violence: Food, Famine and Peasantry in Northern Nigeria,* Berkeley: University of California Press.

Watts, M., 1988, 'Coping with the Market: Uncertainty and Food Security Among Hausa Peasants', in de Garine and G. Harrison (ed), *Coping with Uncertainty in Food Supply,* Oxford: Clarendon Press.

Watts, M., 1991, 'Entitlements or Empowerment? Famine and Starvation in Africa', *Review of African Political Economy,* X.

White, P., and Cliffe, L., 2000, 'Matching Responses to Context in Complex Political Emergencies: 'Relief', 'Development', 'Peace-building' or Something In-between?', *Disasters* 24 (4): 314-342.

Wilson, K., 1992, 'Thinking about the ethics of fieldwork', Ch.12 in Devereux, S., and Hoddinott, J. (ed), 1992, *Fieldwork in Developing Countries,* Hertfordshire: Harvester Wheatleaf.

World Bank, 1990, *World Development Report 1990: Poverty,* New York: Oxford University Press for the World Bank.

World Bank, 2001, 'Dynamic Risk Management and the Poor', *African Region Human Development Series* 21961, the World Bank.

World Food Program, 2018. "South Sudan – Food Security and Nutrition Monitoring Bulletin". Rome: World Food Program.

Zimmerman, F. and M. Carter, 1996, "Dynamics Portfolio Management Under Risk and Subsistence Constraints in Developing Countries", *Staff Paper* No. 402, University of Wisconsin-Madison.

ABOUT THE AUTHOR

Luka Biong Deng Kuol is the Dean of Academic Affairs at the Africa Center for Strategic Studies at National Defense University in Washington, USA. In addition, he is the faculty lead of three academic programs: National Security Strategy Development and Implementation in Africa, Managing Security Resources in Africa, and Emerging Security Sector Leaders in Africa. His work focuses on national security strategy, security sector budgets, social contracts, food security, vulnerability and resilience, and the security-development-governance nexus.

Dr. Kuol is also a Global Fellow at the Peace Research Institute Oslo (PRIO), a Fellow at the Rift Valley Institute, and an Associate Professor of Economics (on leave) at the University of Juba in South Sudan. He also sits on the editorial board of the Disasters Journal, published by the Overseas Development Institute. Prior to joining the Africa Center, Dr. Kuol served as director of the Center for Peace and Development Studies at the University of Juba in South Sudan. He was also on the teaching staff of the Faculty of Economics and Rural Development at the University of Gezira in Sudan.

He was a resident fellow at Harvard Kennedy School and a Visiting Fellow at the Institute of Development Studies in the United Kingdom. He served as Minister of Presidential Affairs for the Government of Southern Sudan and as National Minister of Cabinet Affairs for the Republic of Sudan. He has also worked as a senior economist for the World Bank in Southern Sudan. He was the founder of the New Sudan Center for Statistics and Evaluation that became the South Sudan Bureau of Statistics.

He has published scholarly articles in a wide array of prestigious international journals and contributed with many peer-reviewed chapters in various books. He is a co-editor of a book entitled "The Struggle for South Sudan: Challenges of Security and State Formation" and co-editor of a book entitled "Abyei: Between Two Sudans".

He received his BSc (Honors) from the Faculty of Economics and Social Studies at the University of Khartoum, Sudan, an M.A. (Distinction) in Economics, an M.B.A.(Distinction) from the Catholic University of Leuven, Belgium, and a Ph.D. from the Institute of Development Studies (IDS) at the University of Sussex in the United Kingdom.

www.ingramcontent.com/pod-product-compliance
Lightning Source LLC
Chambersburg PA
CBHW041255040426
42334CB00028BA/3028